"WE WERE THE NINTH"

General W. S. Rosecrans (upper left), Colonel Gustav Kämmerling (upper right), Colonel Robert L. McCook (center), General August Willich (lower left), General George H. Thomas (lower right)

"We Were The Ninth"

A History of the Ninth Regiment, Ohio Volunteer Infantry April 17, 1861, to June 7, 1864

by Constantin Grebner

translated and edited by
Frederic Trautmann

The Kent State University Press
Kent, Ohio, and London, England

Library of Congress Catalog Card Number 87-3884
ISBN 978-1-60635-029-4
Manufactured in the United States of America

First paper printing 2009

Library of Congress Cataloging-in-Publication Data

Grebner, Constantin, d. 1907.
"We were the Ninth".

Translation of: "Die Neuner."
Bibliography: p.
Includes index.
1. United States. Army. Ohio Infantry Regiment, 9th (1861–1864)—History. 2. United States—History—Civil War, 1861–1865—Regimental histories. 3. Ohio—History—Civil War, 1861–1865—Regimental histories. 4. United States—History—Civil War, 1861–1865—German Americans. 5. Ohio—History—Civil War, 1861–1865—German Americans. 6. German Americans—Ohio—History—19th century. I. Trautmann, Frederic. II. United States. Army. Ohio Infantry Regiment, 9th (1861–1864) III. Title.
E525.5 9th.G7413 1987 973.7'471 87-3884
ISBN 0-87338-337-0 (alk. paper) ∞

British Library Cataloging-in-Publication data are available.

To

David M. Neigher

(F. T.)

First published as *"Die Neuner": Eine Schilderung der Kriegsjahre des 9ten Regiments Ohio Vol. Infanterie, vom 17. April 1861 bis 7. Juni 1864* (Cincinnati: S. Rosenthal & Co., 1897).

Now, as in the war, let our motto be:

Forward—March!

—Constitution of the Associated Veterans, Ninth Ohio Volunteer Infantry Regiment, 4.

"We would be happy if they who follow us and read our book—our children and our children's children—were infused by the same spirit and filled with the same conviction."—infra, 33.

No more they hear the roll of drums,
No more the call to battle comes.

. . . .

Their work is done; [they rest] beneath the sod
Where lilies lean and roses nod.

—W. J. Lampton, quoted by Jacob Smith, *Camps and Campaigns of the 107th Ohio,* 238.

Contents

Illustrations

Introduction by Frederic Trautmann

A Regiment.—Its Veterans' Association.—The Regiment's Historian.—His Book.—This Translated Edition of It.—Books Useful to Reading and Understanding It.—The Editor-Translator's Acknowledgments.—The Book's Purposes: May They Be Achieved!

1

On Friday, April 12, 1861, in Columbus, the Ohio senate conducted business—but not as usual. Anxiety and strain filled the chamber. News from the South had worsened as more states passed "ordinances of secession." Worse, a Southern army, with artillery, had gathered opposite Fort Sumter. Guns were trained on the Federal arsenal; a shot could bring war. The senators worked, but their hearts were not in legislative humdrum. Fear of war and dread for a nation's breaking up preoccupied the senators. What of the Union? What of Ohio, which touched Kentucky and Virginia, both likely to secede? Indeed, a spike of Virginia pointed like a dagger stabbing between Ohio and Pennsylvania, as if to slice the North in half. Would geography and history drive the national epicenter west, beyond the Alleghenies? Would Ohio become "the keystone of the Union," the shield against invasion, or the victim of a Rebel offensive?

On the floor, Jacob Cox, of Trumbull County, shared his colleagues' foreboding. In the gallery, Abby Kelly Foster, the abolitionist, may have rejoiced alone at the dark rush of events. She believed in a solution by the sword: through blood would the slave be freed.

A senator entered from the lobby, excited. Catching the presiding officer's eye, he said: "Mr. President, the telegraph announces that the secessionists are bombarding Fort Sumter!" A solemn, painful hush—broken by Foster: "Glory to God!" Blood would be spilled. The sword, terrible and swift, would strike. The scourge of war would follow. Gloom settled in the senate.

Outside, not senatorial dejection but Foster's fervor prevailed. Ohioans and other Northerners, largely regardless of party, approved Lincoln's call for 75,000 volunteers. More than 75,000 wanted to enlist. "At the first shot from Beauregard's guns in Charleston harbor," Cox observed, "these men crowded to the recruiting stations to enlist for the defense of the national flag and the national union."

The popular enthusiasm, Cox said, "swept politicians off their feet." Judge Thomas Key of Cincinnati, chairman of the senate's judiciary committee, took Cox by the arm, paced the floor outside the railing, and declared: "Mr. Cox, the people have gone stark mad!"[1]

In Judge Key's Cincinnati, Lincoln's call had been heeded. People, if not mad, *were* up in arms. Troops mobilized and, as elsewhere, often into ethnic units. Indeed, from New Mexico to New England, Irish, French, Scandinavians, Swiss, Welsh, Dutch, Poles, and even Mexicans assembled for the Union.[2] Most notable were the Germans. The willingness to fight, of this, the biggest ethnic group, erupted in Cincinnati, where beer and Germans had long flavored a populace 30 percent German in 1860. There, in the German quarter known as Over the Rhine, a German regiment appeared, the first of its kind in the nation, the one that would take martial honors with the bayonet. The regiment needed one thousand men; two thousand applied, and "1,000 pairs of eyes" wept "because they were not permitted to go."[3] Four days after Lincoln's call, the Ninth Ohio Volunteer Infantry—German by ethnic origin and mostly foreign-born, German-speaking, organized along German lines, and run in the German manner—reported for duty, eager for action. *Ohio must be defended, the Union preserved, and freedom extended to all.* This the Germans believed. So the Germans of Cincinnati answered the call of their President.

In June of 1861 "the well-trained Ninth" went to West Virginia to begin "a long and brilliant career in the field" and become "the staunch and trusty old Ninth Ohio."[4] "Dutch devils" Southerners called them, those "bloody Dutch" noted for success with the bayonet.[5] Their steel routed Confederates at Mill Springs, Kentucky, in the first bayonet charge of the war. At Chickamauga, in "a famous charge," one of its "several telling charges" there, The Ninth blunted and bent a Confederate assault.[6] Their battle-cry, a Teutonic *hurrah*—cohesive, inspiring, evocative, savage—raised Union hackles and struck fear into Confederate hearts. Shouting *hurrah,* wielding bayonets, repulsing other attacks at Chickamauga, and "scattering the enemy like chaff," The Ninth became "the pivot point on which our [Union] right swung back toward Chattanooga"; and Chattanooga was held.[7] The Ninth's recapture of Burnham's Battery won an inscription on the monument raised to the battery at Chickamauga after the war. The Ninth was second in the line of attack at Missionary Ridge.[8] When The Ninth left Georgia to muster out in 1864, it had done "excellent service," it "could be depended on in any emergency," and "the division lost one of its best regiments."[9]

For most of its enlistment The Ninth served and fought at points of geographic and strategic significance.

- At Rich Mountain and Carnifex Ferry in West Virginia to protect Ohio in 1861.
- At Shiloh, Tullahoma, and Corinth in 1862.
- To secure Nashville, Louisville, and Cincinnati itself against Braxton Bragg's mobile and dynamic designs and John Morgan's predations, in 1862 and 1863.
- In bloodier battles in 1863 and 1864, as the army of the Cumberland maneuvered for position in what would become Sherman's march to the sea.
- In carnage at Chickamauga, through hunger in Chattanooga, and therefore, in 1863 at Missionary Ridge, mounting but half its numbers and losing half of *them.*

In a word the history of the Armies of the Ohio and the Cumberland is the history of the Ninth Ohio from 1861 to 1864, in Kentucky, Tennessee, Alabama, and Georgia.

Despite hardship and danger, The Ninth never wavered or shirked but did its duty to the end. Though counting their remaining days and calculating the hours before they could leave the war, they set out to engage the enemy at the Etowah River in May of 1864. General Thomas, the corps commander, himself, appeared and ordered them from the front. A few days later they mustered out at Camp Dennison, Ohio. Of those who had taken the oath there in 1861, fewer than half remained to be discharged in 1864.

2

In 1870, veterans formed the Association of the Ninth Regiment. They wanted to remember, and they intended to remind the nation, where they fought, why they sacrificed, how they suffered, and what they accomplished in the Civil War. Accordingly, the association met quarterly, celebrated anniversaries in the regiment's war history, and organized visits to battlefields and cemeteries. The veterans' memories of their first commander, Robert L. McCook, were their fondest, proudest, dearest, and saddest. So, in 1877, to give substance and permanence to what might otherwise be forgotten when they died, the association raised a monument to him in Cincinnati's Washington Park. Likewise realizing late in the century that no record had been made for posterity, and that survivors had not been able to read their own story, the association published a history of the regiment, the book in hand.

3

As the history of the German regiment would be in German, so the editorial committee selected an author fit for the task, Constantin Grebner.[10] True, he had not served with The Ninth or even in the Civil War. But his credentials included university education, military experience, and knowledge of the United States north, south, east, and west—knowledge gained not only by study but also through travel and observation. Moreover, his books and essays distinguished him as an authority on the German language and its literature, and proved him one of the best writers of German in America.[11] In the German language, and especially *his* capable German, the history of the regiment would reach its likeliest audience: America's millions of German speakers. Indeed, theirs was America's second language. For them, a spate of books and magazines and some seven hundred newspapers, all in German, were being published across America.[12] A German-American literature flourished.[13]

Grebner was born in Bronnbach near Wertheim in the south-German state of Baden. His acuity of mind and vigor of body—his mental and physical strength—proved exceptional at the University of Heidelberg and among the revolutionaries of 1848. He suffered the typical fate of a Forty-Eighter when the revolution failed: exile in Switzerland and emigration overseas. But, though scarcely into manhood, this robust adventurer delighted in the thrills of the frenetic career of a political fugitive. Indeed, much of his life seems a determined flight from the ordinary and the humdrum. When barely twenty years old, he arrived in Rio de Janeiro on a burning ship. Mexico and California were next, then back to Europe. He taught German in London and the Netherlands. But that occupation was too tame and those places too sedate for one who had trailed the Conquistadors; he wanted excitement. After learning the necessary Dutch, he sailed to Java in the Netherlands East Indies and worked as a teacher and ran plantations for seventeen years. Then he returned to Europe, touching at China and Japan. He lived in Paris and Brussels in the late 1860s and early 1870s and accompanied two young Belgians on a trip around the world.

In the mid-1870s he headed west again, to the United States and a series of teaching posts. In Ohio he learned what it meant to be a schoolmaster who accepts room and board in small towns and with pupils' parents. He moved to East Saginaw, Michigan. Then, Texas. Next, Baltimore, where he managed an orphans' home. Then he taught in Wilmington, Delaware. At last he settled in Cincinnati to teach and write. He taught German in the public schools. He compiled anthologies of German literature. He wrote poetry in German, textbooks for students of German, and essays in German on the German language. And he wrote the history of the Ninth Regiment. In it the far-ranging anthologist's array of quotations introduce and set the tone of chapters, and decorate and illuminate the skilled and practiced author's limpid, graceful, and vivid prose. After more than twenty productive years as a teacher and writer, he died in Cincinnati, of an accident, in 1907.[14]

4

This book "is intended as neither a history of the war nor a definitive account of battles. Rather, we have restricted ourselves to a straightforward, veracious report of what happened to The Ninth, and to recounting as accurately as possible The Ninth's experiences as a wartime regiment."[15] To that end, Grebner talked to veterans, read their diaries and memoirs, interviewed their survivors, and studied other documents. Captains Henry Metzner and Friedrich Bertsch furnished a lot of information.[16] The result, this book (a comprehensive and detailed work of historical value and literary worth), constitutes a chapter in the history of an ethnic group and tells a part of the story of the Civil War. This "above average" study "of service in the West" is "creditably written" and "a complete and interesting volume."[17] Salient features include

- *Unique ethnicity*—This is a German book—in German, about German-Americans, for German-Americans, and to boost German-Americans. The pride is unabashedly aggressive: "The Germans deserve the utmost praise for their deeds and achievements. We shall not keep mum when it comes to getting their contribution recognized."[18] So here, The Ninth plays at stage center and can do no wrong.

Now, many Germans, probably equally proud of themselves, served in the Union and Confederate armies, perhaps as many as 200,000.[19] Other German units existed—infantry, cavalry, artillery—perhaps as many as 125 of various sizes in every arm and all branches of the Union forces, each probably as convinced as The Ninth of its own merits.[20] Nevertheless, this book, the history of The Ninth, is sui generis, the single one to match subject and language: the only Civil War regimental history published in German.

- *Patriotism*—Though prideful of German ethnic affiliation, The Ninth plumed itself on being American and asserted a passion for the Union. Expressions of nationalistic swagger, chauvinistic fervor, and jingoistic fire punctuate the book. Frau Stöcker of chapter 4, mother of a soldier killed in the ranks of The Ninth, regrets only that he could not take a half-dozen Rebels with him to eternity.

• *Historical Value*—The pro-German apology neither diminishes the book's fidelity to fact nor impairs its detailed, vivid portrait of the regiment's experience. Grebner's delving into primary sources yielded discussions of mobilization, training, organization, logistics, transportation, campaigns, strategy, tactics, and soldier life. There are hints about government and politics, too, including behind-the-scenes intrigues. There are glimpses, with eyewitness immediacy, of notable men and significant events: army officers, for example, such as Robert L. McCook, William S. Rosecrans, and George H. Thomas; and battles, such as Perryville, Mill Springs, and Chickamauga. And there is a sketch, regrettably brief, of a veterans' group, its celebration of fallen comrades, and its efforts to be honored for wartime service.

• *Literary Merit*—Grebner, a German and an anthologist and a teacher of German, must have prized the expository and narrative richness and the symbolic values of that language. A corresponding excellence manifests itself on his every page. Emotions are registered from joy to sadness to horror: from funny to pathetic to grisly: from humorous anecdotes and wry jokes to hunger, injury, and sickness, and to dismemberment and death. (Today's grin may disappear in tomorrow's evisceration by bayonet, or freeze in the next day's decapitation by saber, or vanish in next week's cannonade: blasted to smithereens.) Grebner the anthologist ransacked German literature for the apt and pithy epigraphs that introduce each chapter and set its tone. Further allusions and quotations occur appositely throughout. The prose is compact and terse, even elliptical; rich in rhetorical devices; and ample in figures of speech. Grebner kept a clever and saucy tongue in his cheek and wagged it often in irony, saying one thing to mean and emphasize the opposite. Thus, hardships are "amenities"; soldiers, "we, in our innocence," set fires and wondered how they started; and scanty, repulsive food is "munificent, delectable fare." By adopting the point of view of the enlisted man, Grebner could inject ironic sarcasm with cuts at "our lordly officers." Yet modernity is the outstanding syntactical feature. For the most part calm, simple, economical, direct, and factual, neither romantic nor baroque, therefore unlike other regimental histories, Grebner's style approximates the trim alertness and streamlined sparkle of Lincoln's letters and speeches and the functional lucidity of U. S. Grant's dispatches and memoirs. As The Ninth fought, so Grebner wrote: with *style.*

5

I have tried to turn Grebner's excellent German into representative and readable English. What with the merit of the original, a literal translation would be ideal. Therefore my goal has been a rendition of ideas, and the delivery of all information, in English faithful in meaning and loyal in energy, precision, and grace. Nothing has been omitted, and the translation is as verbatim as I could make it. But *verbatim et literatim,* the Latin paragon of word for word and letter for letter, has been typically elusive here. "A translator does not photograph an original text, he re-creates it through art," obeying the "unwritten law" to "translate not the word itself, but the sense and the style."[21] Thus the title of Grebner's book would literally be "*The Niners*"—unacceptable English, which I have changed perforce. Therefore, as translator and as editor, I have departed from the word when so doing has served sense and style. At the rare points where sense and style collided in English, I chose sense; for, however notable the style, it should be but an aid to sense here, where information through language ought to precede language for its own sake. All in all the integrity of the text has not been merely preserved, it has been enhanced in the edited translation; and readability has not been simply retained, it has been improved.

Syntactical changes accordingly signify, not inadequate or incorrect German, but the remolding of Germanic traits into English, and the remodeling of the one language's rhythms into those of the other. Words imported as transitions, or to round the rhythm, or to complete meanings, or that otherwise exceed translator's license have been bracketed [thus]. Short poems and brief quotations of verse, which do not contain essential information, have been translated to retain their flavor and therefore to impart their intended touch. Long poems, on the other hand, have been put into "semiprose" to avoid distorting their essential information.

Editorial changes include rearrangement of the book, occasional shifts in sentence sequence, and infrequent alteration of paragraph length and position. The book has been resolved into three parts. For proper emphasis in the right places, chapters now respect both chronology and logic. Notes indicate each chapter's location in the original. A few documents and some lists have been moved from the text into notes.

English words and phrases in the original have been kept in the translation, even when not *le mot juste.* Often they have been enclosed in quotation marks. These words and phrases appear in a list infra. Misspellings and old spellings of names of towns and other geographical features have been corrected or updated. Supplemental topics have been provided to the lists at the heads of chapters and enclosed [thus]. Since Grebner's statistics (chiefly of casualties) either coincide with or deviate insignificantly from the standard sources, they have been let stand without comment.[22]

6

This book is best read in parallel with the histories of the heavily German units that served on friendly terms beside The Ninth through most of The Ninth's enlistment: Frederick W. Keil's of the 35th Ohio and Judson W. Bishop's of the 2nd Minnesota. To these should be added Henry M. Cist's on the Army of the Cumberland.[23]

7

I didn't, I couldn't, produce this book on my own. Kind, congenial, intelligent, generous, considerate, thoughtful people helped—more than they might guess. Thanks therefore

• To Joe Zucca and staff at Inter-Library Loan, Temple University Libraries. Had they not served me well, I might now be hunting something somehow somewhere between Point Lobos and Cape Cod.

• To Don Heinrich Tolzmann of the German-Americana Collection, University of Cincinnati Libraries. He answered questions soon and right.

• To Gary J. Arnold, assistant archivist, Ohio Historical Society. He supplied basic and essential information abundantly.

• To Elizabeth Delano Whiteman. She is my best reader, an author's dream.

• To Maxwell Whiteman. His energy, scholarship, and passion for learning remain an inspiration.

• To Beth Trautmann. She knows, she understands, always.

I also acknowledge with gratitude the research leave granted by Temple University for the academic year 1984–1985.

8

If clarity, fidelity, and readability have been realized together with enough of Grebner's excellence, this edited translation bids fair to achieve in English the purposes laid down by the editorial committee three-fourths of a century ago in German.

> To commemorate the dead,
> To inspire the living,
> To enrich posterity, and
> To foster the highest ideals.

Here, then, in English at last, is the story of Ohio's "bloody Dutch."

F. T.

Glenside, Pennsylvania
Winter Solstice, 1985

Chronology

1860 (November 6)—1861 (April 11): Abraham Lincoln is elected President; seven Southern states secede; the Confederate States of America adopt their constitution; Jefferson Davis becomes president of the Confederacy; his incipient nation continues to organize, seizes Federal installations, and prepares for hostilities; and Lincoln says in his Inaugural Address, "In *your* hands, my dissatisfied fellow countrymen, and not in *mine,* is the momentous issue of civil war."

1861. April—12: Confederate artillery bombards the Union garrison, Fort Sumter, at Charleston, South Carolina.—14: The fort surrenders.—15: Lincoln, calling for volunteers, requests 75,000 militia from the loyal states.—17: Virginia secedes.—18: Union military action to secure West Virginia begins; McClellan moves to West Virginia the first Ohio troops, later to include the Ninth Ohio Infantry.—22: The Ninth, mobilized and eager for action, takes the ninety-day oath informally in Turner Hall, Cincinnati.—24: The Ninth leaves for Camp Harrison, Ohio, where it will be formally sworn-in for ninety days.

May—6: Arkansas and Tennessee secede.—18: The Ninth leaves Camp Harrison for Camp Dennison, Ohio.—20: North Carolina secedes.—27: The Ninth takes the three-year oath at Camp Dennison.

June—16: The Ninth, ordered to West Virginia in the strategy to save West Virginia for the Union and protect Ohio and Pennsylvania, leaves Camp Dennison for Camp Putnam near Marietta, Ohio.—19: The Ninth is ordered to Parkersburg, West Virginia.

July—11: The Ninth takes part in the Battle of Rich Mountain, West Virginia.—21: The Battle of Bull Run (Manassas), Virginia.

August 10: Brigadier-General Franz Sigel and his German troops are defeated at Wilson's Creek, Missouri.

September 10: The Ninth takes part in the Battle of Carnifex Ferry, West Virginia.

November—1: Major-General McClellan, an Ohioan commanding the Department of West Virginia, succeeds Lieutenant-General Winfield Scott as General-in-Chief, Union forces.—26: West Virginia secure, Union strategy shifts to the Mississippi valley and the middle border, and The Ninth leaves West Virginia for Kentucky.

December 8: The Ninth enters Kentucky.

1862. January—15: Edwin M. Stanton is confirmed as Secretary of War (Union).—19: The Ninth distinguishes itself with a bayonet charge in the Battle of Mill Springs (Logan's Cross Roads), Kentucky.

February—6: Fort Henry, Tennessee, falls to the Union.—16: Fort Donelson, Tennessee, falls to the Union.

March—2: The Ninth arrives in Nashville, Tennessee.—7: The Battle of Pea Ridge, Arkansas.

April—6 and 7: The Battle of Shiloh (Pittsburgh Landing), Tennessee.—8: The Ninth, joining operations of the Department of the Mississippi, arrives belatedly at the scene of battle, Shiloh. General Henry W. Halleck takes field command of the Department of the Mississippi.

May 30: Confederates evacuate Corinth after a month's siege.

June—6: The Battle of Memphis, Tennessee, a Union victory.—

23: The Ninth leaves Corinth for Iuka, Mississippi, and Tuscumbia, Alabama.

August—5: The Ninth's Colonel McCook is ambushed near Athens, Alabama.—6: He dies.—7: The Ninth, after taking revenge, returns to Tennessee.—9: The Battle of Cedar Mountain, Virginia.—28: Union and Confederate Tennessee/Kentucky campaigns begin.—29 and 30: The Second Battle of Bull Run (Manassas).

September—16: The Ninth returns to Kentucky from Tennessee.—17: The Battle of Antietam (Sharpsburg), Maryland.—19: The Battle of Iuka, Mississippi.—22: The preliminary Emancipation Proclamation is announced.

October—3 and 4: The Battle of Corinth.—8: The Ninth takes part in the Battle of Perryville (Chaplin Hills), Kentucky.—24: William S. Rosecrans replaces Don Carlos Buell in the Tennessee/Kentucky command and heads the new Department of the Cumberland, in whose army The Ninth will remain for the rest of its enlistment.

November (early): The Ninth returns to Tennessee from Kentucky.—5: Burnside replaces McClellan as commander of the Army of the Potomac.

December—13: The Battle of Fredericksburg, Virginia.—31: The Battle of Murfreesboro (Stone's River), Tennessee.

1863. January 1: The Emancipation Proclamation is issued.

March 3—: The Enrollment or Conscription Act obligates to military service nearly all men of age 20 to 45.—10: Lincoln proclaims amnesty for soldiers absent without leave who report by April 1.

July—4: Vicksburg surrenders to Union forces.—8: Port Hudson falls to the Union, and the Union controls the Mississippi River.

August—16: The Ninth leaves Winchester, Tennessee, on the Chickamauga campaign.

September—9: Bragg's Confederates evacuate Chattanooga, Tennessee.—22: The Battle of Chickamauga ends on its fourth day, and until November 6, Bragg besieges Chattanooga, where Union forces (including The Ninth) have withdrawn after hard knocks.

October 13: The Ninth, which despises the Copperhead Vallandigham, votes for his opponent, John Brough, a War Democrat on the Republican (Union) ticket. Brough wins the Ohio gubernatorial election.

November: The Ninth fights in the three-part Battle of Chattanooga: Orchard Knob (23), Lookout Mountain (24), and Missionary Ridge (25).

December 6: The siege of Knoxville, Kentucky, ends when Sherman relieves Burnside.

1864. February—22: Union strategy commences to strike southeast and plunge a torch into Confederate vitals, and The Ninth begins to move toward Atlanta.—24: The Ninth engages Confederates near Tunnel Hill, Georgia; and such skirmishes continue into May.

March 10: Grant assumes command of the armies of the United States.

May—2: Sherman's Atlanta campaign begins.—5 and 6: The Battle of the Wilderness, Virginia.—7: The Ninth is among the Union forces that test from now until the 10th the strength of the enemy at Buzzard's Roost and Rocky Face Ridge, Georgia.—19: The series of battles known as Spotsylvania end in Virginia.—20: The Ninth leaves Sherman's army at the Etowah River and sets off for Cincinnati, to be mustered out.—27: The Ninth arrives—home to stay—in Cincinnati.

September 2: Sherman's troops enter Atlanta.

November—8: Lincoln is reelected.—9: Sherman's march to the sea begins.

1865. February 17 and 18: Charleston, South Carolina, evacuated, surrenders.

March 4: Lincoln delivers his Second Inaugural Address.

April 9: Lee surrenders the Army of Northern Virginia, to Grant, at Appomatox.

1870. January 14: Veterans of The Ninth found their regimental association, in Cincinnati.

1877. August 23: The monument to Colonel McCook is unveiled in Cincinnati's Washington Park.

1878. January 19: Veterans of The Ninth visit the battlefield at Mill Springs, Kentucky.

1895. September 18: The Ninth attends the dedication of the Chickamauga and Chattanooga National Military Park, where there is a monument to The Ninth.

1897. Veterans of The Ninth publish the history of the regiment.

Preface by The Editorial Committee[1]

Two years ago [in 1894] the decision was made and the committee appointed to prepare a history of our regiment. Our comrades of The Ninth Ohio wanted a comprehensive and an authentic account of their share in what happened, and a memorial to what they felt and did, as well as an example and a model to guide future generations. But obstacles blocked and delays hindered even a beginning. At last the way was cleared, and the committee could start its work. Our goal has been to satisfy our comrades as much as possible. Their ideas and opinions, mentioned often in this book, constitute its presuppositions and the principles that guided its composition. Have we met the standards and fulfilled the expectations of everyone, at least approximately? Let the judges be the men who were there and who influenced the events described in the following pages!

To the people who very kindly supplied diaries and other documents, and to those who furnished additional information orally and in writing—thanks for your help!

Let the book be received with favor and evaluated with forbearance. May it achieve its purposes—

To commemorate the dead,
To inspire the living,
To enrich posterity, and
To foster the highest ideals—

as long as we and our children and our children's children believe in patriotism and manly dignity, and in freedom and justice.

And, in praise of a job well done, a richly deserved thanks to the author of this book:

Constantin Grebner

It is a book of history, based in part on faulty documents and contradictory accounts, "official" and private. All errors that could be eliminated have been eliminated. Nevertheless it cannot be error-free, of course, any more than it can agree with diverse opinions that remain in vogue. Although the author did not write as a participant or an eyewitness, he has produced the best book possible, at once clear and interesting, and as impartial as it can be.

Surely every reader will therefore agree implicitly with what we have just said, and not put the book down dissatisfied.

The editorial committee for the history of the Ninth Regiment:

C. W. Herman Lübbert
Gustav Bergmann
Friedrich Bertsch

Cincinnati, Ohio, October, 1896, and January 4, 1897

Foreword by Gustav Tafel[1]

[Events Leading Up to the Outbreak of Hostilities.—News of War Arrives in Cincinnati.—McCook Wants a Regiment of Cincinnati Germans.—The Regiment Is Formed in the Turner Society, Begins Training, and Looks Forward to Fighting for the Union.]

"Our century produced one grand epoch."

The United States, developing rapidly and on a grand scale, had become the marvel of the modern world. Yet the North and the South had long been antagonistic. Clearer and clearer, and more and more precisely, the issue came into focus: slavery.[2]

In 1856, Fremont represented the new [antislavery, Republican] party and, after an exciting campaign, lost [the presidency] by only a few votes. In 1860, Lincoln [a Republican], America's second Washington, was elected. Winter months passed, tensions increased, and the year was 1861. As long as Buchanan remained President, however, open hostility by the South was out of the question, because the Southern vote had been decisive in putting him into the White House.

Despite plots to the contrary, Lincoln took office. Stephen Douglas, pugnacious representative of the northern Democrats, was at Lincoln's side during the inaugural address [signaling to the South that it could fear anti-Southern unity in the North]. Lincoln, speaking to the Southern states, denied their right to secede. Earnestly he told them that if they left the Union, they would be responsible for the consequences.

But the South was not to be stopped, the situation worsened, and the first shots rang out on that memorable April 12, 1861, when Southerners bombarded Fort Sumter and its Federal garrison. Late Sunday evening [April 14], newspaper extras spread the word of Lincoln's call for 75,000 volunteers [including thirteen regiments from Ohio, the third-largest state levy]. War was certain.

Our story, how Ohio's first German regiment originated, would be incomplete without this brief historical sketch of the American political situation at that time, and a glance at the relationship of Cincinnati's Germans to that situation. In Cincinnati the news [of war] caused an uproar beyond description.[3] The focus of German social life there, Turner Hall on Walnut Street, hummed like a beehive.[4] Now, the German people in America had always and fervently opposed the slaveholding party—an idealistic predisposition true especially of the new German immigration after 1848. Accordingly [in answer to Lincoln's call for volunteers], the head [and founder] of the Turner Society, Gustav Tafel, immediately proposed enlistment. Quickly the roll filled with signatures of men eager to join the fight against the slavocracy.

In those days the opinion still prevailed [from the time of the Mexican War] that the best [way to mobilize] was to organize companies of volunteers as fast as possible [in the states]. Companies in turn were to join [state] regiments, which would take shape equally fast. Only in that way would delay be minimal and troops reach the field speedily and confront the enemy forthwith. As to an *all-German* regiment, Robert Latimer McCook thought of it first.[5] He alone deserves the credit for the idea.

An American attorney in the prime of life, he had been in partnership for several years in a [Cincinnati] law firm with Johann Bernhard Stallo, a German.[6] True, McCook was not identified with the Republicans, the party born of antislavery agitation. But he did belong to the northern Democrats. Led by Stephen Douglas, they had turned vigorously against the southern Democrats, over the abomination of slavery, when the southern Democrats announced they would rather wreck the Union than allow slavery to be infringed or even questioned.

McCook traveled in Europe in the summer of 1860. This energetic and sensible American [keen on learning about armies] had chosen to study Europe's firsthand—French, Austrian, Italian, and Prussian. He liked Prussia's and returned to America enthusiastic about the Prussians. His inborn understanding of such matters thus proved brilliant. For, while Americans notoriously fancied everything French—indeed, favored anything non-German—he bluntly declared he preferred the Prussian military system.

On April 15 [1861], by accident, he met Tafel. They spoke of the salient topic.

McCook: "The men who voted for Lincoln [the Germans] should now back him and fight!"

Tafel: "They are ready to fight!"

McCook broached his idea for a German regiment. He would sacrifice everything to realize it, he said, and closed with "I know the Germans will fight! Our American boys of course mean well enough, but they don't know how."[7]

On Tuesday, April 16, Tafel circulated a call to a mass meeting on Wednesday, April 17. "In order to take the necessary first steps toward forming a separate all-German regiment, we the undersigned, adopted citizens of Cincinnati, herewith announce a meeting for 8:00 P.M. in Turner Hall. Herr Stallo and several other gentlemen will speak. Especially invited are [German] commissioned officers, as well as enlisted men of all-German companies: come one, come all, to show how necessary and important it is to create a separate regiment under German command."[8]

The hall was jammed, Tafel served as secretary, and Medard Fels presided.[9]

Stallo the attorney expressed eloquently the sense of the meeting: "Although the blessings of our free institutions have been enjoyed longer by native-born than by adopted citizens, the adopted shall rise all in a body, united to defend the Union and protect the Star-Spangled Banner. The Tree of Liberty wilts unless watered from time to time with blood."

A committee of twenty was assigned to solicit funds to defray the [regiment's] initial expenses.[10] Recruiting stations were designated: Turner Hall, J. Zeltner's Tavern, Lafayette Hall, the Mohawk Firehouse, Weyand's Brewery, Flattich's Hall, the Courthouse Exchange, and Schiller's [Beer] Garden.

Everybody involved in this early agitation had thought all along that of course General August Moor, a German veteran of the Mexican War, a proven soldier, should take command of the new regiment. Moor, however, seemed unexpectedly to doubt that the regiment could even be formed; he had seen such attempts fail during the Mexican War. But he had promised to attend the meeting.

Stallo's fervid speech produced a tumult. Immediately the cry resounded from every side: "Moor! Moor!" The admired veteran and tested warrior came forward and without seriously opposing the project, expressed his view that it could not succeed. A German regiment was impossible: any effort to form one would fail unless instantly successful. In other words, he concluded, "If a thousand men have not signed up by tomorrow evening, the regiment is an idle dream!"

Tafel took the platform and brought before the assembly the name of McCook. Tafel praised McCook's energy. Furthermore, Tafel declared, McCook had connections in Washington and Columbus; he could most quickly organize a regiment and offer its services to the state.

By popular demand, McCook rose and in burning words set forth why he believed in an all-German regiment. Once again he was stating his case in his distinctive and often bold style.[11]

A commissary was needed to direct the mobilization. Tafel proposed McCook. A committee, named at the beginning [of the meeting] and headed by F. J. Werner, concurred. Finally the assembly approved McCook unanimously, dignifying Tafel's proposal as the opinion of everyone present.

That very evening, Cincinnati's patriotic [German] men and boys crowded around the Turners' sign-up sheets. All the next day, men eager for war thronged the recruiting stations [and 200 were quickly enlisted]. Soon the rolls were full beyond the maximum [of 98 men per company, and still many were turned away]. By evening on the 18th of April, Ohio's first German regiment was an accomplished fact.

Tafel telegraphed the Turners' old instructor, Karl Joseph, and he returned from Indianapolis and at once took charge of the [regiment's] first company, which [like the second, third, and fourth] was composed of Turners. From Evansville, Indiana, came August Willich, well known as an ex-Prussian officer who had later led volunteers [in the German Revolution of 1848] in Baden and the Palatinate. He went to Workmen's Hall [in Cincinnati] and in almost no time organized four companies of Germans. Then the Jaegers [a militia unit of sharpshooters] and the Lafayette Militia, commanded by Herr [Georg] Sommer and Herr [Frank] Link [respectively], all good Germans and true, were added [as companies], to round out the ten needed for a regiment.

Thus, from the start of the mobilization of The Ninth, experienced and capable men could be entrusted with heading and training the companies. Indeed, if at the beginning of the war the South boasted more officers schooled at West Point, the North enjoyed a countervailing advantage. Among its people was a force trained in the armies of Germany: many former commissioned and noncommissioned officers, not to mention the numerous erstwhile common soldiers. Accordingly, German veterans soon became captains in The Ninth and led the companies into the field.[12]

Training began at once and in earnest. The outdoor gymnasium behind Turner Hall on Walnut Street, though spacious, soon proved too small. So we trooped to the "orphanage lot" [the Orphan Asylum lot, the city's parade ground] at Fourteenth and Elm. The majestic Music Hall is there now. At that time, however, the sounds were military, as the 5th, 6th, and 10th [Regiments] joined us; and commands crackled in German and English from morning till night. We drilled, marched, and became soldiers with a vengeance.

On Friday, April 19, the Turners from Hamilton in Butler County [Ohio] arrived, led by [Wilhelm C.] Margedant [who would become a company commander].[13] They were integrated into the second company [Company B], because Turners from Newport and Covington, Kentucky, had already been attached to the first.

The regiment's initial parade at full strength took place on Sunday, April 21.[14] Directed by McCook, and following the Turners' band, it marched along several streets and created a sensation. A number of regular-army officers, watching from the Post Office, judged the regiment's appearance and bearing to be excellent.

On Tuesday, April 23, officers of the companies elected officers of the regiment. As expected, four companies [the ones Willich had organized] wanted Willich for colonel [and commanding officer], while the first five and the tenth favored McCook. Willich would then have become lieutenant-colonel by unanimous vote but chose to be adjutant instead. (He mistakenly thought that in America the adjutant was the commander de facto of a regiment.) Unfortunately, another man had all along been the one for adjutant: Tafel. Yet, without a doubt, had Willich not had his way, he would have left the regiment and taken his four companies with him.

Hesitating not a moment, Tafel [therefore] withdrew in favor of Willich. The positions of lieutenant-colonel and major went respectively to a former Prussian officer, Karl Sondershoff, and the captain of the fifth company [Company E], Frank Link. All discord [over leadership] was forestalled when Willich proposed and the regiment agreed to make the vote for McCook unanimous.

The Ninth Ohio, the Union's first all-German regiment in the West, [had been informally sworn in on April 21 and] was mobilized for a three-month tour and ready to fight for The Good Cause. How well was the promise kept? The following pages tell the story.

Cincinnati, October, 1896

I

The Men and the Struggle

1

Our Leaders and Comrades-in-Arms[1]

Robert Latimer McCook.—August Willich.—Gustav Kämmerling.—Karl Joseph.—Raimund Herrmann.—Martin Brunner.—Joseph Gräff.—Anton Kurtzleb.—George H. Thomas.—William S. Rosecrans.—The Iron Brigade: The 2nd Minnesota, 35th Ohio, 87th Indiana, 105th Ohio, 75th Indiana, and 101st Indiana.—The 28th Ohio.—Willich's 32nd Indiana.—The "Fighting McCooks."

"And there comes a time
When one man finds himself
A mainstay to the many—
He stands like a stone wall
And behind him they can serry the ranks
And feel secure."

Robert Latimer McCook
(Portrait: Frontispiece, center)

Our revered colonel (shamefully snatched too soon from us!) first saw the light of day in New Lisbon, Ohio, on December 28, 1827, the fourth son of Daniel McCook. Daniel had left his native Pennsylvania in 1826, to settle in Ohio and begin the older branch of Ohio's Scotch-Irish McCooks.[2] Robert studied law in Steubenville, in the firm of Stanton & McCook: [Edwin M.] Stanton (later the famous secretary of war) and Robert's older brother [Alexander McDowell] McCook (later a major-general). Robert then moved to Cincinnati; became a partner to Judge J[ohann] B[ernhard] Stallo, the German attorney; shared a lucrative practice; and thus grew to know the city's other prominent Germans.

In 1860 he visited the major countries of Europe, studying especially their armies and military systems. He concluded—and returned home to proclaim without reservation—that the Prussian army was Europe's best and the closest to his ideal.

Hostilities began between the North and the South [on April 12, 1861]. A day later, people in Cincinnati spoke of the immediate formation of an all-German regiment. McCook was one of its most eloquent supporters. Inside of two days the plan for the regiment had been brilliantly formulated. By the evening of the 22nd—that promptly—1,000 men were provisionally enlisted. Initially, McCook was elected commissary; and a few days afterward, colonel.[3] With his great energy and grand spirit, and aided by experienced drillmasters, he created an exceptionally good unit in the shortest possible time.[4] Soon, Cincinnati's first German regiment, later called the "Ninth Ohio Volunteer Infantry," *his* regiment, was held up to all others as the model.

Scarcely had he brought the regiment to the West Virginia theater than he was entrusted with a brigade, which he commanded to the end of that campaign. Because of the *way* he commanded the brigade, The Ninth congratulated themselves on having elected him their leader, the only Anglo-American among more than 1,000 Germans.

He never stopped loving and caring for his regiment.[5] In a notable act of kindness, when his men were en route from West Virginia to the new seat of operations in Kentucky, he arranged a three-day layover in Cincinnati; and an earnest wish on the part of his men and their families and friends was fulfilled. They had wanted to see each other one more time, perhaps the last. Furthermore, on the march, and bivouacked, and in camp, he would make the frequently tough situations easier, and the extreme hardships more bearable for his men, by interpreting and obeying orders as humanely as possible. He never hesitated to have serious words with his superiors, in the interests of the health and battle-readiness of his troops. He would and often did ignore something if he could thus improve the fitness of his men and thereby do them a good turn without harming The Cause.

In the Battle of Mill Springs, while his brigade and especially his regiment were earning glory, he was wounded but did not leave the field until victory was ensured. And he returned before his wound healed, though he could not yet mount a horse. Promotion to general and the command of a division were to be payment for his outstanding service. Quietly he accepted the promotion, but in name only, for he highmindedly rejected the command [though he later led the brigade in which The Ninth was one regiment]. He did not want to leave his Germans; he wanted to return with them to Cincinnati when the war was over.

In Chapter 3 [i.e., 7] we have told at length how this exceptional man, this brave yet circumspect warrior, met his end: cowardly murdered near New Market, Madison County, Alabama, on August 6, 1862. We have described, too, the sorrow of his regiment and his brigade, and their revenge. The entire country cursed the foul act and mourned him. His body was brought to Cincinnati and buried in Spring Grove Cemetery.[6] In August, 1877, the survivors of his regiment and his dear friends raised a monument to his memory in Cincinnati's Washington Park.

To know him was to respect him: a soldier who always did his duty; a leader whose men would have followed him to the ends of the earth; honest, straightforward, and without ostentation; tireless; easily aroused and easily calmed; brave to the point of being foolhardy; and yet cautious and calculating. He was "an officer and a gentleman" in the best sense of that phrase. On behalf of his men he exposed himself to fire in battle whenever he could benefit them. In return (as he once said) he expected them to go with him and for him "to Hell itself."

When the final note of "Taps" sounds over the grave of The Ninth's last veteran, personal memory of this venerated man [McCook] will be dead, too. But his name shall endure as long as the Civil War has a place in the history of our nation.

August Willich
(Portrait: Frontispiece, lower left)

August Willich was born in Gorzyn, Posen [East Prussia], in 1810.[7] At the age of eighteen he was already a second lieutenant of Prussian artillery. In 1846, when stationed as a captain in Wesel on the Rhine (but inspired by that era's ideas of freedom), he requested and received his discharge. He learned the carpenter's trade, took part in the social-democratic movement in the Rhine provinces, and consequently fell out with his family, every last member. In 1848, having joined Hecker in Baden, he commanded a free corps at Kandern in April and, soon after, at Hüningen.[8] Then he lived in Besançon, France, until the spring of 1849, a fugitive among [other fugitive] German Social-Democrats. They were largely of the working class, tolerated and [even] supported by the French government. When rebellion broke out in the Palatinate, he and his "men of Besançon" went there. He took charge of a free corps of students, turners, craftsmen, and former [government] soldiers. When the Palatine uprising failed, he led them to Baden, where they fought in most of the engagements. When the Revolution ended [everywhere in Germany], he brought his corps to Switzerland.

From there he went to London and immediately became prominent in the radical wing of the "Red International."[9] They sent him to America in 1853, to prepare an invasion of Germany. But, calming down quickly after crossing the Atlantic, he picked up his hammer again without a second thought, and worked as a ship's carpenter in the Brooklyn Navy Yard. Soon he accepted a job with the Coast Survey; in Washington he made the acquaintance of Cincinnati's Judge Stallo; and at Stallo's request he moved to Cincinnati. In 1858 he became editor of the workers' newspaper there, *Der Deutsche Republikaner*.

When the Civil War began, he was among the earliest to enlist in the "first German regiment."[10] He aspired to be its colonel but lost to the lawyer Robert L. McCook. Willich was adjutant and then major. Largely because of the way he drilled and trained it, The Ninth grew into one of the Union's best. In West Virginia with The Ninth in the fall of 1861, he answered a call by the governor of Indiana [Oliver P. Morton] to raise a German regiment of Indiana volunteers. He, as its colonel, led his 32nd Indiana to Kentucky to join the Army of the Ohio. He distinguished himself wherever he served: Munfordsville, Shiloh, Murfreesboro (a prisoner there), Liberty Gap, Chickamauga, and Missionary Ridge. At Chickamauga, as a brigadier-general, he headed [a brigade] in [Richard W.] Johnson's 2nd Division XX Corps. At Resaca on May 15, 1864, he took a bullet in the right shoulder. Unfit for service in the field, he commanded the District of Cincinnati for a while, then followed his corps, the IVth, to Texas and served there until October of 1865. He then left the army; rank: major-general.

In 1866 he was elected auditor of Hamilton County, Ohio, and remained in the post until 1869. When the Franco-Prussian War started, he hurried to Berlin and offered his services to the king of Prussia. The king thanked him but declined the offer. Willich spent some time in Berlin, attended lectures on philosophy at the university, and made up with his older brother, a Prussian officer and commandant at the garrison at Erfurt. Willich then returned to America and at the urging of his friend and former adjutant Karl Hipp, he settled in St. Mary's, Ohio. There he enjoyed his declining years in peaceful comfort, devoting himself to study, good works, and keeping company with children. He considered all the children of the town "his children" and they loved him. His busy life ended in a stroke on January 23, 1878. The size of the funeral procession, 2,500 people, proved his popularity in his last home. Many of "his children" followed the procession for their "papa."

He was an original, unique in many respects, often eccentric, easily aroused and as easily calmed. Always fair, he demanded and expected the same undeviating fairness from others. We of The Ninth were grandly favored to enjoy his services when we were getting started, for he did much to help us. He was able to do it, and to do even greater things earlier and later, because of his motto, which he lived up to and liked to expound. "I am a *man* because I finish what I start, and throw heart and soul into my endeavors."

Gustav Kämmerling
(Portrait: Frontispiece, upper right)

An exceptional individual led The Ninth to battle at Mill Springs, Chickamauga, and Missionary Ridge. The Ninth was generally recognized as one of the Union's finest; and according to the official word of a competent authority, General [George H.] Thomas, the personality and discretion of this individual were notably responsible for helping The Ninth achieve that distinction.

Gustav Kämmerling was born on December 9, 1819, in Mülheim on the Prussian Rhine. His own notes say he first entered public life in 1848 when his fellow-citizens elected him commandant of the municipal militia. But the revolution was unexpectedly and speedily suppressed; a powerful reaction set in; and he and many others had to flee. He joined Willich's free corps in the Palatinate. At the end of the uprising there, he went with the corps to Baden [where the uprising continued]. He fought in the people's army to the end [of the revolution in Germany], seeking refuge at last with others [like himself] in Switzerland.

Forbidden to return home, he emigrated to America in 1850. He arrived in Cincinnati in 1852 (after nearly two years in Pennsylvania), found a suitable position with a meat-packing firm, and worked there until he joined The Ninth in April of 1861. He was immediately chosen captain of Company F, promptly promoted to major on November 1, then lieutenant-colonel on March 8, 1862, and then colonel of the regiment, August 6. Because he and his troops received such favorable mention in the reports by his immediate superiors after the battles of Mill Springs, Chickamauga, and Missionary Ridge, he was named brigadier-general in January, 1864.[11] He declined [to command a brigade], however, and stayed with his regiment to the end [of its enlistment] and led it home [to Cincinnati].

He has since moved to Tell City, Indiana, where he lives in the bosom of his family, a respected old soldier, hale and hearty in his late seventies.

During the war he was always serious; indeed so grave as to be taciturn. Ever "on" and awaiting orders from superiors, he required the same conscientiousness and unqualified obedience from subordinates. He did not achieve popularity among his men, in the usual sense of that word. But they entertained the greatest respect for him and maintained unshakable faith in his leadership. For nobody exceeded him in cold-blooded resolve and an opportunely ferocious courage. A born soldier, he was a model of all soldierly virtues, with acute vision and a phenomenal ability to choose the right action in every situation and to make quick decisions. These qualities outweighed his lack of formal military training, and ensured him always the greatest admiration from superiors. Thomas, the master soldier, held him in great esteem.

Kämmerling [with the rest of The Ninth] abandoned military rank and trappings on the road to Atlanta, and his martial severity and reserve along with them. Thus, since his return and ours to civilian life, we have enjoyed the other side of his character, which is affable, talkative, and charming. As we revered him earlier as a soldier and leader, so we love and respect him now as a man, a citizen, and a friend.

Karl Joseph

Karl Joseph was born in 1833 in Kösterbeek near Rostock in Mecklenburg-Schwerin. The son of a farmer, he learned farming; but at the tender age of eighteen he volunteered for the Jäger battalion of Schwerin and soon proved to be an outstanding member, especially in physical training. He was a military instructor in gymnastics, swordsmanship, and swimming, in Schwerin and Rostock, until 1856, when he took his discharge and returned briefly to farming.

In 1857 he emigrated to the United States. He stopped briefly in the East, then came to Cincinnati and learned cigar-making. Meanwhile he was an avid Turner, there and in Indianapolis, whither he moved in 1860. At first word of the outbreak of hostilities, he helped organize a company of Turners for the Zouave regiment. He hurried next to Cincinnati as soon as he heard of the inception of the German regiment there, joined it, and at the first election of officers, was chosen captain of Company A. In November of that year [1861] he advanced to major and led part of The Ninth's left. Wounded, and the wound not fully healed, he did not rejoin the regiment until it was at Pittsburgh Landing [Tennessee]. In November, 1862, he became lieutenant-colonel. When the colonel [Kämmerling] was ill, Joseph commanded the regiment on the march to Louisville and in the Battle of Perryville; and his leadership satisfied everyone. Later his wound reopened. Unfit for service, he left us in May of 1863. We lost a capable officer.

He settled in Cincinnati and, until about ten years ago, ran several businesses and held local public office. Then he went into insurance and remains active in that line. He is an esteemed citizen now, and still admired by old comrades. He likes to look back with satisfaction on his honorable military career and distinguished wartime service.

Raimund Herrmann
(Portrait, page 89)

An outstanding, a distinguished personality in our regiment: Raimund Herrmann. Birthplace: Dresden [Germany]. Although of a family of scholars, he served in the Saxon, Russian, and French armies, seeing duty with the French Foreign Legion in Africa. He was in Cincinnati when the Civil War broke out. He joined The Ninth immediately, one of the first to enlist in it, and was elected sergeant-major. In September, 1862, he advanced to second lieutenant of Company D. At Chickamauga on September 19, 1863, during the bayonet-assault and the recapture of Burnham's Battery, a cannonball struck Lieutenant Herrmann full in the chest and he died a hero's death.

He was a soldier from head to foot, almost painfully strict and exacting with subordinates (but no less with himself), superior in endurance to everyone in the regiment and acknowledged as the best man on foot in the brigade (despite his fifty years), often scorned and laughed at, but generally respected if not exactly loved, mourned after death, and only then truly appreciated. His comrades called him the Grand Crusader. Though handsome neither of face nor form, he exemplified the true soldier, and seemed to embody the soldierly ideal, especially in combat. Therefore, if we are to name our best men, he must be named. He made a place for himself in The Ninth, and he was a leader.

Martin Bruner

This machinist's son, born in Cincinnati, received an excellent education and was with Egly's law firm when the war started. Though very young, he was immediately elected second lieutenant of Company F, then promoted to first in September, 1862. Colonel McCook treasured him for his virtues—he was capable, bright, reliable, versatile, and good natured—and McCook assigned him a variety of tasks, which he accomplished though many were hard. He was the brigade's "acting quartermaster" several times, and "acting commissary," and leader of escorts, and other things. He proved to be especially talented at drumming up and bringing in supplies. He fought bravely at Chickamauga, was wounded on September 20 [1863], recovered, and mustered out with the regiment in June of 1864.

After the war he returned to the law in Cincinnati and went into politics. He developed consumption in a few years, however, and the malady ended his life prematurely. As a boy he had been a Young Turner, a pupil of Friedrich Bertsch's (Bertsch was then a Turner instructor), and equally distinguished in physical and intellectual achievement. All his life he was liked and admired for congeniality and lack of prejudice. He hated gloom, obscurity, mystery, and arrogance. The regiment remembers him yet, and the memories are good.

Joseph Gräff

Joseph Gräff was born in Bamberg, Bavaria, and trained to be a merchant. He came to America in the 1850s. At the start of the war he was head bookkeeper at Katzenberger's big clothing store, as well as a member of the Turner Society and the Turner Guards. From the beginning he championed the preservation of the Union and the abolition of slavery; he was one of the fifty who signed up for the army first, that day in Turner Hall [April 17, 1861]. Soon after election as second lieutenant of Company I, he became regimental quartermaster and remained in that post until the mustering out, advancing to first lieutenant and captain meanwhile.

After the war he ran various commercial establishments in Cincinnati but died prematurely—too soon mourned by a widow and three children. He had been a boon companion and a respected businessman, always ready to speak or act on behalf of friends and comrades. Before the war he belonged to the Turners who in 1855 were imprisoned and endured miserable prison food for a week in Covington on the charge of sedition and attempted murder.

The Ninth delighted in having him as quartermaster. Proud of his regiment, he did everything possible to procure it the necessities whenever he could—often a difficult matter in the field, as is well known. Frequently he served also as quartermaster for the garrison, the brigade, and the division under Generals Rosecrans and Thomas. He so satisfied them that they several times offered him the positions permanently, and the rank to go with them. He declined; he wanted to stay with The Ninth. Never shall The Ninth forget him. May his memory be honored!

Anton Kurtzleb

Kurtzleb was young when he came to America from Frankenhausen in Schwarzburg-Rudolstadt and promptly joined the Turners: a Cincinnati Turner and gunsmith and an early volunteer for The Ninth when the war began. He served as a brave and faithful soldier in Company B until the mustering-out. By nature somewhat eccentric, he was nonetheless good-hearted and always ready to risk his life for a comrade. Because he hated slavery with a vengeance, he often thought the Union's prosecution of the war far too lethargic and much too lenient to the Rebels. Thus, being open and forthright and in favor of changes, he often became embroiled in arguments, which he sometimes lost.

Wounded in the arm the first day at Chickamauga, he nevertheless reported for duty at Chattanooga before fully well—despite the admonitions of his company commander: "Recover first and meanwhile let the healthy do the work." Then Colonel Kämmerling appointed him temporarily as regimental bugler. At the colonel's side at the head of The Ninth at Missionary Ridge, he rode in the attack across that mile and a half of open field under a savage Rebel cannonade. His wounded arm had not yet healed, and now a cannonball ripped it off.

Obviously unfit for his old trade after the war, he studied law and became an attorney and a notary in Louisville, Kentucky, where he lives today with a big family. He is still popular in the regiment as a fearless, plucky, and broad-minded comrade.

George Henry Thomas
(Portrait: Frontispiece, lower right)

Thomas remained true to the Union though a Virginian by birth and [before the war] a major in the 2nd U.S. Cavalry, which supplied the Confederacy a number of outstanding leaders. He began his glorious career in that great war as colonel of the 2nd and a brigade-commander in the first Shenandoah campaign. Named general of U.S. Volunteers, he served in one after another of the various armies in the West. He became our "Pap Thomas" as the head of our division at Mill Springs. He commanded the right wing of the Army of the Tennessee at Corinth, and the center of the Army of the Cumberland at Missionary Ridge. He was the "Rock of Chickamauga" who led us in the Atlanta campaign: the man we followed without grumbling, always, wherever he might go. Like an old friend and true, he personally relieved us of picket duty at the Etowah [River] on May 20, 1864, and brought us back to camp, whence we began the march home.

He meant what he said to us on the second anniversary of Mill Springs, January 19, 1864: "It will ever be a joyful memory to have had the good fortune to command the brave men who compose the Ninth Ohio Regiment." We of The Ninth, for our part remain as firmly convinced as always that the honor and the privilege of serving under such a man contributed richly to the achievements on which we so rightfully prided ourselves.

His grandest deeds were the defense of Horseshoe Ridge and the defeat of [General John Bell] Hood at Nashville [December 15–16, 1864]. He was often criticized for an almost bullheaded tenacity and a dogged determination. The history of the war teaches that those feats—indeed, all his renown as a battlefield commander—resulted from those qualities as well as his ability to seize the moment to strike profitably in the right place and with irresistible force. Yet his virtues were usually construed as sluggishness and irresolution, and the case against him would have been considered clinched—only, the results in each instance proved him correct in how he interpreted and implemented in his own way the plans and orders of superiors. He never left any assignment undone. If he often deviated more or less from the prescribed manner, the outcome always vindicated what he did: he won the battle. Few leaders on either side could plume themselves on being as consistently victorious as Thomas. No leader could more rightfully claim to be not only revered but also loved by his troops.

He himself explained this, the supreme achievement a great soldier can attain, in a letter of November 26, 1869, to a meeting in Indianapolis of the Society of the Army of the Cumberland: "It was my hearty desire, from the beginning to the end of the late war, to accept with cheerfulness and do with zeal and honesty, whatever duties devolved upon me. At the same time it was my constant endeavor to impress those who were with me and under my command with a sense of the importance of the services they had undertaken to perform."[12] At the dedication of the Thomas Memorial in Washington on November 19, 1879, General [William Tecumseh] Sherman said: "Nothing can ever shake the name and fame of Thomas."[13] We would add: "Monuments of marble and brass, army orders and Congressional resolutions, noble speeches, yes, but something else honors more this unforgettable man and classic hero; and that honor is the name given him by his men: 'Pap' Thomas."

William Starke Rosecrans
(Portrait: Frontispiece, upper left)

The high-ranking officer we of The Ninth knew best—after Kämmerling, "Pap" Thomas, and "our own" McCook—was another Ohioan: Rosecrans. From Rich Mountain to Gauley Bridge, from Bowling Green [Kentucky] to Chickamauga, and in the armies of West Virginia and the Cumberland, we were his and we always deemed it an honor to serve under such a general. Highly educated and a capable engineer, he was the Union's finest strategist. Many a commander owed victories principally to the wholesale slaughter of America's sons on the battlefield. Rosecrans, innocent of that widespread defect, never won a battle for that reason. Indeed, he was a master at outmaneuvering, he knew how to use terrain, and he did not let his plans and the details of their execution be broadcast months in advance for the enemy easily to foil.[14]

Rosecrans had been the victor at Stones River and Corinth. He had prevailed in the battle to occupy Chattanooga. Yet, to his misfortune (as we quote him in Chapter 6 [i.e., 10]), a powerful enemy opposed him in Washington. The General-in-Chief [Henry W. Halleck] obviously tried to make things hard for him and thus hurt The Good Cause [of the Union]. Still Rosecrans rightfully earned fame as a circumspect officer and battlefield commander; and he deserved his popularity as a humane and an amiable leader. In addition [further to his credit], he emphatically retained those honors despite the disfavor he shared with other generals when he and they did not enjoy the rare good fortune of winning all battles as planned. So he voluntarily ended his military career as early as 1867 and the age of forty-eight.[15]

To us of The Ninth, officers and men, he was always a friend. Therefore we still remember him most kindly.

The Iron Brigade[16]

> "Only when you have risked your life
> Will life indeed be yours."

Nothing binds firmer the ties [of friendship] than dangers mutually shared. Of times spent with a friend, we remember best those moments when the two of us pluckily stared death in the eye. So it was that, to its original regiments, our brigade became more than a mere military unit formed for the duration; we became a true confederation of friendship, whose unwritten statutes endure yet among comrades. The first and foremost is:

> Put me back at the cannon's mouth.
> If another man is to be lost,
> Let me not stand by and watch.

Our brigade, when organized as part of Thomas's 1st Division of the Army of the Ohio, consisted of four infantry regiments: 2nd Minnesota, 35th Ohio, 18th Regulars, and our own. After about a year the Regulars left, and the 87th Indiana joined us. Following the Battle of Chickamauga the 105th Ohio and the 75th and 101st

Indiana were added. Our first brigade-commander was Robert L. McCook, our own colonel. After his death, command passed to James B. Steedman, colonel of the 14th Ohio; and then, following the Battle of Perryville, to Colonel [Ferdinand] Van Derveer of the 35th Ohio. The distinguished and meritorious Van Derveer held the post until forced by illness (during the Atlanta campaign) to yield to Colonel Newell Gleason of the 87th Indiana, who headed the brigade until the end of the war.

We need not recount here the brigade's feats of arms. In the [official] reports of the war, probably few units were praised more often than the "Iron Brigade," as "Pap" Thomas dubbed it after Chickamauga. Let us add only these words from General J[ohn] M[ilton] Brannan's battle-report of September 20, 1863: "This gallant brigade was one of the few, who maintained their organization perfect throughout the hard fought passes of that portion of the field."[17]

The 2nd Minnesota[18]

Originally intended for service in the East after being organized at Fort Snelling [Minnesota], this regiment joined the Army of the Ohio instead, and was integrated into our brigade immediately [at Lebanon, Kentucky, in December 1861].

The Ninth and these Minnesotans remained together [as part of the brigade] for the duration of the [Ninth's] enlistment. It was a fond brotherhood-in-arms, formed and strengthened by joys and sorrows shared—a brotherhood perhaps without parallel [in durability] in that protean war. Each regiment looked out for the other, attending as much to honor as to essential needs. "As if they are part of me" was the mutual watchword.[19] In the early days of January, 1864, our Minnesota comrades took the furlough given them because they reenlisted for another three years. When they left the brigade, they and The Ninth acted as if parting permanently. For who dared say how many of us they would find alive when they returned? But we met again. Honorably and joyfully we received our good comrades [at the end of their furlough]. They in turn saw us off in the same spirit a few months later when we departed for home (nevermore to trade the fireside for the battlefield.)

The 2nd Minnesota was as good as any regiment in the [Union] army—a fact acknowledged sincerely by the often and extravagantly praised Ninth Ohio.

The 35th Ohio[20]

This regiment came from Hamilton, Ohio, to Buell's Army of the Ohio and was at once assigned with us to McCook's brigade. The 35th too [like the 2nd Minnesota] remained with us throughout our three years in the war. In camp, on the march, in battle, they were good and true comrades ever and everywhere: ready for anything, always courageous, and never failing to answer a call in a crisis. Like us, they chose civilian life over another three years in arms; and they left the army before Atlanta, to devote themselves again to peaceful occupations. They brought home a high, an unblemished reputation. Veterans now [in 1897], they still manifest the old friendship for us, and we for them, from the bottoms of our hearts.

The 87th Indiana

This regiment was scarcely two months in existence when it joined us [in the brigade] in September, 1862. The young and naive are always teased as newcomers, and the brigade teased the 87th a little then.[21] But as early as Perryville and in every hazardous hour thereafter—during the days of bloody struggle—these brave Hoosier comrades proved to be intrepid and sterling warriors beside us "old-timers" of 1861. Their record is perfect.

The 105th Ohio and the 75th and 101st Indiana

These fine, courageous regiments did not join the brigade until Chattanooga. They brought good reputations, which they sustained superbly. But their main achievements in our brigade occurred after The Ninth mustered out [so we can say nothing about them here].

The 28th Ohio

This, Cincinnati's second German regiment, was organized in June, 1861, under the veteran of the Mexican War, August Moor, who had originally been expected to command us [Cincinnati's and Ohio's first German regiment]. Ordered to West Virginia in August, the 28th joined us at Sutton on September 4. They, the 47th Ohio, and us, together with Schombeck's Dragoons, composed the 2nd Brigade of Rosecrans's corps. (This was McCook's brigade.) We fought side by side at Carnifex Ferry; and we remained good comrades together until the end of November, when our regiment left Camp Anderson [West Virginia] for another theater of war.

The 28th stayed in West Virginia a long time thereafter, and distinguished itself at every opportunity: Droop Mountain, West Virginia; South Mountain, Maryland; Antietam, Maryland. Early in 1864 the 28th joined the Army of the Shenandoah and fought under [Major-General Franz] Sigel and [Major-General David] Hunter at New Market [Virginia] and Piedmont [Augusta County, Virginia]. The 28th brought back from three glorious bayonet-assaults 1,300 prisoners and 72 holes in regimental colors riddled by bullets and shrapnel.

This handsome and valiant regiment returned to Cincinnati a month behind us, to be welcomed back and mustered out with the highest honors. They are still firmly united [in 1897] and highly respected in their regimental [veterans'] organization; and they remain ever in good comradeship with us of The Ninth.

Willich's 32nd Indiana

"The holy bonds of language unite us."

We never fought shoulder to shoulder with this regiment in the same brigade. But we did serve in the same corps and were intimately linked by common sympathies and one language. Brotherly love therefore demands that we remember Willich's unit here.

The courageous old warrior, [once] our drillmaster and regimental linchpin, formed it in the late summer of 1861. When he left us in August of that year, he intended to bring his future regiment together with us into one brigade and under his leadership. With us as the model, he molded the new unit in the German way, using the German method of drill and the German system of command. But [as for the all-German brigade] the winds of war blew otherwise: "It was not to be."

In the Army of the Cumberland, the two regiments were close enough to visit one another and be boon companions in the friendship of mutual military service. The solidarity owed in part to the common influence of Willich's personality, and in part to the shared feats of arms. We did not separate until the start of the Atlanta campaign. And even then, though we saw the 32nd no more, we never forgot them.

Our regards to the valiant 32nd! Let these words convey our feeling of having been at one with them!

The "Fighting McCooks"

"The feat, the true achievement, is rooted in the soul."

In any book on the Civil War the "Fighting McCooks," a large Ohio family of military distinction, deserves more than brief mention. In a history of The Ninth, the parents and siblings of our esteemed Colonel [Robert] L. McCook must be commemorated in as thorough a discussion as space permits. The older branch, the "tribe of Dan," consisted of Major Daniel McCook (the father) and his nine sons, from seventeen to forty in age when the war began. Merely a glance at the accompanying family portrait will prove them a group of men and youths ideally suited [to the profession of arms]. They provoke automatically a comparison with the distinguished military families of antiquity.

The portrait's caption identifies the ten McCooks.[22] [Let us add that] "Father Daniel," in Washington when the war started, offered his services at once to President Lincoln. This patriarch of McCooks was killed on July 21, 1863, at the age of sixty-six, while fighting the guerrilla-leader [John] Morgan near Cincinnati. [His death occurred] after Brigadier-General Robert L. McCook, our original colonel, had been murdered on August 6, 1862, and Charles Morris McCook, private in the 2nd Ohio, killed on July 21, 1861. Daniel McCook, Jr., also a brigadier-general, died of wounds on July 21, 1864.

"The Fighting McCooks"

Before the war, most of Daniel's sons had been respected in civilian occupations. During the war they distinguished themselves on every battlefield and under all generals in the several campaigns.[23] And three died in honor in battles for the preservation of the Union.

We have mentioned that all these noble McCooks shared antiquity's ideal [of the martial family]. Daniel McCook, Jr., the sixth son, colonel of the 52nd Ohio and brigadier-general in the Army of the Cumberland, best exemplifies the ideal. General W. T. Sherman, his former partner in a law firm in Leavenworth, Kansas, chose him to lead the assault on Kennesaw Mountain [Georgia] during the Atlanta campaign [July 3, 1864]. He disposed his brigade into a front of four waves. Awaiting the order to attack, he recited them a few lines of [Thomas Babington] Macaulay's splendid "Horatius":

> Then spoke brave Horatius,
> The captain of the gate:
> "To every man upon this earth
> Death cometh soon or late;
> And how can man die better,
> Than facing fearful odds

For the ashes of his fathers
And the temples of his gods?"[24]

Then: "Forward!" A few minutes later, McCook fell, mortally wounded. He died July 21, 1864.

The eighth son, Charles Morris McCook, a seventeen year old, refused a lieutenancy in the regulars and served as a private in the 2nd Ohio. Father and son met—the father was then a medical orderly—during the retreat from [the first battle of] Bull Run [July 21, 1861]. When they separated, the son intended to hurry after his regiment, but enemy cavalry surrounded him. He shot their leader and defended himself with the bayonet against the rest. The father, situated where he could see everything, shouted to the son to give up: "You're outnumbered!" The son answered: "Never shall I surrender to a Rebel!" In a minute he was dead.

We know how Dan McCook's fourth son, our colonel, suffered his untimely end. In the picture he stands behind his aged father. [Surviving members of] The Ninth will recognize him at once.

As to the other six brothers, suffice it to say here that—in war and peace, as soldiers and citizens—they did their duty in their inimitable style. Each in his own way distinguished himself. Some still hold respected positions.

The younger branch of the McCooks—Dr. John McCook [1806–1865; army surgeon] of Steubenville, Ohio, and his five sons ("the tribe of John")—served the Union, too. Though spared the horror of death in battle, they dignified the name nonetheless, in various posts and offices, and achieved honors after the war.

Both branches of the McCooks enjoyed priceless good fortune in the influence of amiable and accomplished women—affectionate mothers who cared. Their elevated character and magnificent example molded sons into high-minded men revered by us and all who followed them.

Martha Latimer of Pennsylvania, model wife and venerable mother, seemed pleased to part with husband Daniel, and nine sons, for service to the Union. But what did she really feel, this rare woman who, every year [of the war], with any news of a battle, at each report of another campaign, could expect word of death or mortal injury to a loved one? We think too often of the famous

Colonel Robert L. McCook's mother

matrons of antiquity—to the neglect of the equally great women of our own time [such as Martha Latimer McCook]. For she bore her suffering with heroic sacrifice equal to theirs. Her picture has [therefore] been published together with this discussion.

In August, 1877, she was present at the unveiling of the memorial to her dearly beloved son Robert, colonel of The Ninth. And, at that time, an exceptionally warm relationship formed between her and the veterans of The Ninth. She delighted in their calling her "Mother McCook." Her daughter, also there then, a Mrs. Dowling, gladly accepted the office of "Daughter of the Regiment." Touchingly the mother displayed her love for her departed son. Happily we recall her words: "Whenever you decorate Robert's grave, don't forget that of his mother!"[25]

* * * * *

We should point out, as we end this chapter, that space does not permit our mention of other brave men we chose as leaders and officers. They either died the hero's death on the bloody battlefield or mustered out at Camp Dennison. In any event, few are still alive. But The Ninth honors the living and the dead: soldiers, comrades, champions. Arisen from our midst and named by us to be commanders, they remain in charge, though time and distance have intervened. For

> In battle what price glory
> If the leader is forgotten?

2

North against South[1]

[Causes of the War, Why We Fought, and What Was Achieved.—The South Secedes.—Fort Sumter.—Lincoln and Davis Call for Volunteers.—Bull Run, the Atlantic Blockade, and Other Early Action.—The War in 1862.—The Emancipation Proclamation.—The War in 1863.—The War in 1864.—Lincoln Wins a Second Term.—The War in 1865.—Its Consequences.—Lincoln's Hopes for a Reunited Nation.]

"War has begun, civil war, the uncanniest of all wars."

For many years the North and the South disagreed on principle. In the foreword to our book we saw that the fatal question of slavery turned the disagreement into a national calamity to be neither averted nor forestalled. Let us here suggest briefly, then, how the question could have achieved such all-consuming significance. We will thus learn the reason the disaster of a devastating civil war persisted beyond the predicted three months and dragged out to three *years* and at last to four. Accordingly, in the short discussion that follows, we outline the war's chief events and characterize its leaders and soldiers, the sons of a fatherland fortunately reunited now. It will then be easily understood how 600,000 could be sacrificed on the battlefield, 400,000 crippled and invalided for life, and four billion dollars spent during the fighting and afterward. Sacrificed, maimed, spent—for what? At first to quell a "little fraternal strife," later to prevent the collapse of a nation that had grown so powerful, and finally to punish those who rebelled against the nation's established government.

World history tells of other civil wars, comparably sad, equally unavoidable. How tragic our great one would have been, how vain its result in comparison with them, had nothing but those three aims been fulfilled! Something more was achieved. During its last two years the combatants' eyes fixed on a glorious principle, an idea grander and more humanely pure than any for which mankind has ever fought and suffered, an apotheosis sustained by the pillars of justice and braced by the strong arms of human dignity and illuminated by the crystal light of freedom. Victory's reward was the realization of that goal: the abolition of slavery everywhere in the United States, and the liberation of a race from shackles more disgraceful than any known to the barbarism of centuries past.

Because of that triumph we forget our sorrows [caused by the war], we feel less sharply the pains over friends lost [in the war], and we would be happy if they who follow us and read our book—our children and our children's children—were infused by the same spirit [as inspired us] and filled with the same conviction [as moved us]. Yes, there are comprehensive histories of the war; and from them anybody can easily learn of the war. Plenty of monuments and additional memorials exist to recall the feats of arms. Nor can our purpose be to impose, as uniquely correct, our point of view and our way of thinking, to the exclusion of others, however sure we may be of ours. But we know that a passion burns yet like sacred fire in our breasts, the passion which called us to war, the passion for The Good Cause of freedom and human dignity; and that passion empowers us to speak a word, plainly and sincerely, on that horrific, lamentable war and the men who fought in it.

Now it would be wrong [in a thorough discussion of the war] merely to consider its direct and immediate cause, Negro slavery. For [such an oversimplification] would leave unexplained the unquestionably savage hatred, the rancor that existed in a spacious land with "room for everybody and everything," and the detestation that prompted Northerners and Southerners, not only to slaughter one another in a bloody civil war that grew more vicious as it lengthened, but also to persist until the weaker must surrender unconditionally. Hence the origins of the war are older and more fundamental [than slavery].

Centuries ago the Puritans came to New England, the Dutch to the Hudson, the Swedes to the Delaware, and the Germans to Germantown [Pennsylvania], driven by the desire to retain or acquire personal freedom and the right to their own opinions. English, French, and Spanish aristocrats and adventurers came to Virginia and the South Atlantic and Gulf states for other reasons: gold and empire. The swashbucklers by and large had never eaten their bread in the sweat of their faces in the lands of their birth; and they were not about to work to feed themselves in the New World, either. So (in our view), from the beginning, two distinct people [occupied this country], not firmly united even at the time of the Revolution, but merely associated tenuously by commercial interests and a sketchy national pride that (as was soon proved) must bow to selfish enterprises. Nor did all subscribe to the republican form of government. Our conjectures are confirmed by the history of the land and its people as they developed from Washington's time to the opening shot at Fort Sumter. So we believe without a doubt that a conflict, a violent act of purification, was unavoidable; though perhaps it would not have broken out so soon had Negro slavery never existed here.

Slavery did exist, however, and Northerners were as much to blame [for it] as Southerners. But the North must be credited with recognizing the disgrace and deciding that the United States should not remain the only civilized country where (in the words of the founder of Germantown, noble [Francis Daniel] Pastorius) "one person inflicts bondage upon another."[2] And the South is to be condemned for opposing that high-minded goal and wanting to wreck the Union instead. Right or wrong, each side risked everything to put across its beliefs; each side fought as bravely as the other; and each side extended with equal sincerity the hand of reconciliation, after the Confederacy was beaten and the god of war issued a peremptory "Enough!"

Lincoln had been elected on November 6, 1860. Four days later, South Carolina called upon the slave states to secede. Secession followed: South Carolina (December 20), Mississippi (January 8), and Florida, Alabama, Georgia, Louisiana, and Texas by February 1, 1861. At Montgomery, Alabama, on February 4, 1861 [at the convention of Confederate states] they became the Confederate States of America, with the Kentuckian Jefferson Davis as president, because (as stated in their proclamation) "fifteen states of the United States had been denied their constitutional prerogatives for years," and because "a man unfriendly to slavery had been elected to the high office of President of the United States."

The day the Confederacy was founded, southern troops under General P[ierre] G[ustave] T[outant] Beauregard invested little Fort Sumter in the harbor at Charleston, South Carolina. On April 12, 1861, Confederate cannon began bombarding the fort and the United States forces who held it: eighty men of the 8th U.S. Artillery under Major Robert Anderson. On April 14, the fort surrendered. The next day, President Lincoln called for 75,000 volunteers, to serve three months. But on May 3 he requested 82,000 more, "for the duration of the war."

On April 25, Virginia seceded.[3] Arkansas, North Carolina, and Tennessee followed by June 8. The Confederacy then counted eleven states. Kentucky and Missouri, their people divided, were represented in the congresses and armies of both the North and the South.

The South, too, answered the summons by its president, Jefferson Davis, and sent its sons to volunteer at arms. Both parties labored under the delusion that the war would be brief. Northern statesmen, overestimating Union strength, were sure the rebellion would be suppressed within ninety days, hence the "three-month enlistment" of the first volunteers [often called "ninety-day men"]. The South, counting on sympathy from many kindred spirits in the North, anticipated no vigorous action by the Federal government. The South furthermore trusted that England and France would take its side as soon as an extended war interfered with cotton exports to Europe. North and South were both wrong.

The first thought by each of course was to capture the other's capital while defending its own. Therefore the battle-cry in the South: "To Washington!" and in the North: "To Richmond!"

The enemies met at Bull Run [July 21, 1861], about 30,000 on each side, those of the Union under General [Irvin] McDowell, and of the Confederacy under General Beauregard. The Union lost and retreated in confusion across the Potomac. The battle's first consequence was a clear and valid insight into the true state of affairs;

both sides now knew that war, bloody war, was unavoidable. Still, neither expected it to last for years.

The Federal congress approved a half-million men and appropriated 500 million dollars; the Confederacy mobilized 400,000 men; and the armies were organized and equipped with the greatest of care. Meanwhile the Union navy busied itself installing an effective blockade along the Atlantic coast; and the Confederacy commissioned privateers and fitted out blockade runners. In the beginning, Confederate generalship—by the likes of Beauregard, Johnston, Lee, Jackson, and Bragg—outclassed that of the North. So: old Union generals retired [such as Winfield Scott, the general-in-chief] and new ones—McClellan, Rosecrans, Thomas, Grant, Buell, Sigel, Curtis, and others—took their places, the purpose being to increase the prospects for success.

At the end of 1861 the Union had recovered some important places on the Atlantic coast and retained Missouri and West Virginia; and the government could announce on December 1 that it considered the Union strong enough not only to defend itself but also to attack any foreign power that dared meddle in our affairs.[4]

The Federal government set itself three immediate goals: to secure the entire Mississippi River, to occupy the whole Atlantic coast, and to capture Richmond. The Confederacy intended to thwart those intentions as well as win Kentucky, take Washington, and penetrate the northern and eastern states via the Ohio valley.

Without question, therefore, a clear distinction was to be drawn between the eastern and western theaters in 1862. In the East the great battles that year—Fair Oaks, Cedar Mountain, Bull Run, Antietam, Fredericksburg—decimated the Union armies without bringing them a step nearer Richmond. Operations along the coast were of similarly questionable success. But the Union managed brilliantly in the West. In Kentucky, victory at Mill Springs and Perryville; in Arkansas at Pea Ridge; the capture of Forts Henry and Donelson on the Tennessee and Cumberland rivers; in Mississippi the occupation of Corinth (a sequel to the bloody battle at Shiloh); and finally, on the last day of the year, triumph at Murfreesboro, Tennessee,—were the happy result of bold yet circumspect warfare that taught the Confederates a clear lesson: the Union was able and ready to carry the war from the southwest [i.e., from the western Ohio and upper

Mississippi valleys] to the heart of the Confederacy and would soon cut the Confederacy's lifeline.

The year 1862 also saw new faces among Union generals. Halleck was commander-in-chief of all armies east and west now. [Ambrose E.] Burnside and [Joseph] Hooker, meteoric phenomena [who had rocketed to stardom], plummeted to the commonplace equally fast. Grant, Sherman, and [Philip] Sheridan, heroes of the future, were foreshadowing what they would become.

But what were the military successes of a year, compared with the farthest-reaching of the Union government's measures in those momentous times? Lincoln's proclamation of September 22, 1862, declared slaves free in the states out of the Union, as of January 1, 1863; and slavery in our country was abolished.[5] Of course the Confederacy was thus driven to extraordinary and desperate efforts.

Union war aims continued from 1862, and the Federals were once again considering strategy for them in the coming year [1863]. But then the Confederates in the East successively defeated the new Union commanders-in-chief [of the Army of the Potomac], Burnside and Hooker [promptly after each had been appointed]. In midyear the Confederates attempted to carry the war into parts of the Union they had not touched before. But at Gettysburg, Pennsylvania, their commander, General Lee, met his master in General George C. Meade and was forced to retreat back into Virginia. Meade had succeeded Hooker, who had recently been beaten at Chancellorsville.

In the West the Union triumphed again. The city-strongholds of Memphis and Vicksburg were forced to surrender, and with them Port Hudson [Louisiana]; and the Union held the Mississippi from Minnesota to the Gulf. The Confederacy was split, its supplies from the West cut off. The Confederates [moreover] had intended to create a new base of operations centered around Chattanooga in the mountainous areas of eastern Tennessee and northern Georgia. But Chattanooga was occupied for good [by Union forces], after the region became the site of Union successes: the two-day battle at Chickamauga [a tactical victory but a strategic loss for the Confederacy], which prepared for the brilliant [Union] win at Missionary Ridge. Union operations in the West [abundant of triumph] would have been of significance and exerted effect on the course of the war, only Washington negated much of it. For a year the high command in the Federal capital had issued regulations that put cliffs in the way of the generals in the field, hampering their plans and hindering their movements.

In 1864, Grant was promoted to lieutenant-general and named commander-in-chief of the Union armies: the year's first and most blessed gift to the Union. Though divided in opinion of this man so favored by the fortunes of war, the nation approved his advancement [to that post] and its wisdom was quickly demonstrated. The first splendid consequences were coherent plans and unity in carrying them out. A single will and one man to impose it—therein lay a decided advantage: the basis for success. Ways and means, money, armies, and thousands and thousands upon thousands of lives meant nothing to the man! At Vicksburg he had demanded "unconditional surrender";[6] and now, inspired by the same doggedness, despite grave losses in the battles of the Wilderness and Spotsylvania Court House, he spoke winged words: "I propose to fight it out on this line, if it takes all summer."[7] His lieutenants Sheridan and Sherman knew and endorsed what he wanted and were willing and able to carry out the parts assigned to them. They ignored the cost, braved every sacrifice, and completed their tasks brilliantly.

Grant and Sheridan took on Lee and his Confederates in the East. Sherman meanwhile addressed Johnston, Hood, and their forces in the West. Fortune again smiled first on western operations. In May, Sherman broke loose and drove the enemy to Atlanta. Enormous casualties [were suffered] on both sides. In July he captured the city and with it the whole of Georgia. The state had been storehouse and factory for everything the Confederates needed for war—and [those essentials] were lost to them at that moment. Still not satisfied, he burned Atlanta. In mid-November he led 60,000 men straight across enemy territory and through Georgia to the Atlantic coast and South Carolina. His Christmas present to President Lincoln: 25,000 bales of cotton and 150 cannon, captured in Savannah on the South Carolina [i.e., Georgia] coast. Meanwhile at Nashville, General Thomas [Thomas the Invincible] had annihilated the Confederate forces in the West: 40,000 men under Hood, who had hoped to draw Sherman from Georgia to Tennessee.[8] With respect to large-scale operations, the war in the West was in fact over and [the Union had] won.

In the East, however, the stiff-necked general [Grant] had to suffer the terrible losses at Cold Harbor [June 3, 1864]. But they only hardened his determination to "keep hammering at Lee" until Lee was destroyed.[9]

The Union navy's blockade had sealed the Atlantic coast. At the end of the year, Lee was surrounded in Richmond. Yet, not at all downhearted, [he took hope] because the people of the North were dissatisfied. They thought the rebellion was not being suppressed fast enough, and the sacrifice of men and money excessive, indeed colossal. The national debt was two billion dollars! In July, $1.00 in gold could not be got for less than $2.90 in paper. But Lincoln and his lieutenant, Grant, stood firm, unshaken. The end (victory) was near. In November, Lincoln won the presidency by 400,000 votes, defeating [the man who might have softened Union policy toward the South,] McClellan.

In 1865, there could be but one plan by the Union, one [two-part] goal to be reached: (1) Richmond must be forced to surrender. (2) The armies of Lee, Johnston, [Richard] Taylor, and Kirby Smith, still operational, must be disarmed.

The iron ring tightened around Richmond. Wherever Rebel forces remained under arms, their situation grew more and more desperate. They turned now to the last resort, self-destruction. Witness the ruins of a Charleston torched by General [William] Hardee.[10] In the end, Richmond itself would suffer this fate. General [Richard] Ewell ordered the warehouses burned before Union forces at last entered [the city] on Monday, April 3.[11] Lee meanwhile headed west, pursued by Grant. At Appomatox Courthouse, Virginia, on the 9th, forced to admit he must give up, Lee and 28,000 men surrendered: the sad remains of the Confederacy's strong and brave Army of [Northern] Virginia. Johnston and the other generals soon followed Lee's example. Kirby Smith and the Trans-Mississippi Army did so on May 20. However, as the first engagement of the war had been a Confederate victory (Big Bethel [Virginia], June 10, 1861), so was the last: General [James E.] Slaughter's Confederates over the Union forces of Colonel [Theodore H.] Barrett at Boco Chico on the Rio Grande in Texas on May 13, 1865.[12]

The great Civil War was done. Four million slaves were free. The defeated South quivered at the feet of the triumphant North.

The Men and the Struggle

The antagonists had still been locked in bloody struggle when Lincoln referred to them in his second Inaugural Address on March 4, 1865. He spoke perhaps in the certainty of victory, perhaps in a petition of hope:

> Both read the same Bible and each prays to the same God for help against the other. . . . Both cannot expect their prayers to be heard. . . . Neither will be heard entirely. . . . The Almighty has His own plans. . . . With malice toward none, with charity for all, unshaken in the right, as God has given us to see the right, let us bring our work to an end and bind up the nation's wounds. . . . To do everything that will create a just and lasting peace between us and among all nations.[13]

The abolition of slavery became the law of the land in the thirteenth amendment to the Constitution. On April 14, the anniversary of [the Southern attack on] Fort Sumter, Lincoln proclaimed a national day of thanksgiving for the end of the war. That evening the actor John Wilkes Booth assassinated him. This sacrifice on top of all the many others exacted by the Civil War! Had the man not already been called to the country's highest office, he would certainly have served in the war; yet he must die at the hand of an assassin. He saw the war through to victory but was forbidden to see victory's rewards.

"What will they do to us, the many hundreds of thousands of discharged soldiers, used to a frequently harsh camp-life but alien to peaceful occupations?" That question was often heard, directly the war was over. We knew the answer, as we knew it to another, asked when the slaves were freed:

> Fear not the slave who breaks his chains,
> The free man is not to be feared!

Neither the soldiers who returned to civilian life, nor the slaves who became citizens for the first time, justified the fears that they would disturb and harm the nation. They merged into a nation reunited and peaceful again. Today, if the "old soldiers" still feel like men-at-arms and pride themselves on having served, it is because they helped achieve that beautiful and enviable state of affairs [reunification and peace], and because they and their comrades [who died] proved in a four-year war the truth of what Lincoln said in March of

1861: "The union of these states is indissoluble. There is no line, straight or crooked, that can serve as a border if they are divided."[14]

According to official sources, the Union had put 2,650,000 men into the field. Ohio alone (population 3,000,000) contributed 330,000. The annual depletion of forces averaged a third of the total. Half of the third were discharged because of wounds. The Union counted 316,000 dead: killed in battle and victim to illness. Confederate war statistics are incomplete and unreliable. However, we find 549,000 [Confederate] men called to the colors in 1864. Casualties were estimated to be as numerous as those of the Union. The war scarcely over, 800,000 [Union] men were paid off and mustered out.

In the spring of 1865, Congress passed the law [i.e., proposed the Thirteenth Amendment] which we mentioned above. On December 18, two-thirds of the states had ratified [the proposal] and the amendment became legally binding [and a part of the Constitution], abolishing slavery in all the states and territories of the United States—forever.

Reconstruction, begun at that time, ended in 1868 with the readmission of the states that had seceded.[15] The nation was again united!

II

The Ninth at War

3

April 17 to June 16, 1861[1]

The Three-Month Enlistment.—Camp Harrison.—Camp Dennison.—Reorganization and Reenlistment for Three Years.—Definitive List of Officers.—Accepting the Colors.—Life in Camp.—Ordered into the Field.

[Regiments Are Organized among Willing Volunteers of Several Nationalities in Cincinnati.—Rosecrans and McClellan, Ohioans, Direct the Strategy to Protect Ohio.—Ohio Troops Are Assembled to Fight the Confederacy in West Virginia.]

"Loyal to one another, absolutely and without end."

Devotion to the Union's noble cause prospered in Cincinnati and grew by leaps and bounds among people of every national origin. Americans, Germans, French, and Irish vied, organization against organization, to equip members as regiments [for active duty] or as "home guards."[2] City Council allocated $250,000 for support of dependents of men going to war. Women—young and old, married and single—formed associations for the procurement of stockings, underwear, and the like. To soldiers in the field, manufacturers and merchants supplied small but essential pieces of equipment, gratis or at slashed prices. The school board granted indefinite leave to teachers who intended to enlist forthwith. Gustav Bergmann, the public schools' first German teacher to answer Lincoln's call for volunteers, enlisted in our German regiment and became one of the early members of Company A.[3] He stayed with it until November, 1862. Today [1897] he is a teacher again, and an avid and a popular member of our Associated Veterans of the Ninth Regiment.

Meanwhile [1861], drilling intensively, we soon turned into seasoned, single-minded troops who promised to be a regiment with brilliant prospects for excellence on tomorrow's battlefields. At least part of the regiment passed the first test of German readiness, German fitness, and German attention to the fine points of soldiery. A man of the regiment, who took part in the curious incident, says:

> On an evening between April 19 and 22, Company A was summoned to Turner Hall in an allegedly important matter. People spoke darkly of the approach of steamboats intending to land secessionist forces. According to another version, Rebels were to rise in the city itself. Again, arms were to be seized [by Rebels].[4] A Zouave company of that time had an arsenal in the lower part of the city and we quietly proceeded to occupy it. We laid hold of the weapons and armed ourselves—we did not yet have firearms and swords of our own—and after about an hour, girded and prepared, we marched to Jefferson Hall.
>
> It had been transformed. Sentries, patrols, guards being mounted and relieved, war cries, passwords: everything was strictly military [here and] now. The pandemonium agitated us to quite a warlike excitement. Sleep was impossible. But we nonetheless cared for the stomach as conscientiously as we defended the city (or was it the Union? I no longer recall just which had been threatened). Throughout that night of glory, humanitarians and a soldiers' aid society kept food and drink always at hand. Jolly old Münzenmeier's plum brandy and cheese sandwiches were in great demand. Morning therefore dawned on general merriment. Then, by platoons, morale high, we attacked breakfast. An astounding maneuver after such a night of fasting! The breakfast had been prepared for us near this scene of our first heroic exploit. We were hailed for our performance, admonished to care for those borrowed weapons, and dismissed.

That episode, which at best we never fully understood, at least benefitted us in one respect. The men involved "came to know their own worth" and to realize that, at any moment, the situation could become deadly serious.

On April 23 we elected officers.[5] Of course this German regiment also had its excellent band: twenty musicians under Günther Seidensticker.

Thus within ten days after the call for volunteers, Ohio's first German regiment was at full strength, awaiting weapons and equipment, ready to serve the government, and impatient for the order to march. We believed we had mobilized 1,000 German-Americans so well, and chosen officers so wisely, that they would lead us, with high hopes and brave hearts, to honor and fame.

At headquarters it fell immediately to Willich [the adjutant] to be our de-facto drillmaster and father to this military family. In the shortest possible time he improved the regiment to its generally recognized excellence. True, its admirable physical traits and moral attributes extended to every last man. But without the superiority in military science [inculcated by him], the Ninth Ohio would not have been held up so often as a model to brigades, divisions and, yes, entire corps. Nor would it have been regarded as eminently competent in every respect.

Our smooth and rapid mobilization did more than produce universal praise for us. At that time, Cincinnati saw 15,000 men—Germans, Americans, Irish—enter infantry, cavalry, and artillery regiments.[6] Thus our example exerted a beneficial influence on units formed and forming inside a scant three months.

It was no reason for surprise, then, that the desire for uniforms and arms manifested itself so fast and turned so soon to impatience. Moreover, close-order drill and the movements of men learning to march, though conducted amid the greatest enthusiasm, were seeming more and more peculiar. For, under stern injunction to become soldiers, groups were turning into military units but doing it in a city [and in civilian clothes and unarmed].

Orders to transfer therefore pleased and gratified all concerned. Destination: Camp Harrison, a meadowland and [the county] fairgrounds, the so-called Trotting Park between Spring Grove and Carthage [seven miles north of Cincinnati], commanded, for the time being, by General [William Haines] Lytle. On April 24 a multitude assembled at the station of the Cincinnati, Hamilton & Dayton Railroad, to see us off with their best wishes.[7]

At the camp we found other [Ohio] outfits [from Cincinnati and environs] already in place, such as the Guthrie Grays [i.e., the 6th Ohio] and the Continental Regiment, Korff's Sharpshooters, and the Steuben Artillery. New units and recruits were joining them daily.

We arrived to nothing by way of shelter: neither tents nor anything with which to make camp. Some blankets had been delivered via the private road, however, and there was the bare ground. On it,

Camp Harrison

with blankets provided to each company, we spent a most cozy first night. Still we retained part of our [original] jubilation. It, together with our ever-prevalent patriotic ardor and our German sociability and good nature, helped us through this predicament.[8] Everything turned out well enough.

Next morning, bright and early, we started to build small wooden barracks [also called cantonments] on the southeastern side of the camp, each to accommodate eighteen to twenty men. In a few days we had roofs over our heads. Unfortunately our lodging had nothing but roofs to recommend it. We slept on meager straw on the ground. A scant sufficiency of woolen blankets was delivered—but not for a while.[9]

So we lavished all the more care and affection on our barrack-city. Narrow streets between the rows were named Main, Walnut, Race, Elm, etc., and boasted such edifices as Turnhalle, Deutsche Republik, Arbeiterhalle, Sängerhalle, and the like.[10] English-speaking regiments tried to throw these proud names into the shade of their own: Pike's Opera House, the Burnet House, and so forth.

Progress was slower in provisioning the stomach. At first a dearth of cooks and culinary utensils prevailed in some quarters. Indeed, many such things were in short supply. But humor and goodwill abounded. Therefore, slowly but surely, order and a cautious practicality obtained, too, in this, the principal question of housekeeping. Even the most dissatisfied of mortals gradually gave in (those for whom everything had been wonderful "once upon a time") and rarely did you still hear that, with Cincinnati so near, it would be a lot simpler to have at least the day's main meal brought to us by the express. Good cooks were found, field kitchens erected, and three meals a day put out on quickly improvised serving tables. The men ate by companies or platoons, or brought the meal into the barracks and ate it there according to the dictates of each individual appetite.

Provisions, which were purveyed to us, often left something to be desired. Indeed, the best of company cooks frequently had to use the rifle if he wanted to set a satisfactory meal before his hungry comrades. Accordingly, very soon, complaints were heard about purveyors, accusations leveled against officials, and curses hurled at real or imagined traitors, thieves, and other scoundrels. The lack of know-how on problems of this nature [feeding an army in the field]; ignorance of laws and obligations, on the part of high echelons and low; and the downright unwontedness of such a life [of soldiers in camp] certainly would have soon rendered the disagreeable situation unbearable.

But then, with vigor, the Cincinnati newspapers took up the issue. An English-language one said: "We're tired of these complaints. The evils must be corrected as fast as possible. Official fraud is somewhere at the bottom of the problem. The guilty must be tracked down and called to account."[11]

In that time of unnecessary want, Cincinnatians made great sacrifices. Especially the Germans. Those people were tireless in their expression of sympathy and their concrete efforts to help. Food and drink, and underwear and blankets, were delivered in quantity and distributed in the regiment. Many a doubter was thus restored to faith; he now believed that Ohioans were patriotic, and he wanted to fight for the Union. He might otherwise have served not one day beyond his stipulated three months, and perhaps he would have quit sooner. For, as has been said, the best of humor must, in such conditions, turn to bitterness, like "the milk of human kindness to rankling poison"[12] unless things changed and for the better.

Things did change: Duty called!

The regiment had already [been inspected and examined and] mustered in (April 26) and taken the oath for an enlistment of three months [in United States service] in proceedings supervised by Captain [later, General] G[ordon] Granger, U.S.A. The rigorous medical examination culled more than 300 men, and they were let go. New recruits would replace them to the extent they had not been surplus. Replacements arrived May 6.

Drill, kitchen police, and fatigue were carried on assiduously, despite weather continually cold and damp. They stopped only when the camp was under water, a sorry sight that occurred more than once, caused each time by faulty workmanship [and defective construction of flood-control devices], and by blunders on the part of officers of all ranks—blunders not always to be excused. Many a man's zeal, not yet fully ablaze, was thereby doused.

On May 16 we got training rifles at last, *Schiessprügel* or *Kuhfüsse,* rightly called.[13] Also on the 16th a deputation of Cincinnati burghers gave Colonel McCook and Major Link each a sword and a scarf, together with the usual speeches. Thus we learned indirectly of the order to exchange Camp Harrison for the main rendezvous of Ohio troops, Camp Dennison. There General Rosecrans had set up shop for three brigades, about 12,000 men. They would be leaving soon for McClellan's army in [West] Virginia.

That news did not disturb us—not at all! True, greater rigor could be expected in a large assembly of troops; but more system and organization would be enjoyed, too. Besides, we had enlisted to fight. So: the closer to the enemy, the better!

Let us look a last time at life at Camp Harrison. A comrade glimpsed this panorama on one of our final days:

> We see hustle and bustle everywhere. Over there a unit drills, profoundly intent. Meanwhile, farther on, a cluster of soldiers—still motley in a hodgepodge of dress—strolls about, having fun con amore. A group of men and women [civilians] are speaking affably with the young warriors.[14] Another fighting-man walks arm-in-arm with his

one-and-only. A third, in the company of wife and child, exchanges a few casual words with him. To the right of the main road, ball players romp amid happy shouts. Mealtime approaches; already a few companies are assembling, to eat their morsel, standing at the long tables. In a different place a detachment is still busily at work on a barracks, to make it prettier and more comfortable and tighter against rain. Elsewhere a Master of Personal Beauty clips and grooms bearded faces. A few yards from there, guard is mounted; the march is in step. Some prisoners and detainees, under escort, amble to the guardhouse; the march is not in step. Looking into barracks we see a game of cards in one, hear anecdotes and jokes in a second, and observe political discussions or intimate conversations in a third. In a fourth, two old campaigners square off before an audience of comrades who lie on their beds and watch with bated breath; at battle's end they will decide which was the better boxer. From another street a joyful song rings out, accompanied by a guitar—proof that, even in an army camp, beauty and grace can be cultivated. Turning our attention outside again, we watch several guards variously busy near the fence. One paces with measured tread and meanwhile looks as stern and serious as if he were protecting a powder magazine. Another sits at ease on a mound of earth, his gun over his knee, whittling. Nearby, his partner, no doubt as green as the Emerald Isle whence he came, hammers with stones on the lock of his gun, then fills the barrel to the top with pebbles and bits of grass, delighted that he has a gun that's fully loaded. In the evening the distinguished music director G[ünther] Seidensticker strikes up his regimental band, the only one left here. An audience gathers. And that splendidly poetic touch finishes our picture of a day in camp.

The order to march was given on May 17. Next morning at 8:00 we left for Camp Dennison. After a five-hour, eighteen-mile trek [via Carthage and Pleasant Ridge], the regiment entered its new home on the Little Miami between the towns of Milford and Miamisville [or Miamisburg]. Here, as at Camp Harrison, no shelter had been prepared; which, by this time, caused little grief. We set to work at once and had finished our quarters [of rough pine lumber] by the following evening, Pentecost. Tents did not arrive until June 15. They were pitched along the railroad at the edge of camp.[15]

Initial inconveniences notwithstanding, this place soon pleased us. Led by Willich, our worthy drillmaster, we converted a big cornfield to a training area where he allotted his time and ours so well that we were soon unquestionably the best-trained regiment in camp, an achievement universally known. Our field became the chief attraction for visitors. Every evening [elsewhere in camp] a "dress parade" was held; but we whipped into formations and cut evolutions with such infinite precision that visitors, one and all, would rather watch us than the parade. (We had no great liking for the parade ourselves.)

Of course the newspapers dug up all sorts of things to say about us. For example the Cincinnati *Commercial Gazette:*

> In two respects the Germans take to life at Camp Dennison like ducks to water: lager beer and military drill. There is little of the first but the second pullulates. Training incessantly, exploiting boundless tenacity, they have already achieved extraordinary precision and skill. An old English-speaking officer said recently that the Ninth is one of the best regiments he had ever seen.

And we intended to remain among the best!

Word now arrived that the governor of Ohio [William Dennison] would ask troops on three-month enlistment to reenlist for three years.[16] On May 23, during training, Willich ordered the regiment into square formation, went to the center, and gave a speech. Yes, what we had heard was true; and he discussed the matter with us, explaining it in more detail. "The country desperately needs us and all the citizens presently in arms." He ended with the hope that not one of us would back out now, especially since three years would undoubtedly be required to crush the rebellion. He needed no more of the art of oratory; the men (except only a few) declared they were ready to serve for three years.

The governor's proclamation arrived in a few days, promising a bonus—i.e., a "bounty" of $100—and the rights to (1) a pension for the crippled and the victims of incurable diseases contracted in the field and (2) support for survivors of those killed in battle.

Still the German regiment stayed in uniform less because of such prospects and promises, but more out of a sense of duty and a passion for honor, which told the men: "As you have left home to fight the Rebels, so you should not return until you have matched word with deed. Stand by the Star-Spangled Banner until it is out of danger." Nobody then thought that three years, long though they seemed, would not suffice to end secession.

On May 27, Colonel Robert Anderson, "the hero of Fort Sumter," appeared and swore in the troops for three years. The governor himself had been there the day before, to inspect and praise us. Shortly after the swearing-in, we received uniforms and rifles (including some Springfields).[17]

Able recruits were still enlisting in the regiment. Why? Let us hear from one of them.

> At that time a friend and I were working in Lexington, Kentucky. We heard something of events in Cincinnati now and then, of course, but did not know exactly what was going on, as we were not reading the newspapers much. Then one day a trader told us that every young German in Cincinnati had joined up and more were wanted.
>
> Well, that was enough for us. A few days later we were in Camp Dennison trying to enlist in the Ninth Regiment. But they had enough men. Up and down we went, to company after company, asking and being rejected.
>
> Captain Kämmerling of the 6th Company [i.e., Company F] had just told us he could not use us. My friend said, "OK, then we'll just have to give it a try with the 6th Regiment." Hearing those words, an old bearded officer whirled. With sharply critical eyes he inspected us. He barked: "What! The 6th! See that fence? Jump it!"
>
> Both of us were turners: a running start, each a hand atop the fence, and we were over. With equal speed we vaulted back. The officer met us: "You're both accepted!" To Captain Kämmerling: "We're taking these fellows. There'll be room. Some of those on leave will probably not come back." That officer was Major Willich.
>
> A justice of the peace, resident in camp, swore us in at once. He wrote my good German name with heart-rending mistakes. Only the first letter and the last were right; all others, wrong. I pointed out the flaw to him. He answered calmly: "That don't matter a bit! You are sworn and registered by that name, and it will be yours until you are mustered out of the service again. Mind that, and don't worry about it."[18]
>
> It never occurred to me to worry about it. Today I appear on the "Ohio Roster of Soldiers in the War of the Rebellion" under that alias.[19]

When we reenlisted, we retained the right to elect officers, to be commanded in German, and to follow the Prussian method of training.[20]

On June 11 we elected officers [to lead us during our three-year enlistment]. A lively poll, because some of the incumbents, even in the short time they served, had disgraced themselves: some by incompetence and some by shabby treatment of subordinates and other reprehensible behavior.[21]

On May 10 a number of men from Cincinnati, on behalf of Cincinnati's German women, had come to give us a flag [the regimental colors]. Thirteen gold stars rode in a field of blue silk above a pennant inscribed, on one side, "To Cincinnati's first German regiment," and on the other, "Fight bravely for Freedom and Justice!"

The colors were the result of one-day's effort by the Misses Elise Arnold and Karoline Greslin. With words of pure patriotism, Dr. Bauer handed the colors to the colonel [McCook], who [expressed regret that he could not say thank-you in German but] accepted them for the regiment and pledged his sincere intent that they be carried ever forward to victory and to German honor. Sergeant [Philipp] Fitz [of Company I], named standard-bearer then and there, received the beautiful colors with appropriate dignity.

At the same ceremony the men of the regiment presented a sword of honor to Willich, their "beloved father." He accepted in his unique style: at once honest, simple, and passionate; and with a stirring speech.[22]

The rite closed with a parade to additional pleasures at Wagner's Tavern in Milford. There—not to mince words!—people let themselves go: with music, singing, speeches, and beer.

Unfortunately, during those days, a drop of bitterness tainted our cup of overflowing bliss. Dr. [William] Krause, of Cincinnati, had rendered yeoman service in raising the regiment and had been the medical examiner at our reenlistment. He applied to be regimental physician. According to regulations, such applicants must take a state test, and the results would be of principal importance in making the appointment. Because he had long been known as a good physician, Dr. Krause did not want to take the test. Therefore he was not appointed. Cut to the quick, pride wounded, this revered man killed himself. In Cincinnati and here in camp: grief.[23]

On June 2, Governor Dennison had sent from Columbus another gift for the regiment: a drum. A woman, he said in his accompanying message, had provided it in recognition of the initial three-year enlistment by an Ohio regiment. In other words, [to honor] *us*—Ohio's first German regiment [and first to take three years].

Thus, at the middle of June, 1861, we had been given generous gifts and issued uniforms and weapons. Well trained and capably led, morale high, we were prepared for life in camp and ready for duty in the field.[24] We wanted only to be ordered to the theater of war.

Orders came the evening of June 15. Sunday, June 16, at 6:00 A.M., we were to proceed to the field, to help drive the Rebels out of northwestern [or west] Virginia.[25] We were 1,135 strong (plus the twenty-man band) and battle-ready in every respect.

Also on the evening of the 15th, many Cincinnatians bought tickets in advance, for the next morning, Sunday. The Turner Rifles, organized as a German militia company in Cincinnati, left for Camp Dennison on the 15th at 10:00 P.M. They wanted to be ahead of everybody in meeting with their friends and fellow turners one more time.

Ebullience prevailed among the Germans in Cincinnati. A newspaper said: "It is an honor for the German regiment and the German element itself, that, recognized as ahead of all others in combat readiness during the last review, the regiment was therefore the first to be sent from Camp Dennison to the theater of war. We are convinced that the regiment, as it shone as a model to the others in training, so it will lead them, with good examples, to victory and honor in battle. Accordingly, as they depart, we shout after them: Hurrah! Farewell! Until we meet again!"

4

June 16 to November 26, 1861[1]

Departure from Camp Dennison to the West Virginia Theater.—Camp Putnam.—Our First Rebel Flag.—Webster.—Philippi.—Our Baptism of Fire and Blood: Rich Mountain.—Willich Leaves the Regiment.—Carnifex Ferry.—Big Sewell Mountain.—Discord.—Camp Anderson.—Departure to Jeffersonville, Indiana.

[The People of West Virginia and Their Attitude to the War.—Soldier Life.—McClellan.—The Heat of Battle and the Chill of Its Aftermath.—Honor to German Troops.—Rosecrans.—Duty in an Army of Occupation and Defense.—"Eel" for Breakfast.—We Leave West Virginia, Mission Accomplished.]

"Into the field and to freedom."

Incredible hustle and bustle prevailed at Camp Dennison on the morning of June 16, 1861. At 5:00 the first Cincinnatians (the Turner Rifles [who were staying behind as a home guard] and others) were already there. At 6:00, when we were putting the finishing touches to our preparations to leave, the multitude of well-wishers crowded in. Some wanted to bid husbands, brothers, other relatives, and friends adieu. And some wanted to be present at the departure of the popular German regiment, and to shout: "Farewell until we meet again!"

You could sympathize with individuals as they said good-bye; and their feelings can be understood; but those scenes are not to be described. As the purpose for hurrying to war was at hand, so may departing soldiers' hearts have been ready to overflow with joy and the happy expectation of combat. Perhaps the soldiers were proud of what they had set about. And the pride, of men and lads alike, did not flag in the presence of relatives and fellow Cincinnatians and the others who had come to see them off. But the pride was mixed with melancholy, grief [and apprehension]. Who could blink the fact that we were journeying on a serious mission? Who wanted to face squarely the prospect of travail? Who would dare predict how many of us would return from dances with death in the war ahead? Yet an inspiring thought triumphed: "What will be, will be! This splendid German regiment, Ohio's first, now hastens to the theater of war and shall do its duty consummately. We are proud of our regiment!"[2]

Meanwhile our band played stirring, beautiful airs; and the grand lieder, the old favorites, were sung. They raised many a tear, some happy, some bitter.

The regiment fell in, executed a few precisely turned evolutions, and with the spectators crowding after, marched to the train station. A last kiss, one more handshake, a final hug, and at 10:00 A.M. the first battalion boarded the waiting cars. "Farewell!"—again—from a thousand throats. Handkerchiefs waved. Slowly the train pulled out.

> Dawn, O Dawn of the reddish sky:
> Light my way so soon to die[3]

boomed from the departing cars, and the people who remained behind took up the song.

The scene was repeated when the second battalion left at noon. And so we were

> On our way to fight and die for our country.

Obviously Colonel McCook and the other officers had taken pains to ensure the comfort and safety of their men, impressing the relatives, friends, and fellow Germans who remained behind. Unanimously they believed that, under such leaders, the regiment would win laurels for itself and bestow the greatest honor upon the German name.

Our first destination: Marietta, Ohio, four to five hours [east] across the southeastern [i.e., southern] part of the state, a most pleasant ride [on the Marietta & Cincinnati Railroad]. At every station, and especially Chillicothe, we were warmly and heartily received. In Chillicothe there were lavish refreshments at the station and a friendly welcome by a populace that included many Germans.

This reception pleased us all the more because we had curbed the unexpected but natural and unpleasant thoughts [that rose] during the farewell [at Cincinnati]. The atmosphere in Marietta, however, sobered us a bit. By and large the people acted so blatantly cold that we had reason to doubt their patriotism.

We entered quarters immediately at Camp Putnam and remained in a continual state of readiness. The camp lay about a mile from the city, in a fairground. Beginning the day after we arrived, we trained hard from morning until night and always under full pack. For us to bear up willingly, in oppressive tropical heat, demanded all our devotion to duty and every jot of our irrepressible good humor.

Without bloodshed we captured our first Rebel flag. Company A, marching out to training, passed a house with Secession's notorious four-star banner hanging from the fence.[4] Captain Joseph ordered a halt and sent inside a detail that demanded surrender of that rag. Initially the women in the house indignantly rejected the demand. But soon they complied and added some lame excuses. Carrying guns reversed, as if in a cortege, the company brought the flag home to the hearty grunts of the regiment in camp.

On June 19 we were overjoyed to be ordered to Parkersburg, West Virginia, and Major-General McClellan's army there.[5] Four companies, led by Major Willich, left at 11:00 A.M. by train [south-southwest on the Marietta & Cincinnati and Baltimore & Ohio railroads], to prepare quarters. In the afternoon, six companies and a detachment of artillery, under Lieutenant-Colonel [Charles] Sondershoff, followed by steamboat [on the Ohio River].

Mariettans treated us surprisingly well when we left town. (We had suspected them of unfriendliness if not downright hostility.) At our departure they entertained us royally and showered us with flowers and wreaths. Women, once stone cold, now enchanting, taught many a young warrior's heart how it could be heated instantly to a boil. Especially Germans [of Marietta] seemed proud that such an excellent regiment could be made up of "distinctly outstanding" countrymen. Had our enthusiasm brightened patriotism [here], like a breath on embers glowing beneath ashes?

Pretty hands had decorated our colors with wreaths. To them an old German cavalryman of the Napoleonic Wars attached a poetic dedication. Because of its truly astounding originality, let it be entered accurately and in full:

To the Good Officers and Men, Germans, of the 9th Regiment,
in Marietta

Wherever peepul speak the dutch,
  Wherever the lieder are sungg so much,
Then it be as it were to be,
  With German voicis in harmuny.
Fear not the flash and roar,
  Of big and liddle guns galor,
Nor even the power of an inimy host,
  And the balls and bullits that whiss and bust.
Wheel and tirn, you German men,
  And defent yerselfs.
Obey yer offisirs,
  Holt that line, and then hit bak
With brafery—attak.

Marietta, June 19, 1861.—C. D.

(By an old vetteran of the struggle for freedom, from 1813 to 1817, in the caffelrie of Emperor Nabolion an King of Prussia. Carl Doehler of the province of Saxony, near Naumberg on the Salle—to the Germans [of the Ninth Ohio], with love).

We arrived in Parkersburg [about fifteen miles south of Marietta] in the evening [of June 19] and encamped until June 22. Troops already there, and many civilians loyal to the Union, greeted us heartily.[6] Then we went through Rebel-occupied territory [about seventy-five miles southeast] to Webster [County] and pitched a field-camp under Rebel eyes. We pulled outpost duty and it was difficult. Rebels swarmed about us continually, disappearing as fast as they appeared, and (especially at first) astonishing us with their mobility and seeming ubiquitousness. These characteristics, which had long made the Rebel army seem bigger than it was, resulted from its superior numbers of men in the saddle, a decided advantage. Only after a succession of misfortunes did Union leaders perceive the dire need for a large and competent cavalry.

We belonged to General Rosecrans's brigade, together with a Michigan artillery detachment (called the Coldwater Battery)[7] and the 5th, 6th, and 19th Ohio Regiments. Other units of McClellan's army, about 30,000 men, were ever on the move around us.

The populace was unreliable. The governor of Virginia [John Letcher], after extended hypocrisy, had unmasked only a few days before [and led Virginia out of the Union] and summoned the mountaineers of northwestern Virginia to join the war against the Union. He exhorted them to assert their right "to institute a new government, laying its foundations on such principles, and organizing its powers in such forms as to them shall seem most likely to effect their safety and happiness."[8]

Fortunately the simple mountaineers did not fully understand those phrases; outright support for the Rebels was not to be so easily achieved. Unionists, however, likewise not sure of the meaning, were confused about where they stood with [Union and Rebel] troops.

The upshot [of those unsettled circumstances] was that in those days we enjoyed many a treat when we approached a house and the occupants fled, often leaving a newly prepared meal. Nor did we lose sleep over their hunger. Moreover, somehow or other, since we happened to be in wooded mountains, we had to roast ourselves a juicy haunch of venison (or so at least one of our captains thought). One evening he went still-hunting alone; his stand was beyond our string of outposts. Soon a shot rang through the woods. Mr. Captain had dropped his stag. And, next day, how lips smacked over that splendid roast! But misfortune travels fast. It strode up in the form of a farmer who complained to the colonel: one of the men had shot one of his tame deer. The facts of the case were soon established, the bold sharpshooter had sinned against fauna, and he must pay $15. Long was that roast decried as an exorbitant morsel of venison.

On June 25 we put ourselves to the test. Fully loaded with bag and baggage for the field, how well would we march in a tight four-file column with advance-guard and rear-guard and flank-guard and all the other impedimenta and appurtenances peculiar to an army on the move—and fifteen freight wagons besides? We went from Webster to Philippi, our destination, about fifteen miles, in three hours.

Many such oscillations on that military chessboard followed. They might have dragged on longer, had breaks in supply not occurred often. And so we [of The Ninth] took it on ourselves to begin foraging and soon became expert at it. In the eyes of men of other regiments we raised the good name of The Ninth to that of Elite Forces.

We camped in Philippi and Buckhannon until July 7. Clashes between patrols abounded but we [of The Ninth] took part in none at that time. Under a new camp regulation adopted then, a civilian could enter [camp] at will but not leave until he swore loyalty to the Union. After the word spread, many annoying curiosity-seekers stayed away from us.

Important irregularities occurred at that time in several regiments. Yes, cases of insubordination, too. Even in The Ninth we experienced occasional tiffs among lordly officers. The men watched or heard them usually with fiendish delight. Some of the junior officers, in the few months of their vocation as warriors, had acquired downright astounding military talents and tactical expertise, and did not hesitate to boast and carry-on accordingly—to the detriment of discipline. But those mostly childish attempts to win attention failed against our general good sense. We also applied a good-humored procedure (so well understood by Germans) of putting vainglorious egotism in its place.

On July 2 our officers paid army commander [i.e., head of the state forces of Ohio] General McClellan a visit at his general headquarters. On July 3 he returned it and inspected the regiment. Visibly pleased with our appearance and our drills, he said he had never seen, here or in Europe, a militia regiment better trained or made up of men so strong and fit.[9] For a long time after that day, when the army marched, we were in the vanguard.

To us, July 4, 1861, was drab and boring, what with practically everything lacking for a proper celebration. At last we resorted to target practice.

On the 7th we moved to a new camp at Middle Fork Bridge. Alarms, now, every day and every night. We marched here and there, we reconnoitered and skirmished [and routed the enemy] as needed, we heard cannonades and small-arms salvos nearby: in short, we were in the middle of a war.[10]

On July 10 [after moving to Roaring Creek] the regiment received its baptism of fire and blood.[11] *Reconnoiter the forest immediately before you, and to Rich Mountain; and ascertain the enemy's position and the nature of his fortifications near Roaring Creek:* those were our orders. Companies A and K advanced on either side of the [Buckhannon-Beverly] road [the main enemy position]; B and D covered the flanks; and the rest proceeded in column. Soon, however, at the first bend in the road, it was discovered that a continued advance meant marching into a concentrated crossfire from Rebel artillery. No doubt about it, the road belonged to the Rebels. Furthermore, the companies in the forest [to the right and left] were soon exposed to a withering small-arms fusillade. Company K, on the left, emerged from the trees at another bend in the road and met an abatis. After the exchange of a few shots, the Rebels manning it, forty or so, took to their heels. Part of the company crossed the road, again to enemy entrenchments. Scorching Rebel fire was so powerfully returned that the Rebels fled back into the trees once more. Similarly, Company A, on the right, traded a number of shots with the Rebels. The other companies, partly in reserve, partly posted as flank-guards, did not come under fire and were able to carry out satisfactorily our stated purpose: to scout enemy fortifications for their position and strength. We began our return. The enemy hurled a generous cannonade after us. Aimed too high, it went over our heads and into the trees and against the hills. The regiment regrouped on the road, held by our troops now. The commanding general [Rosecrans], thinking us harshly pressed, had positioned artillery, cavalry, and infantry in reserve, to provide us emphatic support if necessary.

The regiment was not a little proud that it had accomplished its mission fully and without reinforcements. We had also taken our first prisoners. We regretted only that we were kept from attacking and seizing the Rebel position. But we could not have done it alone; some 3,000 Rebels occupied the fortifications and with their cannon could rake practically every approach. Still, from our location, we could have hurt the enemy significantly, had we had good rifles.

The enemy had not expected us; witness his haste to retreat from low-lying entrenchments to positions higher on the mountain and behind ridges. Our losses: one dead, Private Gustav Stöcker; and one wounded, Private Georg Vonau; both of Company I. Just before the engagement, Private [Georg] Büttner of Company K, heading a small patrol, had mixed it up with a superior force of cavalry and was also wounded.

Stöcker, our first fatality, had two brothers, Georg and August, in Company I, and a third in the cavalry. The four stalwart sons' aged mother lived in Cincinnati. Of course, when she heard of the death, she indulged the pain of losing her child. But soon she rallied and said: "The death of my son hurts me deeply, but I regret only that he could not send at least a half-dozen Rebels to eternity before he lay down his life for our country." May the words of that brave German woman endure as long as those of the Spartan mother at the report of *her* son's death: "I bore him that he die for Sparta!"

Next day, July 11 [the main day of battle], at the early hour of 2:00 A.M., General Rosecrans wheeled most of his troops in a ten-mile detour through the forests, to take from behind the Garnett fortifications [i.e., Camp Garnett, the Confederate position] at the back of Rich Mountain. At 8:00 we [of The Ninth] were ready to go, too. Meanwhile the 3rd Ohio and the pioneers had been hacking through the trees a road for the cannon, that they be able to fire effectively from a likely hill. In late evening, however, they were driven back and could not accomplish their mission.

We and the rest of the brigade, drawn up in the forest the whole afternoon, toward evening must advance to secure the advantage that had been won. Companies A and K remained hidden in the forest, as skirmishers, while B and I covered the flanks. The afternoon's downpour had drenched us and left the roads bottomless. A sharp chill gripped the night. The four companies must suffer in spite of it, and listen for enemy movement—*listen,* because the eye could distinguish nothing. Not a sound, now, of the small arms we heard through the afternoon and evening.

At 5:00 A.M. [July 12] the companies were to shift to higher ground where they could later man outposts. Meanwhile the artillery was to position its guns. The previous afternoon [however], Rosecrans came from the rear and smashed the Rebels. His own losses were slight. That engagement produced the firing we had heard—and the enemy's hasty withdrawal. Soon [therefore] the companies that had been sent to higher ground, and the artillery, were ordered to join the regiment at the foot of the mountain and march into fortifications abandoned by the Rebels, [which was done] without opposition. Four cannon had been left [by the Rebels], and all the camp-equipage, even though the fortifications were well constructed on all sides [and could have been defended].

And so the regiment received its baptism of fire and blood [suffered its first casualties, some dead and some wounded, and took its first prisoners].

We pursued the enemy [southeast], finding stout fortifications once more, at Beverly, also abandoned. Huttonsville and the enemy's position on Cheat Mountain had likewise been forsaken.[12] We marched back [from Cheat Mountain, Traveler's Repose, and Tygart's Valley] to Beverly, where we intended to settle-in for a while. We spent Sunday morning, July 15 [i.e., 14], in absolute rest, enjoying the pleasant thought that in our very first skirmish we had done our duty and nobody had done theirs better. Then we started to build ovens and otherwise make ourselves comfortable here. But this idyllic life would not last long.

At [about] this time an overeager young soldier of Company A, a teacher by trade, happened to be near General McClellan at a moment when many Rebel patrols were swarming near our outposts. The youthful warrior skirmished his way to the General's very presence and with an innocent thirst for knowledge, asked him in the friendliest of tones, why he did not send The Ninth over there to thrash the devils. The General smiled. "Our department ends right here, my boy. We have no business over there!"

Then how are we to win this war? our comrade wondered. Prudently he kept the opinion to himself.

As we have already discussed the first of our wounded, so it is proper that we mention our protowounded now. Mind you, this victim was nothing like your usual flesh-and-blood military casualty. Rather, it was of felt: the hat of one of our dear lieutenants. On the night of the 6th and 7th, when the hat returned from a skirmish between patrols, it retained a bullet wound that at first the man beneath thought he had suffered. Aforesaid hat, moreover, was obviously peacock-proud of its wound; it induced its owner to repeat the story afterward, in complete detail, and in all variations. At last the story brought him to grief. The affable Captain [Karl] J[oseph] spoke in the dry manner of a German from Mecklenburg. "Where are you hiding the bullet? It must have perched on your head. The hat has only one hole in it." An unsettling fact, to be sure, and a hard question.

Other things soon demanded to be pondered and discussed.

We had been praised for what we had done at the front. While citing bravery and perseverance, the general failed to mention that we were all quite intelligent. Indeed, at that time, our keenness of mind was as excellent as our other qualities, no doubt about it. To illustrate: At Middle Fork Bridge the inspecting officer [i.e., the officer of the guard] asked one of our sentries for the *countersign.*

"Napoleon," the sentry said. He was a good Swabian [and the Swabians and their dialect are often the butt of humor among other Germans].

"Wrong. It is *Bonaparte.*"

"I know very well it's *Bonaparte,* but *Napoleon* is the same thing. Besides, it's easier to pronounce."[13]

For a while we marched among our former camps [including Laurel Hill and Philippi], from one to another, then returned to Webster on July 25. There the first part of our West Virginia campaign ended.

Meanwhile, General Scott had resigned as general-in-chief. McClellan, called to Washington to replace him, turned over to Rosecrans the command of the army in West Virginia.[14] Shortly before McClellan left us, he issued this general order:

"Headquarters Army of Occupation,
Western Va.—Beverly, Va., July 19th, 1861.

"Soldiers of the Army of the West:

I am more than satisfied with you. You have annihilated two armies, commanded by educated and experienced soldiers, intrenched in mountain fortresses, and fortified at their leisure. You have taken five guns, twelve colors, fifteen hundred stands of arms, one thousand prisoners, including more than forty officers. One of the commanders of the rebels is a prisoner, the other lost his life on the field of battle. You have killed more than two hundred and fifty of the enemy, who has lost all his baggage and camp-equipage. All this has been accomplished with the loss of twenty brave men killed and sixty wounded on your part.

You have proved that Union men, fighting for the preservation of our government, are more than a match for our misguided and erring brothers. More than this, you have shown mercy to the vanquished. You have made long and arduous marches with insufficient food, frequently exposed to the inclemency of the weather.

I have not hesitated to demand this of you, feeling that I could rely on your endurance, patriotism and courage. In the future I may have still greater demands to make upon you, still greater sacrifices for you to offer. It shall be my care to provide for you to the extent of my ability, but I know that by your valor and endurance you will accomplish all that is asked.

Soldiers, I have confidence in you, and I trust you have learned to confide in me. Remember that discipline and subordination are qualities of equal value with courage.

I am proud to say that you have gained the highest reward, that American troops can receive—the thanks of Congress and the applause of your fellow-citizens.

GEO. B. MCCLELLAN, Maj. Gen'l."[15]

The depressing news of General [Franz] Sigel's defeat in southwestern Missouri reached us now.[16] We were moved to reflect on the long-range prospects and likely outcome of waging a war like this. And we imagined what would have happened had our own corps come off second-best.

By contrast, therefore, we were all the happier to learn that even the boastful governor of Virginia held us in unholy respect. During his "strategic withdrawal" from our area [the battlefield at Rich Mountain], he announced that 10,000 "damned dutch" were wreaking havoc up there, by murder and the torch, and 40,000 more would soon reinforce them. Had it been so! According to a story going around then, an all-German corps was to be raised; and one of our wags [playing on what the governor said] suggested that the Union could rest easy after signing with that corps a contract to crush the Confederacy!

In those days a visit by the paymaster and the jingle of his moneybags would have delighted us. For, not only were we by and large broke, but there was also sad news from Cincinnati: the county commissioners had stopped the stipulated allowances to needy dependents of soldiers in the field; and among the needy, considerable unrest [therefore] prevailed. Not a few of The Ninth impulsively decided to break their word likewise, hurry home to their families, and go to work to feed them as they had done before the war. (After all, we were getting no pay, either.) Fortunately the good commissioners thought better of what they had done. And—lo and behold!—a paymaster said he would be around soon.

General W. S. Rosecrans [as has been stated] had replaced McClellan as our commanding officer [of the Federal Department of West Virginia].

On July 27 we moved by train [of the Northwestern Virginia Railroad, northeast, via Oakland, Maryland, across the Alleghenies] to New Creek [Virginia] near the [north branch of the] Potomac, to intercept a presumed Rebel advance on Cumberland, Maryland [and to guard the railroad bridge on the Potomac]. Three of our companies were sent as a garrison to Cumberland, but only one remained and for a month. The rest of the regiment stayed in camp at New Creek. Cumberland was not attacked.

On August 4 a regimental chaplain arrived—to our surprise. This gentleman, Wilhelm Stängel of Louisville, Kentucky, preached us a sermon the same day, and we liked its intelligent and liberal tone. Still, we could see no need for him; we would have preferred that the government apply his salary to the relief of dependents of soldiers in the field. Neither he nor the regiment was too pious, however; for, as we shall see, not a month later a captaincy came vacant, and he took it. "Again we had no chaplain." Everything was fine without one.[17]

On August 10, Major Willich amazed us with the news that he had received orders to raise in Indiana a German regiment modeled on ours. Moreover, after organizing a section of German artillery, he was to be permitted forthwith to consolidate them and us into a brigade. "Then," said the old warhorse, "we shall really see what German patriots can do!"

So our drillmaster left, never to return. Both his excellent plan for a German brigade, and the integration of his new regiment into our brigade, proved to be impossible dreams. But, though his scheme failed and he did not come back, The Ninth remembered and still remembers its debt to him. He was the perfect gentleman and the best of soldiers.

Meanwhile we were leading a most comfortable existence at New Creek. As to the tranquil monotony of life in camp, we were well along in a series of shindigs to pep it up. On August 11 we observed the Universal German Turner Festival being held in Berlin. Gustav Tafel and an invited guest from Cumberland gave fiery speeches. We decided to send the Jahn Memorial Committee in Berlin a beautiful stone from Queen's Rock nearby on the Potomac; and with it an appropriate inscription.[18]

Next we were to receive the ladies of Cumberland. The red-letter day was to be the 18th. They had said they wished to entertain us royally and in our own camp. There would be party foods, speeches, songs, music, gymnastics, dancing, and that indispensable necessity of every celebration: beer. Thirty-eight kegs arrived from Cumberland on the evening of the 17th. On the 18th—early—a telegram from General Rosecrans: At 10:00 A.M., five companies of the regiment must leave for Clarksburg, West Virginia, where Rebel gangs had been getting too big for their britches.

This obviously serious obstruction of our plans [for a party with the ladies] also scattered the regiment, what with Company F in Cumberland, and K a few miles off at the bridge on the Potomac, leaving only C, D, and H in camp. We liked this dispersal not at all, but it could not be changed.

On August 28 we broke camp at New Creek. The companies that had remained there [C, D, and H] went [southwest via Weston] to Bulltown.[19] On September 2 the five that had been detached [and sent to Clarksburg] returned to military honors and a joyful reception. They had spent ten long hard days in the Greenbriar Mountains, pursuing Rebels (often nonexistent ones) and enduring the lack of every necessity, due to poor leadership and execrable weather. Often and unnecessarily they had hungered and thirsted. Now the regiment was overjoyed to be reunited, especially because we knew it likely we would presently face the enemy again and [therefore] we could hope not to have to repeat soon any mindless and senseless marches and expeditions of the kind just completed.

In those days—despite many doubtful orders, much questionable action, and a plague of demoralizing incidents—the regiment carried its heads high and its weapons at the ready, to save the Union and defend humanity and freedom. As ours was emphatically a regiment neither of slaves nor of mercenaries, and neither stupid nor unwilling to think, so our [honorable] behavior demanded every ounce of our German intelligence and our unwavering German senses of duty and honor.

Fortunately for the cause of the Union, there were more troops like us in the corps. We and they together served as leaven. In other words, we and they supplied a true and steadfast spirit that kept the body from decadence and brutalization. And, given our circumstances, such degeneration would have been no surprise. That is, men without money and lacking food for two to three days at a time—worse, men having neither goal nor purpose—men who therefore wander about like forlorn knights-errant and must observe the pointlessness of their behavior—men in those straits might succumb at last to a stony indifference. But we prevailed!

The reunited Ninth coalesced around the figure already dear to us: McCook. And every last one of us trusted that a regiment like ours, physically and morally of a piece, had been called to greatness and would rise to any occasion.

On September 4 we went [southwest] to Sutton [or Suttonville] and [in the concentration of forces preceding the Battle of Carnifex Ferry] joined Schombeck's Chicago dragoons and Ohio's 28th and 47th Infantry Regiments, thus forming Rosecrans's 2nd Brigade, under McCook. At Birch Creek [or Birch River] on the 8th the new brigade assembled for the first time and was inspected. A funny thing happened, worth mentioning here. General Rosecrans, striding among the units, addressed to each a kind word and a quip, sometimes clever, sometimes not, but always apposite to the unit at hand. Passing [our] Company B, he said [in English]: "Company B stings, I hope!" The words brought fury to the face of the company's captain [Ferdinand Müller]. For, still struggling stubbornly and fiercely with English, he was locked in mortal combat with the difference between *g* and *k* in pronunciation. He could not grasp why the general, looking utterly benign, would hurl such an insult at Company B. Clarification followed quickly, providing hilarity at the good captain's expense. Thereafter for a while [poking more fun at the captain] the company said *k* at the end of *sting.*

General Rosecrans soon enjoyed increased trust with every last man of the corps. The word had gradually spread that the recent ordeals [such as befell the detachment sent to Clarksburg] had been for naught, and that the area swarmed again with Rebels [under Brigadier-General John B. Floyd, gathering strength for an assault]. When our General learned of the shortcomings and in particular the blunders behind that state of affairs, he promised an end to the ordeals and turned at once to preventing new ones.

In other respects, however (at least in our opinion), he was often excessively harsh. In those circumstances, our taking it on ourselves to forage was perfectly excusable; yet he opposed it especially. On reflection, however, we had to concede that, even with respect to foraging, he could not budge an inch. Else he would relax discipline, which ought not be done with raw troops, and all of us were raw troops. Thus, soon after the muster [at Birch Creek], when he set himself (revolver in hand) against the plundering of an orchard, he erred only in doing it personally rather than assigning a subaltern; and in being too emotional. We got those beautiful apples anyway; and we did not believe he, deep down, really begrudged them to us.

McClellan's famous general-order arrived now.[20] Sundays were to be strictly observed: work to stop, services to be held, everyone to attend. Thus we would prove ourselves worth divine aid and partake of it for our holy cause. Exceptions were to be allowed: engaging the enemy, for example, as well as other imperatives of a strictly military nature. Since our pugnacious chaplain had exchanged the Bible for the sword and a captaincy, Sunday services [for us] lacked promise for the time being—a fact of little concern to most of us.

McCook, our brigade commander, was nominated for promotion to general.[21] He declined, preferring to remain colonel of The Ninth (which of course put him in good with us). But he stayed at the head of the brigade, with Lieutenant-Colonel Sondershoff as our regimental chief. Although many changes among officers ensued—replacements, promotions, discharges, etc.—order and excellent leadership did not suffer in the regiment.

On September 10 the corps advanced. At Summersville [western Virginia, east-northeast of Carnifex Ferry] we met small detachments of Rebel cavalry and discovered an abandoned Rebel camp [left from the fighting of August 26]. At noon we heard a rage of small arms and learned that the 1st Brigade had encountered the Rebels [in the Battle of Carnifex Ferry]. Off with our packs! Into battle formation! And thus we proceeded until about 2:00 P.M. and soon found enemy fortifications on the edge of a woods where the 1st was already fighting.[22]

Once again McCook tested his flaming eloquence at the opportune moment. Getting the order to lead his brigade at the enemy, he stood tall in the saddle, swung his sword, and shouted: "Now forward, my bully Dutch! We shall walk over these d——d works; and if we must die, let it be on the other side! I know you and I shall lead you. Let us show the traitors, what Germans can do!"[23] His Germans did not disappoint him.

We, The Ninth [his Germans], were to move to the right flank and seize the fortifications there. But misdirected or misunderstood orders caused us to divide. Each part fought bravely and defended itself as best it could, ignorant of whether it was adhering to the overall but unknown purpose. Two companies had split to the right and they stood in heavy fire smack in front of the fortifications until "assembly" sounded at last, calling troops to the left flank.[24] The confusion cleared up then, and the regiment could regroup. We counted Corporal Karl Pachter and Private Konrad Hosbach (both of Company B) dead and eight others wounded. This engagement would be officially called the Battle of Carnifex Ferry.

Evening descended meanwhile. In the dark of night, intense firing broke out. Another clash between Federals and Rebels? No, the 13th and 28th Ohio were shooting at each other by mistake. Both had been hotly engaged all day long.[25]

We bivouacked for the night on a hill facing the woods. Next morning we discovered that the Rebels had made tracks during the night, abandoning much equipment, even flags. We would not have believed that flags had been forsaken, but Colonel McCook went scouting on his own and brought one back from the deserted camp. This time, instead of a unit being designated to pursue the enemy, so-called volunteers were raised across the corps—with clearly no better results.

Indeed, the battle had been premature. Certain commanders, by all-too-impetuous acts, spoiled the battle's proper conduct and ruined the master plan to lure the enemy into a trap. Still the battle did clear secessionists out of the region [and strengthen the Union's hold on western Virginia]. Closer examination of their redoubts proved that General Floyd and his men had been especially strong here. Hence, obviously, the ferocity of the previous day's fighting.[26]

In the following days we were ordered to various reconnaissances; especially the enemy's deserted fortifications and erstwhile camp must be searched. We took much booty, including General Floyd's war chest, containing about $20,000 in Confederate paper. Considered worthless [by Union soldiers], the beautiful "graybacks" [came to grief in our hands]: thrown away, torn up, and used as spills. Yet, at that time [though inflated], they still represented [in terms of their former worth] a value of $17,000 to $18,000—"among (Southern) brethren" of course. Astonishing that none of us thought of [money as] a [profitable] sideline. The corps fed for several days on provisions left behind in the enemy's fortifications.

We searched high and low for Floyd's runaway army during the following week. Occasionally we thought we had nabbed parts of it. But they sneaked off time and again, after vain shooting and futile strategems. For a change we usually camped in the open at night. Rations were accordingly short, but Colonel McCook showed himself [with General Rosecrans] sternly opposed to unauthorized foraging. One evening, while comrades looked on, a few of the men who violated that ban were made to dance a while around a tree stump. The Colonel seemed to have drawn this punishment from old military histories of bygone days; or from our regular army's code of justice, not a notably humane body of laws, as everyone knows.

We were meeting many units from other brigades. Every regiment—and this is a fact—included a minimum of one company of practically nothing but Cincinnatians. You would almost assume a Queen City nearly devoid of men and boys, and the city council to be at least half female.

We were at Camp Lookout when, on the morning of [September] 22nd, at the wee hour of 3:00, abruptly, our pickets were recalled.[27] The enemy was said to be nearby—and 10,000 strong. At dawn we were off after him. We marched two hours and suddenly were at . . . our own camp! In hot pursuit we had gone out the front, described a strenuous circle, and now were entering at the rear. Local farmers, their motives not necessarily clear, had taken our camp for one of the enemy's and reported accordingly.

Then we spent a week at Big Sewell Mountain. Abominable weather, therefore privation.[28] Our table was often badly supplied and foraging not exactly a snap. Still we enjoyed many a meal not to be found in cookbooks but nonetheless sumptuous (under the circumstances). As is well known, white and black inhabitants of the Virginia mountains eat many large nonpoisonous snakes and even rattlesnakes. "When in Rome, do as the Romans do," some of us said. "Snake is a delight." The gullies of Sewell Mountain, as well as the mountainous country all around, fairly teemed with big snakes. Soon the regiment had its renowned snake hunters. Two of them in particular distinguished themselves: Captain Ferdinand Müller [Company B] and Private Eduard Stremmel [Company A]. They have since departed this life.

A comrade still alive describes a snake breakfast served by the jovial, capable captain.

> On patrol in a dreadful region, we struggled up and down mountains, through ravines, and across steep slopes. You kept your balance with the aid of overhanging limbs, and you supported yourself with your rifle or your sidearm, so as not to lose your footing and tumble into the depths, never to return. Certainly not a pleasurable hike. But our good humor heartened us enough to help us over the obstacles. Meanwhile the snakes simply glided along the ground and curled alluringly around trees and branches. Captain M. soon cut off the head of one with his sword, an especially fine reptile several feet in length. Nobody noticed how he carried it or even that he brought it along.
>
> Next morning, after the mailman delivered letters and packages in camp, it being a day of rest, the captain emerged from his tent, smiling contentedly. He invited several of us, who were standing around, to breakfast at 10:00. "I just got in the mail some splendid marinated eel from Cincinnati and I'm cooking it up in grand style." Three of us accepted. Our amiable benefactor hoped we might bring crackers and beverages; and we brought them. We sat down to pieces of superb eel in a tasty sauce. We crumbled and added the crackers and washed down the oily mouthfuls with an occasional pull at one of those renowned flat and square bottles. Our genial host rubbed his hands in glee and urged us to dig in. "We can't have any left over," he said. "What a shame if such good fish spoils or is thrown out."

> Now, even the stomach of a soldier in the field has its limits. And so at last we were sated on those savory morsels. The bottle was empty. Captain M. folded his hands piously across his giant paunch and turned congenially to a lieutenant notorious for being squeamish: "Well, K., old buddy, how about it? Nothing beats a well-marinated Virginia snake!" A leap from the chair, a savage curse, a dash from the tent . . . and let us not say what else!

On October 1, Major Slemmer, U.S.A., inspected and duly praised us.

Meanwhile [in the ongoing but light and sporadic hostilities in West Virginia] the Rebels had been gathering in force in the area again. We did not know whether they had grown too strong for us; they were not to be moved to sortie out of their entrenchments. On October 5 we broke camp at Big Sewell Mountain because the Rebels occupied a height from which they could look down at us too comfortably for our safety. Retreating silently and secretly, we escaped without trouble from them.

We returned to Camp Lookout and enough excitement and work.

On October 7 a regimental order informed us that our dear and popular Colonel McCook had resigned. The men, upset, were convinced that at this time, no better commander could be found for The Ninth. He gave as his reason: disobedience by several officers of the regiment. The men, knowing only too well of certain intrigues and fits of caviling and even insubordination among some officers, determined to side with the colonel. When the men, through a delegation, made their position known to him, he withdrew his resignation—provided somebody competent be put in the position of major, vacant since Willich left.

Willich, we now learned, had been promoted to colonel of his 32nd Indiana, that state's first German regiment. So he was definitely no longer a member of ours. Therefore an outstanding officer, Captain Gustav Kämmerling of Company F, could promptly be elected and promoted to major on October 18. Thus the deadly strife was crushed.[29]

Those times of torturous marches furnish an example of why McCook was so well liked. One day he found three members of

Company D struggling along with travail and nearly collapsing under the onus of their packs—three who were known as good men afoot and had never been left behind. McCook now showed the compassion he held for his troops, proving himself a true and born soldier and leader. To the two who seemed to him the more tired he said, "Tie your packs together," and he hung them in front of him, across his saddle. The third man, whose pack was the heaviest, he sent to the ambulance. Then he rode ahead with a good-natured "All right, let's march! To the bivouac!"[30]

Even that onerous trek dragged to its end. The three made it to Camp Lookout: the one on the ambulance, relatively hale and hearty; the other two, soaked and shivering. Recognized as stout and brave soldiers, the two were well provided for in their tent. Bundled into a mountain of coats and blankets, after the good colonel inquired about them and had them given "something hot," they broke into a powerful sweat. The first man would have liked to share in it. But he was a zealous Methodist and upright before the Lord. (His pack weighed too much because it overflowed with pious tracts.) Therefore the men taking the sweat cure did not admit him to it, and he must come otherwise to terms with fate.

Stop! Look! Listen! Into a beautiful state of rest and physiotherapy—in piercing tones—the *alarm!* Up and out, dripping with sweat, the patients joined a forced march of several hours. Yet all three sick men returned to camp as fit as fiddles. Now, under the circumstances, this last phase of the cure could have come to a drastically different end. As to whether the Methodist lightened his pack this time, by some or all the bundles of tracts, history has not recorded an answer.

Let another incident from that period show just how bad the situation was in those days. (It is granted of course that similar things occurred elsewhere and at the same time in this war. Furthermore, they have occurred in past wars. Moreover, they will probably occur in all wars to come.) I refer to a soldier from Company I, one of the regiment's youngest, about seventeen years old, who had been healthy and robust. Like many in camp at Sewell Mountain, however, he lay racked with fever. In most cases the malady became a nervous disorder. Victims hallucinated almost continuously and in an alarming manner. Caution and vigilance, which needed to be extreme, were urged on all people who cared for the sick. After the chief physician diagnosed nervous fever, our young soldier was sent to the ward of the second assistant physician, Dr. Carpenter. Sick and very weak indeed, yet always lucid, the young man seemed (to Dr. Carpenter) smitten with a different illness. Therefore one day the doctor prescribed Rhine wine and ordered the hospital steward to see that this tonic was taken as directed.

Next morning the doctor asked the patient how he liked the wine.

"I didn't get any," he said, amazed.

The steward, when summoned, declared: "I gave it to him myself. He's usually delirious, so he can't have any idea what he's getting."

"I never got any wine," the patient maintained. "And I was never delirious."

The doctor agreed; the patient was not delirious. And the steward's behavior proclaimed to the doctor what happened to the wine. The steward was ordered to report to the colonel.

"A nervous fever? You have no such thing," the doctor advised the patient. "You have typhus. What you need, above all, is nourishing food."

After inquiring into the young man's private circumstances, he arranged a furlough to Cincinnati; and as soon as the next morning, our comrade was on his way home. He was well cared for there, as his appearance showed when he returned to the regiment following a brief absence. Given a less-humane physician, and there were plenty of them, this soldier probably would not have left the hospital alive. Yet he served in bloom to the end of his enlistment. As for the villain, who had been a hospital steward a very long time, it was he who drank the wine to his own health, and he who suffered for it.

On October 9 we went to a point on the New River about six miles from where it joins the Gauley to form the Kanawa. We called the place Camp Anderson [named for the hero of Fort Sumter]. Our pickets and the enemy's clashed daily.

Our chief task was to devise a means of getting ourselves across the river. We built a superb ferry: a flatboat pulled with a rope. On October 19 the brigade crossed, with our regiment at point, and proceeded toward the little town of Fayetteville, a few miles off. The order—"*March! March!*"—punctiliously obeyed, brought the advance guard (The Ninth, under Sondershoff and Kämmerling) into the town at last. But the Rebels, once again too quick, were gone and with them the occupants of many houses now abandoned. Brigade-Commander McCook directed us to search them. He also allowed us to plunder a little: fruit and other comestibles which we could use.[31]

Shots rang out, source indeterminate. Then several houses and public buildings took fire. This was the first time we were permitted to handle, with something other than kid gloves, the civilians who sympathized with the Rebels. Clearly, nobody in the brigade found this disciplinary action notably hard or grievous.

Reconnaissance (and clashes between patrols) continued. Rebels swarmed on the other side of the river. Many shots were exchanged; few hit their targets. The Rebels cut our ferry-rope on the 21st. On November 4 they planted a six-pounder over there: the last straw. [But] its shelling did little damage.

We were near historic Hawk's Nest. Marching to Gauley Bridge on the 23rd [of November], we dreamed of winter quarters and that sort of thing. For the present, however, we were to be sent from Cannelton (on the Kanawa) to Jeffersonville, Indiana [on the Ohio near Louisville, Kentucky], aboard the steamboats *Silver Lake, Mary Cook,* and *Glenwood,* and to proceed from there to join General D[on] C[arlos] Buell's Army of the Ohio.

So, at the end of our first campaign, we knew we had done our duty truly and faithfully. In our initial six months we had won the respect of comrades-in-arms and all our superiors, and we rejoiced. Furthermore it goes without saying that we delighted in our hope to see home and loved ones again soon, if only for a few hours' visit. We also knew and felt that, during our days at war, we had done everything to prove ourselves worthy of that privilege. If in the enemy we evoked fear and kindled hatred (as newspapers and war reports told us we did), then we exulted in that feat, too. Moreover, the Rebels and their friends had hung nicknames on us: "Dutch Devils" and "Bloody Dutch." Other regiments joined us in taking pride, not only in them, but also in the recognition, honor, and tribute we enjoyed from all quarters.

The purpose of our campaign had been achieved: West Virginia and Maryland held for the Union. To each and every one of us—and not even the memory of myriad ordeals could obscure this truth—the thought was sublime that we had now been called to dispel the curse of human degradation and drive the horror of slavery permanently from still larger and more beautiful areas of our grand and glorious land. Nor did we blink the fact that ahead of The Ninth lay new and perhaps worse hardships.

Those were our thoughts as we left the theater of war where we had been part of the action. Yet something else was on our minds, too: an excusably relished expectation of meeting a paymaster and perhaps even being able to enjoy a few days of deeply desired rest. Then off to war again, of course, and under different circumstances and in new places. We were ready to do our duty.

5

November 28, 1861, to March 4, 1862[1]

A Visit Home.—Jeffersonville.—Lebanon.—General Buell's Army of the Ohio.—"Pap" Thomas.—Mill Springs.—Danville.—Louisville.—[Nashville.]—Camp Cash.

[A Steamboat Journey.—Praise for The Ninth.—With Buell in Kentucky, to Secure That State and Penetrate Tennessee.—Soldier Life.—Our Bayonet Charge, the War's First.—McCook Wounded.—A Hard March Back to the Ohio.—More Praise for Us.—We Rout the Rabbits.]

"Honor to whom honor is due."

On November 26, 1861, the Ninth Ohio Volunteer Infantry Regiment left West Virginia's shores and steamed down the Kanawa. People cheered us loudly and affectionately everywhere along the banks. Naturally we were very proud when we docked at Gallipolis in our home state.

A pause there, then we proceeded downstream. Now the greetings, still loud and affectionate, were from the banks of the Ohio.

In the morning of the 28th, Thanksgiving, we arrived at the Cincinnati riverfront. A regulation forbade us ashore. But we wanted to disembark and thousands waited to welcome us.[2] Colonel McCook, ready as usual to serve his regiment, therefore went to get permission. We plyed the river up and down in front of the city meanwhile. Our band played. Rowboats circled us and presented snacks, cigars, etc. We reciprocated those affectionate gifts with munificent ones from our covetable treasures of food: bacon and crackers. The throngs surged impatiently on the bank. At last the Colonel returned in the afternoon, to say we could visit the city until evening.

And so we did, landing to the roar of cannon and peal of bells. We marched through the city to the canal, which cuts northwest across Cincinnati [and forms a boundary of the German district, therefore called Over the Rhine]. Thus we went straight to our own people "over the Rhine." Exultation knew no limit there. What happened, in the bosoms of a good many families, is not to be mentioned here.

We returned to the pier in fine shape and on time nonetheless, to reembark. The colonel informed us that, still busy meanwhile in our behalf, he had gotten General Buell's permission to wait in Cincinnati with us for further orders. There were barracks on Elm Street then, and we went there [amid cheers and the boom of cannon], but only to deposit our baggage; the Colonel had granted leave to one and all until 8:00 the next morning [the 29th].

We [that is, some of us] reported on the 29th and again on the 30th, to resume our voyage to Jeffersonville [Indiana] aboard the *Jakob Strader.* What of the men absent? The paymaster had not arrived until the prior afternoon, and the night elapsed before his treasure passed into the pockets of all of us. Some men consequently took French leave and did not return until December 1.[3] Then we left at last. At our departure, let it be no secret, things happened out of keeping with military discipline.[4]

The tone [of our visit] had in fact already been set in Cincinnati on the 27th:

> The first German regiment is on its way here! We want to extend to its brave men a joyous welcome. Thanksgiving shall be their day of glory. What prompts us [to raise our voices in their honor] is not only [the spirit of] reunion. We are also proud that we sent such men from Cincinnati to the service of the nation and freedom.[5]

The *Volksblatt* said:

> The brave men have been granted a few hours with us. May they spend the time in good cheer. May they see that we think well of Ohio's first German regiment, and that our best wishes go with it to the next battlefield. May it have the occasion there, largely denied it in [West] Virginia, to show that its men merit laurels in the holy cause of freedom. We know, the regiment wants to come to grips with the enemy; and where it enters the lists, a trail shall be blazed for liberty. Proudly and from the start the people of Cincinnati have had faith in

The Ninth and paid it the greatest tribute [by proclaiming] *The Ninth above all.* And today, whatever the Ninth's destination, Cincinnati remains confident of her sons who compose the first German regiment.

Is it any wonder, then, that we found it hard to leave Cincinnati?

And even after we left, the *Gazette* declared on December 2:

> Honor to those brave men! As soon as the 9th Ohio Regiment reported to its corps in General McClellan's Army of West Virginia, it astonished all the generals with its [soldierly] bearing and superb military deportment. From the beginning, its ability excited great expectations. During reconnaissance and under fire—always—its skill and courage fulfilled the expectations, every last one. Thus the 9th led the way in the occupation of Cheat Mountain and at Carnifex Ferry, Sewell Mountain, and Gauley Bridge.

While acknowledging all that acclaim [for us], it would be unfair not to mention briefly the praise lavished on the man responsible in large part for what we had become: our Colonel McCook. The *Volksblatt* wrote again on November 30: "We know personally so many brave fellows of the first German regiment and they speak with one voice: McCook, the regiment's father, is the man they trust implicitly because he looked after them in every situation and shared with them every hardship. This is the opinion and the tribute of men who would never be toadies, lickspittles, or sycophants."

On the afternoon of December 2 we landed in Jeffersonville, Indiana, and pitched camp in deep snow a half-mile from town. We had hoped for "winter quarters" but now renounced them in all good humor, happy instead to get new and comfortable summer mansions for the winter, the so-called Sibley tents.[6]

On the 8th we crossed the Ohio to Louisville, Kentucky. There the people were cold and formal on the whole, though we enjoyed many a good word and kind glance from Germans.[7] We were therefore happy to be ordered aboard a train of the Louisville & Nashville, arriving late in the evening at Lebanon, Kentucky.

The goals of Union forces in the West: drive the enemy from the Mississippi and secure that artery for the North; clean the enemy out of the states still loyal [but potentially secessionist], Kentucky and Missouri; and deter hostile penetration of Ohio, Indiana, and Illinois. In the beginning, three armies were therefore organized [corresponding to three military departments, designated geographically]: the Army of the Missouri under General [Samuel R.] Curtis, the Army of the Tennessee under General [Ulysses S.] Grant, and the Army of the Ohio under General [Don Carlos] Buell.

Most of Buell's army was in Lebanon and we joined it now. Divisions and brigades were being formed. The 35th Ohio and 2nd Minnesota Infantry Regiments, together with ours, composed the 3rd Brigade under our Colonel McCook, assigned to General George C. Thomas's 1st Division. Thus we got what we wanted: leaders we trusted implicitly and good comrades who stayed with us for the duration. With them we shared manifold ordeals and dangers; with them we fought through many a bloody battle; and with them we won grand victories.[8]

Of course, drills, maneuvers, and inspections abounded in Lebanon. The old year ended in revel and riot. The new began with rejoicing. On January 1, 1862, the brigade left [Lebanon] and on the 3rd arrived in Campbellsville, Kentucky.

A big strawstack bulked near the camp there. At once we planned to demolish it for bedding. To preserve it for the good farmer who owned it, however, it was put under guard. But the guard could not conceal the fact (which perhaps sentries themselves discovered) that a hoard of beautiful apples had been stored for winter in the stack. Or were they there, as seems likely, to hide them from unwelcome military guests? And what could be more natural than that we lust after this forbidden fruit? The farmer, probably seeing how things might turn out, decided to make what he could on our sweet tooth. With the help of his Sambo, he began moving apples into his house and exchanging them [with us] for filthy lucre. Sambo, on the other hand, with every trip to the house, secretly gave away many of them [to us]. Still it was a slow procedure that yielded us [relatively] little. Suddenly the stack burst into flame, by spontaneous combustion of course! We got the apples already roasted and for nothing—certainly healthier and cheaper than buying them from the would-be sly Kentuckian. In cheerful gratitude [to a happy twist of "fate"] we named our place [at Campbellsville] Camp Roast Apple.

The cold was bitter now; our march south, hard. On the 11th we were at Camp Burt. Here one of our lordly captains sought to brutalize his way to immortality. (We did promise at the outset [of this book] duly to mention the bad and the stupid with everything else.[9]) On picket during the night, his company occupied a barn. There was straw in the loft. Men off duty sought protection in it from that Arctic. The stern, punctilious captain did not want to permit this luxury to sentries returning from their posts half frozen. They did not exactly obey with alacrity his order to leave the straw and come to the empty floor below and lie on the bare ground there. With his sword, through cracks overhead, he tickled, pricked, and stabbed the soldiers resting [in the straw] above. A trenchant example of how far a man can go in his madness.

On the following days [pausing at Camps Locust and Hamilton] we proceeded ahead of all other units of the division.[10] On the 18th of January we and the 4th Kentucky, 10th Indiana, and 2nd Minnesota infantry regiments, and the Wolford Kentucky Cavalry [the 1st Kentucky Cavalry, commanded by Colonel Frank Wolford] formed the advance guard [having come from Lebanon, under Thomas]. We spent the 18th in camp in that arrangement, along the highway at Logan's Cross Roads [near the Cumberland River in south-central Kentucky].

On the 19th, early—before breakfast—we were ordered abruptly into battle-formation and set against the attacking enemy of eight infantry regiments, twelve cannon, and some cavalry, under [Brigadier] General [Felix Kirk] Zollicoffer.[11] The enemy also enjoyed strong reserves and excellent cover near several buildings, and capitalized on the advantage. The 4th Kentucky and the 10th Indiana held out for about a half-hour in the face of murderous fire. By then the enemy had seized the position our cavalry held on the left flank. Pressing the two regiments, the enemy intended next to hurl himself at the 2nd Minnesota [ordered up to relieve the 4th Kentucky and 10th Indiana]. The 2nd was already so near that, presently, only a fence separated contending troops. Each side often pushed rifles through it and into faces opposite—and fired—and thrust bayonets and stabbed with bowie knives at one another.

At last we, The Ninth, were commanded to a bayonet-charge against the enemy's flank, which was crowding our left. Our first four companies, under Captain (Acting Major) Joseph, therefore struggled while Major Kämmerling (Acting Lieutenant-Colonel and interim regimental commander) completed the wheeling maneuver and led us ahead on the double with: "If it gets too hot for you, shut your eyes, my boys—Forward!" And forward we went.[12]

Let others tell how and with what success we advanced. Colonel McCook, brigade commander, said in his battle report:

> Along the lines of each of the regiments and from the enemy's front a hot and deadly fire was opened and continued for about thirty minutes with seemingly doubtful results. . . . Seeing the superior number of the enemy and their bearing, I concluded the best mode of settling the contest was to order the Ninth Ohio to charge the enemy's position with the bayonet and turn his left flank. The order was given the regiment to empty their guns and fix bayonets; this done, it was ordered to charge. Every man sprang to it with alacrity and vociferous cheerring [*sic*]; the enemy seemingly prepared to resist it, but before the regiment reached him the lines began to give way. This broke the enemy's flank and the whole line gave way in great confusion and the whole turned into a perfect rout.[13]

"Pap" Thomas, division commander, confirmed McCook: "The Ninth Ohio charged the enemy on the right with bayonets fixed, turned their flank and drove them from the field, the whole line giving way and retreating in the utmost disorder and confusion."[14]

The Rebel commander, Colonel [i.e., Brigadier-General] Zollicoffer, had already fallen. His troops, beginning to retreat, seemed to be regrouping about a mile away and preparing to send cavalry at us. We formed a square [*carré*] but there was no counterattack. So we pursued. In the evening we were ten miles from camp and in front of enemy entrenchments. We spent the night in bivouac there.

Thus ended the Battle of Mill Springs, the first decisive Union victory, east or west, since the start of the war. If Bull Run [July 21, 1861] gave secessionists some measure of right to say, "On the battlefield, one Southerner is worth five Yankees," Mill Springs dashed such illusions and demonstrated the true worth of Union soldiers.

Approximate Rebel losses: 125 dead, 306 wounded, 99 captured. Union: 39 dead, 207 wounded, none captured. Our regiment: 6 dead and 28 wounded.[15]

We expected the battle to continue on the 20th. Our artillery blasted a "Good Morning!" into the enemy's camp. Our infantry advanced. But the enemy was gone, across the [Cumberland] river, leaving 18 cannon, 100 wagons, many horses, and considerable equipment.[16] In Somerset [where a small skirmish occurred on January 8] the situation proved to have been one of much ado about nothing. The booty [left by the enemy], however, except food and fodder, was of little use to our troops. None of our wagon-masters could find a horse for his purposes among those captured, and few were fit for the cavalry. The wagons looked more like circus carts than military vehicles. The cannon were of the most time-honored sort.

The Rebels had fled precipitately on the night of the 19th, when the main force must have been only a few miles away and at the attackers' disposal. Consternation therefore swept the South. Its people had pinned great hopes on Zollicoffer and his plan to employ only his troops to attack and destroy ours.[17] And according to a letter by Jefferson Davis, made public later, the Rebels had been counting on Zollicoffer's and especially Crittenden's brave warriors to inflict once and for all a bitter defeat on the "Dutchmen." For, at that time, many Rebel troops seemed in terror of us Germans. They were to have been shown that the German regiments were mortal, too, and could be beaten. Then, so it was thought, even the fearful would more readily take us on.

Things turned out otherwise, of course.[18] As a Cincinnati poet [unidentified] sang at the time:

> And on the rifles' ends there glittered bright
> The steel, pointed and sharp, in the morning light.
> Then the order, "Men of the Ninth, prepare to attack."
> Bravely, at quick-step, they drove the enemy back.

Our bayonet charge struck the 15th Mississippi, the "Tiger Rifles," a notorious regiment fighting opposite us and justly known for courage. Those gentlemen especially had sworn death and devastation to the "Dutchmen." Come evening, however, *they* were nearly destroyed.[19] In the abandoned Rebel camp on the 20th [the next day] it fell to us of The Ninth, for whom havoc had been intended, to make ourselves at home in the quarters of those very "tigers" and to enjoy a tasty meal of the excellent food we found there. Thus the fortunes of war: how capricious!

Yet it is not to be denied today that at Fishing Creek (as the Rebels called Mill Springs) fortune favored our arms. The Rebel commander [George Bibb] Crittenden was drunk,[20] and Zollicoffer fell when most needed—unexpected strokes of bad luck for the Confederates.

Thus at Mill Springs the North won not only the moral victory already mentioned, but also a strategic success not fully clear to us at the time. The Rebels had been driven off their advantageous front and forced to seek a new one in southern Tennessee. In addition the loss of their army on the right flank kept southeastern Kentucky out of their hands. Furthermore, though indirectly, the fall of Forts McHenry [i.e., Henry] and Donelson [Tennessee] had been prepared. And the keys to Nashville were as good as ours.[21]

The region south of the Cumberland now swarmed with disorganized Rebel units, demoralized [by the Battle of Mill Springs], without leaders or orders, striving haphazardly to escape our sphere. But as early as the 21st, no [coherent] enemy remained [for us] to pursue. We buried our dead beside his and conveyed sick and wounded to Somerset. The sick abounded because of hard marches. In this campaign, indeed, casualties due to sickness and deprivation were twice the number killed and wounded. In Somerset all available buildings had been converted to hospitals. Unfortunately so many brave comrades would not depart them alive.

January 24th found us in good shape in Camp Cumberland on the Cumberland River. There we received [in a general order from the President himself, through the Secretary of War, praise for the skill and valor of Union forces at Mill Springs].[22]

The soldier in the field appreciates the praise he has earned. To take pride in himself is not enough; he wants recognition for his services. Accordingly, the general order fell on receptive ears and was, especially to The Ninth, an inspiration to further achievements. Let us hear from one of the people who confirm what has just been said. H[enry] V[an Ness] Boynton—lieutenant-colonel of the 35th Ohio, historian of the Army of the Cumberland, eyewitness—later accompanied us often into battle.

> It was the bayonet-charge of the Ninth Ohio which turned the fortunes of that day, and contributed largely to making that battle the Confederate Bull Run of the West. It was the first notable victory of the three-year troops. Thereafter the bayonets of the Ninth were a deciding factor, whenever its lines were formed in battle.[23]

How right he was! Our bayonets did not rust; they glittered in action so much they hurt the Rebels' eyes.

Several months earlier we had gotten a new physician, Dr. Konrad Söllheim of Cincinnati; and now we could also pride ourselves on a new chaplain, Rev. Joseph M. Fuchshuber. He debuted with a eulogy on a soldier of Company E, dead of wounds [suffered at Mill Springs] and buried with military honors at Camp Cumberland the 26th [of January]. The chaplain also remembered eloquently the others who fell in the struggle but did not receive such recognition. Yes, near the battlefield they (including the six of The Ninth) had been lowered into the grave and to eternal glory—but without a sound in their behalf.

Graves of men who fell at Mill Springs

Colonel McCook's wound took him from us for a while. Colonel [Horatio P.] Van Cleve of the 2nd Minnesota assumed command of the 3rd Brigade; and Major Kämmerling, our regiment. (Lieutenant-Colonel Sondershoff resigned from the service at that time.)

Ordered back to the Ohio river [to protect Cincinnati and Louisville], we proceeded [north-northwest] in [a series of] toilsome marches. Our column crossed miles-long swamps, snow-covered fields, and swollen streams. Often enough we made barely five miles in a day. Men had to help pull wagons; there were not enough horses. Hardship beat several companies and they remained in what was called Camp Attenuation.[24]

The region's farmers seemed devoid of humor and especially lacked sympathy for foraging. On February 15, near Crab Orchard, a farmer shot a private of the 2nd Minnesota. We could not catch the farmer, but we caught his house—with fire. "In war be warlike."

On the morning of the 18th [having passed Stanford] we gained Danville [Kentucky]. A pleasant surprise awaited us in that charming town. Its loyal Germans gave us a splendid laurel wreath, with streamers, inscribed: "Mill Springs." After attaching it to our colors, we marched in precise order, to music by our band, amid resounding cheers and fluttering handkerchiefs and flags, through that friendly place and on to Perryville and Lebanon.

There we heard the joyous news: Forts Henry and Donelson taken by our troops [February 6 and 16, respectively] and Bowling Green [Kentucky] and Nashville evacuated by the Rebels [February 14 and 15, respectively].

Next we went from Lebanon to Louisville via Springfield, Bardstown, and Mount Washington—another torturous trek, because of a spring thaw. Exigencies finally demanded that, not only regiments and companies, but also officers and the rank and file, proceed individually: "Every man for himself: *Forward*!" Yet you must marvel that anyone advanced at all. The Ninth's Sergeant-Major [Raimund] Herrmann, acknowledged to be the brigade's best marcher, confessed for the first time that even he could succumb to exhaustion. We had been promised rest and pay on Washington's Birthday in Springfield but got neither. Years later, few of the brigade could recall a harder march during the entire war. Official reports of the campaign, and histories of the units, agree: it was tough.

Sergeant-Major Raimund Herrmann

Yet on the 25th [of February], all those afflictions notwithstanding, we arrived in good shape in Louisville. Destination: Nashville. Meanwhile, irrespective of our reputation as "fine-looking soldiers," we were able to betake ourselves to the Galt House. There the regiments most important at Mill Springs—2nd Minnesota, 10th Indiana, 4th Kentucky, and our own—each received a banner [for gallantry in that victory]. Ours was inscribed:

"*Mill Springs, Ky January* 19, 1862.
9TH REG'T OHIO VOL.
Presented in behalf of the Loyal Ladies of Louisville."

A [laudatory] letter [of gratitude] accompanied the banner.[25] Naturally the obligatory patriotic speeches were given. Our adjutant Lieutenant [Georg H.] Harries spoke for us: profound words of thanks.

Proudly—with every right to boast of this latest tribute—we went to the river. The *Jakob Strader* [the largest steamboat on the Ohio] awaited our regiment and the 2nd Minnesota; and until about noon the next day, we occupied ourselves to depart aboard it. Along the shore, good countrymen, German and otherwise, were *so* obliging and helpful: they could understand the needs of tired, half-starved, destitute soldiers. Soon the inner man was cared for, and the regiment's growling belly received honors as great as those awarded the regiment's battle-record. Everything in its own good time!

Once more we were the men of the hour, heroes, the "crack regiment"; and we suspected that this time would not be the last. Others agreed. Witness the Cincinnati *Volksblatt* of January 24, 1862:

> Ohio's first German regiment is made up of the best men: especially the excellent turners and strong, intelligent craftsmen. Willich's superb instruction soon produced flawless military bearing and the ability to fight. When still in Camp Dennison the regiment was already Cincinnati's pride, filling every patriot with great expectations. And the expectations have been brilliantly fulfilled. In the Union's first important success in this war for freedom and against slavery, the Federals carried off the palm because of the Ninth Ohio's valiant bayonet-charge. Yes, it was a German regiment that initially heard in

this war the bold command: "Fix bayonets! Forward march! Double-time!" Though outnumbered, but with a *hurrah* [the abrupt, piercing, distinctly Teutonic battle cry, the apt counterpart to the Rebel yell] that could erupt only from German throats, our band of heroes hurled themselves at a startled enemy who could not withstand such ferocity, broke ranks in shock and fright, and abruptly fled in wild retreat. Victory was ours! Unfortunately the favorite among the troops, the brave Colonel McCook, was wounded. Three bullets hit his horse, a fourth tore at his overcoat, and the fifth struck the courageous man himself.

The signs cannot be mistaken; better times are coming! Our intrepid [Union] soldiers have been indolent, sluggish, and ill-humored; but the evil causes of such behavior are beginning to weaken.[26] Indeed, after a brief but perfidious withdrawal, men of action [in the military, in Congress, and in the White House itself] are again coming to the fore in our national catastrophe. What pride and what gratification for us Germans that a German regiment gained the opening success [at Mill Springs] in this the month of the great turning-point! The deed shall go down indelibly in history; and future generations, enjoying in absolute peace the splendid fruits of freedom won in a bloody struggle, will think back with admiration and gratitude on the heroes of Ohio's first German regiment. Therefore, O soldiers of the Republic, follow the example of those brave men! Hasten to victory on the road of battle and let the laurels of fame and immortality be yours! The eyes of the civilized world are upon you; your deeds are interlaced with the destiny of the century! Freedom is in danger; yours the grand assignment to rescue it! This Republic, born to prophecies of a glorious future, remains a bastion of civilization; and you are to restore it to unblemished purity and undiminished power! May your battle-cry be: "Down with barbarism! Long live freedom!"

The Cincinnati *Volksfreund* was no less enthusiastic:

Our armies have triumphed in the West, and the glorious and memorable Battle of Mill Springs crowns that brilliant feat of arms. Within two hours a small group of brave, well-trained soldiers routed the pride of the Rebel forces in Kentucky, driving them from their fortifications, inflicting heavy casualties, and capturing great quantities of materiel. Zollicoffer, the Rebel general, was killed; and his troops could muster no resistance to our violent assault, especially the daring

> bayonet-charge by Ohio's first German regiment. Someday the pens of impartial historians shall with bold strokes enter this shining military exploit into the annals of American history, an enduring monument that shall forever bear noble witness to the bravery of the sons of the great West.

On February 26, at noon, amid boundless cheers, we left Louisville and steamed down the Ohio. On the 28th we arrived at Smithland, where the Ohio receives the Cumberland. On March 1 we started up the Cumberland. Colonel McCook, General Thomas and his staff, and (best of all) a paymaster came aboard. Always happy to see a paymaster, we unburdened this one to the tune of two months' pay for each of us.

We were a fleet of steamboats headed up the Cumberland, taking shortcuts across flooded banks. Numerous brief races occurred despite a ban on racing. Our *Jacob Strader*, the largest boat, never lost the lead. We yearned to see Fort Donelson; but, unfortunately, the racing put us there at night ahead of schedule, and we could not get a good look at it. The arch-Rebel [Brigadier-General John B.] Floyd had commanded it, shortly before its surrender. He knew us from West Virginia and Carnifex Ferry.

We met everywhere the signs of the reckless vandalism that seemed to have possessed the Confederates after their defeats. At Clarksville we saw that the bridge over the Cumberland had been burned. We arrived at Nashville on the night of March 2nd, to find even the superb suspension bridge largely destroyed, cables cut, wooden framework still burning. We assumed—and our assumption proved correct—that the Rebels had intended to level Nashville, lest it become a Union stronghold. The "eternal God" and us mortals [of the Union army] justified their fear: Nashville never fell into Confederate hands again.

We landed on the 5th of March and pitched camp about three miles outside the city, on the Granny White [or Charlotte] Pike, near the attractive and well-built Fort Zollicoffer. Arriving with fat wallets, we named our place Camp Cash.

On the 7th, in the afternoon, the alarm sounded and we were told to arm ourselves, not with guns, but with clubs: we must go on a hunt, to put an end to the frequent shooting of rabbits by sportsmen in our environs. With McCook there and in charge, the brigade closed in on a nearby field from three sides. Like battue beaters we began driving hordes of rabbits out of the tall prairie-grass and toward the river on the fourth side. We did not catch most of them; they hopped to a miserable death by drowning. Our regiment bagged forty-nine: meat for a frugal meal.

After the Rabbit Battle, we had nothing to do but await the order to advance. How impatiently we waited! The reason was that since our day at Mill Springs—and this is no exaggeration—the patriotic impulses of every man jack of our regiment had remained as fervid as those that brought us into the ranks of Union warriors in April of 1861.

Amenities—a victory, a trustworthy commander, good food, and a timely visit by the paymaster—do [nevertheless] help [soldiers] over many hardships in the field. Rare indeed was the occasion when everything was so nice for us!

6

Life under Arms in Europe and Here in America[1]

[Soldier Life in Europe and America.—Reasons for the Differences.—Transportation on the Two Continents.—Its Influence on Warfare.—Quartering.—Need for Reform Here.—Its Improbability.]

The soldier's life in the field in wartime, difficult indeed in Europe [and here in America], imposes physical hardship and psychological stress. Forced marches under full pack, outpost duty, reconnaissance, and other military exigencies, in Europe and America, demand exceptional will-power together with the requisite unflagging bodily strength. But [when we consider the disparity] between European and American roads and trails, a [consequent] difference is to be noted [in the lives of European and American soldiers]. In America a few big military units, with gun carriages and wagons of provisions and baggage, traverse roads and leave them washboarded and pot-holed. Even some of the infrequent and widely separated highways suffer this damage. Riding, driving, and marching are therefore much harder [here] than on the well-maintained roads and thoroughfares of Europe.

And just how few highways exist in America? The terrible secondary routes or "mud roads" are practically unfit for traffic [and don't count as highways]; a few days' rain turns them into quagmires hardly to be negotiated. The traveler [on a mud road] must soon seek, left or right, a new way, be it over rough terrain, through forests and thick and thorny blackberry brambles, or across swollen streams. Outside the East, there are perhaps two highways in the United States, certainly no more. Worse, they have long suffered disrepair. For, almost everywhere, instead of good roads, railways have been built, which move people, livestock, and freight. And canals and navigable rivers [not roads] remain the railways' strongest competition.[2]

At most the state, or the states respectively, take sporadic care of waterways. Maintenance of railroads is left to railroad companies. Their first purpose being to maximize profits, they are not otherwise concerned if trade and traffic slump and suffer. Thus, in expanses of the West and South, only deficient lines of communication straggle between cities and towns, which usually lie far apart. In this country it is therefore almost impossible to marshal armies so that they strike the enemy at the right time from several directions. And, of course [since troops cannot be moved simultaneously to the attack], the greatest regard has to be exercised with those who arrive early; they must be maintained in such strength that they can withstand a massed enemy's assault, perhaps several days long.

On Europe's good highways and roads [by contrast], armies can be mustered from every direction and speedily forwarded, they and their convoys of wagons. Therefore, in a joint operation, they can be more surely expected to be punctual. In the recent [American] civil war [however], despite strict orders to be in a certain place at a specified time, all sorts of difficulties (some insurmountable) often caused units to arrive [as much as] six days late. Thus, many a well-planned operation miscarried and many a campaign failed.

At Mill Springs, for example, the enemy's right wing, under General Zollicoffer, occupied fortifications along the Cumberland River. Of the Union regiments ordered to attack them, most were still miles to the rear. Wagons mired in a morass, they advanced but slowly and could not be in the right place in the right time. The enemy, seizing the opportunity astutely, hurled from his stronghold a well-calculated sortie with six times the troops we had assembled. Fortunately for us the protracted rains [which had checked us] also delayed the assault on us—several hours longer than anticipated. Therefore the enemy engaged our outposts, not before dawn [as planned], but in broad daylight. That lag, and our brave defense, saved us. So we were permitted another brilliant victory, even though we never allowed for a surprise offensive and were not prepared. At any rate, there was no way we could have been prepared.

Shelter remains a chief and enduring difference [in the life of the European and the American soldier]. The European—however hard he must march, whatever stiff and dragged-out battles he must fight—is quartered in the evening and for the night; and at least he gets protection from cold, rain, and snow. Consequently he rests better and rises more refreshed than if, unable to fix a comfortable bed, he had spent the night the usual American way: forced to lie on bare ground, often even in a swamp, and very often without protection of any kind. Far too frequently the blanket or some sheet or a raincoat was all we had against rain and cold. A little straw or hay, even the boughs of trees (especially cedar), was luxury itself. Not a few times we returned to camp soaked by rain or by wading creeks and rivers, only to have to sleep in the open. A fire for cooking or to dry our clothes? Fuel—so scanty on many an occasion—must be hunted up first. Of course, clothes were dried on our backs. How often we burned holes in clothes and roasted our shoes!

What, then, in the matter of nocturnal shelter, is so very different for the European soldier, no stranger to hardship in every other respect? He [unlike us] usually enjoys a roof over his head, and fuel is available where he is quartered. If nobody else is willing or able to prepare his food, he can repair to the kitchen for everything he needs. He can change clothes if necessary, and dry them properly.

[Did we have] even so much as a tent to pitch in the evening, especially after a long and hard day's march, and after battles, here in America? Fact is, particularly at such times, the wagons would not appear, or not until everyone, exhausted, had bedded down and fallen asleep.

Yet, even then, you could be happy—if coffee could still be made and a few crackers enjoyed with it. So: Hail, all hail to the coffee! Though not always the best, it kept everyone on the ball. Many and many a time you would lie down, soaked to the skin or chilled to the bone, thinking: "I'm sure I won't be able to lift a foot tomorrow." But what happened? A good helping of coffee and crackers in the belly and you slept well and got up promptly in the morning, ready to march again.[3] If your clothes were still somewhat wet, every last stitch would dry during the day's trek.

European soldiers, as mentioned above, are quartered on civilians. Try it in this country and you'll be in a pickle! In America, there is no quartering of soldiers on civilians; not even American soldiers will be accepted by their own countrymen. The principle, "My house is my castle," protects the sovereign citizen from having to quarter soldiers. Even a volunteer, a fellow-citizen in arms, will be considered a uniformed "tramp" and, in any event, be treated like one. So, once again, the soldier is left to his own devices, forced to get what he needs by cunning or by force. Thus, charges of "looting" and all sorts of theft are usually unjustified; nothing was removed but essential food and drink. [In our case, such removal was necessary because] our "fellow-citizens" would have chosen to give us nothing (they disliked us too much). He is barking up the wrong tree who thinks otherwise. They would rather have poisoned us.

Can it be such an incredible notion that the soldier's life in the field cannot be improved and made more tolerable here? In Europe the citizen boards the soldier. That is, the householder must take in the number appropriate [to the size of the dwelling], for which he is reimbursed a stipulated sum by means of a tax deduction. Cannot the same arrangement be adopted in a land where, at the present time, every citizen, able-bodied and mentally fit, is supposed to participate in the nation's defense? Or must men who defend this country be always seen and treated as pariahs?

Under prevailing conditions, what a veritable miracle that the volunteers who served continuously, in three to four years of war, did not grow wild and become depraved! Unlike their counterparts in Europe, they enjoyed almost no relationships with civilians and families. Now, as the European soldier, in friendly and hostile territory, is quartered on civilians, so he maintains some contact with families and, of his own accord, forms affiliations that save him from brutalization. Nothing of the sort happens here. Only high-level officers take quarters with civilians, if even those officers are able to get them. It must be borne in mind, of course [in fairness], that miles may be traveled in the South and West, and not a farm or even a log cabin seen. And then a camp in the open cannot be avoided.

To some extent, Turners and veteran soldiers stood better the hardships imposed by the war, being accustomed to physical training, practice marches, and military exercises. And for that reason, it is said, Turner disciplines will be adopted everywhere in this country, and with them [will come] the Turners' extended hikes on frugal rations and with primitive accommodations and beds of straw.

Perhaps that rigor will appear—but not until hypocrisy comes to an end and a joyful, unconstrained view of life replaces it.

7

March 25 to November 3, 1862[1]

To the Cumberland.—A Visit with Willich and the 32nd Indiana.—Shiloh.—Corinth.—Tuscumbia.—New Colors.—Florence.—The Death of Colonel McCook.—Dechard.—Chasing Bragg in Kentucky.—Perryville.

[The Ninth a Part of Union Strategy against the Confederate Mississippi Valley, Locus of Half the Confederacy's Territory, Power, and Wealth.]

"They have buried a good man but to us he was more than a good man."

From day to day the truth grew plainer and plainer. It required no gift of prophecy to predict that this calamitous war was nowhere near its end but in fact had just begun. Outcome: uncertain. By now we [of The Ninth] had accommodated ourselves accordingly, having dismissed silly illusions. When duty called we took the bull by the horns and held fast and did not worry about the future.

On March 20 we began the advance to the Cumberland River.[2] The 18th Regular U.S. Infantry Regiment had recently reinforced our brigade. For the first time, Buell's Army of the Ohio marched in one compact mass of four divisions: [William "Old Bull"] Nelson's [4th], [Ormsby McKnight] Mitchell's [3rd], [Alexander] McD[owell] McCook's [2nd], and Thomas's [1st]. The last, ours, was the rear-guard. Destination: Corinth, Mississippi, where General [Albert Sidney] Johnston had concentrated his Rebel forces.[3] We traversed a magnificent landscape [via Franklin and Spring Hill, to Columbia, Tennessee]. Spring and divine serenity seemed to have come together to the countryside. Here and there [however] a blocked road or a wrecked bridge reminded us that in those years, peace bestowed its beauty on only that which was not human.

Willich's German regiment, the 32nd Indiana, had to rebuild one of those bridges before the bulk of the army could proceed. The 32nd, part of McD. McCook's division, was camped near Columbia, about two and a half miles from us. On March 30th, taking advantage of the pause [at Columbia], we paid the 32nd a visit. Willich himself met us a half-mile from camp and led us back with music. And there—what grand goings-on! Each company in Willich's regiment hosted its counterpart in ours. When "assembly" sounded about 6:00 P.M., the 32nd formed a square [*carré*], we marched into it, and Willich gave a brilliant speech. He explained why, contrary to his promise made in West Virginia, he could not return to us: his new regiment asked, and higher-ups ordered, that he stay with them.

"I found in the 32nd Indiana," he said in closing,

> a regiment of Germans as brave and tenacious as you, comrades of The Ninth. They made me their leader, I could not leave them then. But I'm convinced that, come what may, wherever you and the 32nd Indiana are engaged, honor will redound to the German name. The bayonet-assault by The Ninth at Mill Springs, and [in early fighting in Kentucky] the 32nd's defeat of the Texas Rangers at Munfordville [on December 17, 1861], will be remembered forever.[4] And there will be plenty of other opportunities to show that we are Germans and always ready to fight—and if need be, die—for liberty and justice. The war is not about to end; it has barely begun. Therefore be steadfast, persevere, keep your spirits up, and remain true to the Noble Cause and to yourselves!

After the evening meal the two regiments went together to serenade the division commander, General A. McD. McCook (a brother to our colonel) at his headquarters. The songfest closed with our German *hurrah* of farewell. Thus the day ended. We separated [from the 32nd]. "When shall we meet again, brother?" An idle question in wartime! [At any rate] that day [of our visit with the 32nd] was one of rejoicing, a shining moment in the life of struggle and danger before and behind us.

The brigade [after passing Mount Pleasant, Henryville, and Waynesboro, Tennessee] did not resume its advance until April 6, on terrible roads, to the matutinal thunder of cannon. We of the rearguard could not tell: had our advance divisions stumbled onto the enemy? Or had Grant, nearby with his Army of the Tennessee, come to grips with Johnston?

Covering forty hard miles the 6th and 7th, we fetched up in Savannah [Tennessee] on the right bank of the Tennessee River. There we learned what had happened. Johnston and about 50,000 troops had fiercely attacked Grant's approximately 40,000 at Pittsburgh Landing [usually called the Battle of Shiloh].[5] April 6 ended with mutually heavy casualties and the outcome undecided. Fighting started again on the 7th, after Buell's first three divisions arrived in the nick of time. Finally the Rebels withdrew. Both sides seemed to have made gross errors. Of ours, the one that limited Grant to 40,000 men was of the gravest consequence.[6] The battle, known as Shiloh, cost the Union 1,754 dead, 4,408 wounded, 2,885 prisoners, therefore a total of 13,047.[7] Rebel losses, never fully determined, amounted to no fewer than 10,000.

We, the fourth division [in the order of march] and the rearguard of Buell's army, approached the battlefield by steamboat about noon on the 9th. The field was an ugly sight, and bivouacking unpleasant.[8] But we had to bear it for ten days.

On April 12 the Commander-in-Chief of Union armies in the West [i.e., commander of the Department of the Missouri], General [Henry W.] Halleck, came from St. Louis to direct further operations against Corinth himself. On the right, then, Thomas and the Army of the Tennessee; center, Buell and the army of the Ohio; left, Pope [and the Army of the Mississippi]. Grant was not in charge of any unit in particular, though by rank he was second in command. He and Halleck were not friends, as was well known.[9]

On Sunday the 13th the mayor of Cincinnati [George Hatch] appeared with twenty-five policemen and supplies of all kinds, to tend sick and wounded Cincinnatians. Fortunately we [of The Ninth] had suffered neither wounds nor sickness, at least thus far, because we arrived at the battlefield late. But the supplies and gifts were nonetheless gladly received and distributed to the sound and healthy, who did not object.

Our colonel [McCook], promoted to general already three months ago, was now supposed to take command of a division. Again he declined and begged for the privilege of keeping his brigade and staying with his Germans. He wanted to share joy and sorrow with them, and return home with them when the war ended. Unfortunately the future held something else!

For five long weeks we worked at the siege of Corinth and skirmished daily with the besieged.[10] Lordly generals and overbearing colonels thought up all sorts of "necessary and useful" trivia for the greater education and finer discipline of the troops. Rational interpretation and humane implementation blunted most of these aberrations, however, at least in McCook's brigade. McCook, if need be, would not hesitate to ignore an order if he believed it destructive.

A certain General Sherman was a terrorizer of subordinates and an authentic martinet. (He is not to be confused with the famous commander of the same name, General W[illiam] T[ecumseh] Sherman, who later led us to Atlanta.) The other Sherman headed our division at Corinth and of course tested on us his talents as a tormenter. Our colonel McCook therefore took a dim view of him. For example, when Sherman directed that roll-call be answered three times a day under full pack, McCook said calmly: "If there is anything to do, boys, we are always there without having roll-call all day. Nonsense!"[11] And we continued to do as we had done.

We "Niners" were entering our second year of service now, and looking forward to it with perfect peace of mind. Meanwhile, though the city was fortified, and despite recent and serious skirmishes between patrols, we extended our works to within 1,000 yards of Corinth. Any day we could expect either the order for our general assault on the fortress or a sortie by the besieged against us.

During the night (29 May) the enemy bustled: trains seemed to come and go continually. Everything signified a Rebel evacuation when at 4:00 A.M. a muffled explosion told us the city's magazines and other installations had been blown up. At last we Union forces advanced. McCook's brigade approached to within 500 yards and then secretly penetrated the city itself. Probably even today nobody can say who gave the order. Certainly when "the old woman" Sherman looked for our brigade, he could learn nothing but "Yes, we were in Corinth!"

Sherman: "By whose orders did McCook move forward?"

Sherman still awaits an answer to that question.[12]

Another question remains unanswered. Why, at Corinth, was the enemy unfortunately allowed to escape again? And we asked especially: Where would such policies lead, when the Rebels were always permitted thus to withdraw instead of being attacked and smashed as could well have happened at Corinth?

We pursued the fleeing Rebels for about a week [as far as Rienzi and Ripley], getting for it nothing worth mentioning but much fruitless marching to-and-fro. Thus the same old story in the West: many cooks under a worse-than-doubtful chef.[13] No wonder, then, that the soup was often spoiled with a vengeance.

We camped at Corinth again, and stayed until June 23rd. Beautiful drill fields were laid out; nearly every company [of The Ninth] had erected a bakery; and the paymaster had turned up. The Ninth's sutler received from Cincinnati a full load of beer and the snacks to go with it. In short, prospects were rosy; everything was shaping up so pleasantly that a delightful summer encampment on the Tennessee could be counted on as practically certain. Consequently, much was accepted placidly into the bargain when, under less-favorable conditions, a stir might have been made instead.

Take for example the peculiar practice of brigade inspections in our army—*peculiar* because the brigade's regimental commanders conducted them. Naturally these inspections did not amount to much; the inspectors were too well known.[14] Events of June 9 included another of the inspections, conducted by a certain presumptuous pipsqueak (or *Fenzmaus* as he was called), the staff officer of the 2nd Minnesota who stood four feet six in his boots. His inspection that day was of the strictest rigor. Now, the Minnesota Mouse could no more find fault with us on June 9 than the Mississippi Tigers could defeat us a few months before. We passed his inspection with the honor of being the division's tidiest regiment. That kind of inspection would have meant more, had a staff officer of another brigade or division conducted it; and we would have valued higher the inspector's stamp of approval.

Pentecost being barely over, our noble Sherman did not want to miss a chance to visit his division with extra-special torment.[15] On the 10th [of June] he marched us several miles to the rear of where we were camped in tents, and we spent the night without shelter. His own precious self did not go unprotected, however, for he ordered that his tent be brought along. Such eccentricities—to put it mildly—provoked his staff, and especially our McCook, to scenes with him. They remonstrated with him for such unnecessary harshness. In vain. So McCook resorted to a different measure. At 7:00 A.M. on the 11th, already back from our night of exposed bivouac, we faced the prospect of another trek. McCook commanded us to do all our laundry the minute we returned. Thus, when the order to depart would eventually arrive, he could plead wet clothes as an excuse to remain in camp. The order, as frivolous as the last, did arrive. In vain. McCook and his laundry brigade could not march, and Sherman and his entire division had to stay put. Finally on June 13, Sherman was relieved of his post. "Pap" Thomas took charge again, and the division became the first in the Army of the Ohio.

The division's turn [to go to war again] came on the 22nd with orders to march to Alabama. Just when things had become so nice for us! But we had no choice. More the pity that so much delightful beer remained on hand. The historian of our sister-division, the 35th Ohio, remarked: "The only way to take the beer along was to take it inwardly; and it can be said the boys fell to and did good duty, but with all that large quantities had to be left, to the disappointment of many."[16]

We marched—it was literally forced—to Iuka and Tuscumbia, Alabama, pausing en route at (among other places) Dickson's plantation [and at Tomkins's farm near Bear Creek]. The plantation belonged to the Rebel Quartermaster-General and we spared nothing there. Then we camped three weeks at Tuscumbia, to guard railway bridges and protect the construction of the Memphis-Charleston line. The Fourth of July was celebrated at "Pap" Thomas's divisional headquarters at Tuscumbia, with the usual national salute at noon and, in the evening, speeches, like Declamation Day at school. Colonel Fry of the 4th Kentucky read aloud the Declaration of Independence and then offered us an oration much concerned with "southern brothers," who were to be treated mildly, and that sort of thing. Then Colonels Steedman and Connolly of Ohio, as well as Harlan of Kentucky, gushed and gushed. But we and our McCook disliked the effusions so much that McCook finally sprang to his feet and stated our position—in *his* style. "The Union must be preserved, the rebellion crushed. The secessionists are our brothers no more, they are enemies: ours and the nation's. If they will not submit peaceably, they must be exterminated. My men and I are ready to do just *that,* even if it means the South is to be laid waste."

"Pap" Thomas listened quietly to the oratorical tournament. But when the tides of bombast rose to a flood, he said it was time to go home. "If the boys" (the good colonels) "can't keep within bounds, they must omit celebrating the Fourth of July hereafter!"[17]

On Sunday, July 6, at 11:00 A.M., The Ninth answered "assembly" by forming a square. Colonel McCook entered it with new regimental colors just delivered by a delegation from the Cincinnati city council. He presented the colors to us with an apt, eloquent speech. They were of splendid blue silk with the American eagle encircled by the inscription: "Mill Springs. From the City of Cincinnati to the 9th Reg't. O.V.I. U.S.A. Col. R. L. McCook." The colors remained with the regiment, together with the national flag.

Several reconnaissances to the east, in frightful heat and without results, made us wonder why in the world such apparently senseless behavior continued, especially as many men of the corps were ill. Sunstroke was no longer unusual among us. Colonel McCook himself took sick and Colonel [Ferdinand] Van Derveer of the 35th Ohio assumed provisional command of the brigade. But McCook never left our regiment; stayed always as near as possible, now in the ambulance, now in a sedan chair.

On July 22 the governor of Ohio [David Tod] named Gustav Tafel of Cincinnati, a second lieutenant in our Company A, to be a lieutenant-colonel of the 106th Ohio Volunteer Infantry. A good officer, he brought honor to our regiment and his new one. Indeed, plenty of changes among officers occurred in the regiment then, as six lieutenants resigned and eight noncommissioned officers were promoted to fill vacancies.

The local residents who had not fled were arch-secessionists. Nevertheless we fed Uncle Sam's delectable rations to women and children left behind—even though, often enough, we had scarcely anything to eat ourselves. In gratitude a preacher in the pulpit one Sunday in Florence, in the presence of many of our officers and men, called down the wrath of God "on the heads of the Yankee hordes whose presence was polluting the South." That diatribe signified "God's repayment" for the mystifyingly generous forbearance of the Unionists! Colonel Harlan nabbed the fellow in the pulpit, and General Thomas packed him off to the workhouse in Nashville.

Fires sometimes broke out in local Rebels' houses. Of course we, in our innocence, never knew how they started. In our honest way we helped with rescue and salvage; and the 35th Ohio was our staunch ally in this work of mercy. We carried beds out-of-doors, for example, and threw glasses and porcelain out of windows, and were passionately solicitous to save from incineration the beehives in yards and gardens. As to the honey in question, our history and that of the 35th are silent.[18]

Day in, day out, local hostility swelled into more and more assaults on some individual soldiers, and increased cruelty to others, by farmers and villagers. Hence reason enough to assume that bushwackers (also called by the pet name "guerrillas") were operating here, albeit in secret for the present.

On August 3 we arrived in Athens [Alabama, via Florence, Elk River, and Hopkinsville]. Here a short while before, Colonel [John Basil] Turchin [or Ivan Vasilevitch Turchininoff and formerly] of the 19th Illinois [and then commander of the 8th Brigade, 3rd Division, Army of the Ohio], a Russian [who had served in the Crimea before emigrating to Illinois], allegedly told his men he would "close his eyes for two hours or so" while the men tried to discover which residents of the little town were supposed to have jostled some soldiers. During the search, it seems, the "southern brothers and sisters" were not treated with perfect gentleness. General Buell therefore ordered the colonel court-martialed. Found guilty (of God knows what crime), he was to be discharged. But President Lincoln did not confirm the verdict. Moreover, at the first opportunity [at the intercession of Madame Turchin], he promoted the distinguished colonel to brigadier-general.[19]

On Tuesday, August 5, we left Athens and headed for Tennessee. We had gone about four miles when two soldiers bounded up at a gallop. Their news was heart-wrenching. Rebels had ambushed and captured Colonel McCook![20] As we of The Ninth were and remain parties to this case, so let another, the historian of the 35th Ohio, tell what happened and what we did.

> On the 5th of August, our regiment had the advance; Col. Van Derveer was temporarily in command of the brigade, which was mov-

ing under the guidance of the brigade topographical engineer, who was not as well informed as to the route to be taken as he might have been. At a point where the road divided he led off on the wrong one. Col. McCook came after us at a short distance, and seeing we were on the wrong track, sent an orderly to recall us. He in the meantime drove ahead, lying on his cot in the carriage, and was now in advance of his troops.

An hour or so later, as the regiment was marching up a hill, it was fired into by some guerrillas. McCook was ahead and of course had fallen into their hands.

Col. Van Derveer took Company C, and moved on a run after Col. McCook, whose wagons were found on fire; and his fine horses taken; and the ambulance in which he was being conveyed overturned, lying by the road side; while he was found in a cabin near by, wounded; left in charge of the family, all his attendants captured and taken away. His wounds were mortal and he could not be moved; so the brigade went into camp.

The outrage was keenly felt by the men of the brigade, and particularly so by McCook's old regiment, the Ninth Ohio. It was one of the finest regiments in the service; and no better disciplined body of men was found anywhere; but this act of perfidy so aroused them, that they broke over all restraints; and could not be controlled. They were bound on revenge and proceeded to work.

It was said that the guerrillas were cheered, as they dashed by after some of McCook's attendants, at a Baptist minister's house, situated on the road we were passing. The inmates were given thirty minutes to get out whatever effects desired; after which the house would be given to the flames. The wife and grown daughters scouted at the idea of burning the house.

When the time had expired the flames broke out from all sides, and in an hour a smoking ruin was all that was left; the flames, seemingly, licked the very earth. The work of destruction did not stop here. The houses of those reported by "intelligent contrabands" as members of the guerrilla band, were sought out and given to the flames. All that day and the next, the black curling smoke could be seen rising heavenward, marking the spot where a guerrilla lived; the lines were smoked effectually. The cavalry sent out from Dechert scoured the country for miles, but no guerrilla band was found; it had disbanded, and members appeared as citizens, until ordered out by the commander for another raid.

The murder of McCook was a cowardly act. He was lying on his bed in an ambulance, unable to rise, being reduced by sickness—they shot him in this helpless condition.

The revenge taken by the regiment on the country around, may have been severe; but in strict accordance with the usages of war. The citizens were in accord with the acts of the guerrilla band and boldly avowed the same, as did the Baptist minister and family.

McCook lingered nearly two days and died. The brigade was placed in motion at once to convey the body to the nearest railway station, so as to be sent thence to Cincinnati for interment.

The fame of the Ninth Ohio as "avenging angels," spread rapidly; and when the citizens of Winchester heard that we were approaching that place, they petitioned the military authorities for extra guards to protect their town. We noticed, on entering the place, that an unusual number of sentinels were stationed on both sides {of} our line of march; and numerous inquiries were made: "Which is the Ninth Ohio?"

That regiment was then the rear of the brigade; and when it reached town, the band struck up a well-known Prussian air, and every man fell into place. The regiment marched through Winchester in fine style; more orderly troops never passed the streets of any city. It

Dr. Beatty's house, near Newmarket, Alabama, in which Colonel Robert L. McCook died on 6 August 1862

was not known until afterward, that extra guards had been placed to protect the citizens against the Ninth Ohio. Had that fact then been hinted, there would have been trouble.[21]

Thus wrote the historian of the 35th Ohio. His account must be true and faithful because, as the brigade's advance-guard, the 35th can be called eyewitnesses to the tragedy. So we have only to add that an inexpressible grief seized us at the loss of our beloved leader. A foul and murderous hand had canceled his keen desire to return, as our colonel, home to Cincinnati. Guerrillas and their leader, Frank Gurley—murderers, bushwackers, thieves, and soldiers and militia not in the [direct] service of the Confederacy—had robbed us of a revered man, and deprived the country of a very promising officer. Our reprisal was justified; we have no reason to reproach ourselves for it.[22] Indeed, we regretted only that our entire regiment was not allowed to accompany the body of its colonel to the train station, and that the body was relegated to the rear-guard.

We have spoken several times of McCook's grand virtues, and shown why he was popular.[23] Therefore, in the way of the soldier, let us advance and not look back!

Gustav Kämmerling became our colonel. We have observed what he did at Mill Springs. As our narrative unfolds [from here], you will see clearer what kind of man *he* was.

We [passed Salem and Winchester and] pitched camp on the 7th [of August], near Dechert Station [i.e., Decherd, Tennessee], on the Louisville & Chattanooga Railroad. Erecting fortifications, we put to work the Negroes who had come to us for protection, and all the others in the area besides. We would stay here quite a while, so it seemed.[24]

Brigadier-General Johannes [i.e., James] B. Steedman took over the 3rd Brigade [on August 8, replacing the dead McCook]. At the personal request of the division commander [Thomas], our regiment received the following message as a regimental order. Thomas directed the regiment's commander [Kämmerling] to tell his officers and men that he [Thomas] shared their grief at the death of Colonel McCook.

I sympathize with the regiment in their sorrow over the bitter loss they have suffered. I know how much they loved their leader, so I can

> understand their desire for retaliation and revenge. I believe, however, that they will best express it by confronting the enemy in battle. I believe, too, that the regiment shall soon have the privilege of launching that very attack [of retaliation and revenge]. Therefore I presume that despite its anguish, the regiment will remember discipline and mind regulations. Without discipline and regulations, no happy result can be expected against an enemy who could use the helplessness of the grievously mourned colonel to murder him.[25]

Thomas's words were blunt but fair. He further ordered thirty days of mourning for McCook, to be observed throughout the division, another proof of esteem for the murdered man. It seemed that we were to be reminded time and again of our beloved leader.

In the aftermath of his brother's slaying, General Alexander McDowell McCook visited us in Pelham [Tennessee] and suggested we might have ourselves transferred to Willich's brigade, which belonged to his division. Thus Willich's wish—and ours, so McCook had heard—would be granted: that we serve under our old drillmaster and major, and side by side with his German 32nd Indiana. McCook promised to take it on himself always to care for our regiment as well as his brother had cared for it. Almost all the men favored the proposal, but the officers divided over it. Did the officers better appreciate the [likely] consequences; or did the men, always easily talked into anything? Let us not discuss that question now. McCook's suggestion was debated with considerable agitation. (Germans are notoriously thought to be phlegmatic, yet when are they not agitated?) Result: "Let well enough alone! Keep things as they were! Stay with Pap Thomas!"[26]

Food was an acute problem again; eventually we were put on half rations. Still, this region [of Tennessee] was fertile. Besides, the "poor, abandoned families" of bushwackers and other Rebels received ample quantities of Uncle Sam's rations. So we foraged assiduously—as individuals, as companies, as regiments. Fields of ripe corn, and smokehouses, for miles around, were hit for contributions. Now and then we could be almost happy for the shortage [of regular rations].

An army-wide order of that time was intended to force secessionists and their friends to recognize the merits of Union paper money, "greenbacks." That is, when buying things from those people, Union soldiers were to pay in greenbacks; and the sellers would be obligated to recognize and accept good paper as legal tender. Gold or silver coins were to be used only in a transaction when change must be made. Well, soldiers were not involved in making change very often!

Meanwhile [in the Confederate campaign to retake Tennessee and Kentucky] the Confederate commander [of the Army of Tennessee], General [Braxton] Bragg, had begun his march on Nashville [from Chattanooga].[27] We also set out [from south-central Tennessee]. We intended to keep him company [and cross his purposes]. Mountains [ranges of the Cumberlands] lay between his army and ours, so our main goal was to "plug the gaps"; that is, prevent the enemy's slipping through narrow passes from the east and interrupting our advance. And thus we proceeded [racing with Bragg] for some time.

General Steedman, our new brigade commander, knew well when to wink, even when to shut his eyes, if rations grew more or less short. (Short ones, by the way, were normal then.) On August 20, near Decherd, we stumbled onto a large peach orchard overflowing with ripe fruit. The general discovered immediately that the brigade needed rest and he stopped for it where the entire brigade had access to the orchard. What happened to the fruit has no place in our story, but let us mention that he seemed happy with the proceedings and did not interrupt until the peaches had served their purpose. An incident like this often produces more results [in building morale] than an army-wide order pages-long. And perhaps the general foresaw the one that appeared on the 22nd. It put us back on half rations because the Rebels had wrecked the railway and blocked all shipments to us. But the countryside abounded with food and, using our talents, we were able to recoup the losses.

Still our morale left something to be desired; we longed for decisive action, for *battle*. Yes, guerrillas were provoking quite a stir with their considerable numbers hereabouts. And The Ninth, certainly having a score [the murder of McCook] to settle with those bushwackers, wanted nothing more than the chance to give them a sound thrashing. But our wish was not fulfilled; no changes were made [and we did not pursue the guerrillas].[28]

Meanwhile our half-ration menu boasted diversity; and on September 2 there shone in camp another example of the infinitude: heaps of that sweet fruit of the South, pawpaw. Many of us ate too much and were sick. Yet, deferentially, the place [at Beech Grove] was named for the cause of the internal disturbance: Camp Pawpaw.

On September 4 [after Pelham, Hillsboro, and Manchester] we reached the well-provisioned Murfreesboro [Tennessee], and [on the 6th, Lavergne and] on the 7th, Nashville, ahead of the Rebels, after fourteen days of hard and often dangerous marching. If Bragg's intent had been to take Nashville, we beat him to it and occupied it ourselves.[29]

The city had changed much since the Rebels evacuated it six months before. Life bustled now. Business and commerce throve, even though under military control. People who had fled were back. The news pleased us that, under Thomas, we were to stay a while; that is, in Fort Negley nearby.

The government had announced by general order that it would no longer salary the army's musicians, and on the 11th our regimental band left us. We let our musical comrades go, but reluctantly, not only because of our long and happy association with them, but also because we sorrowed at the thought that we of The Ninth, we music-loving Germans (we of all people), now had to follow the drum and nothing but the drum [and the fife]. [Must] *we* be satisfied with what we had so often scorned as barbarous: the drum and the fife? We sighed: "Such is the fate of beauty in the world" and "Times change, music changes [and we sing a different song]."

In the meantime we had been busy fortifying Nashville. Simultaneously we had provided for our own welfare and built ourselves ovens. Now the fortifications and entrenchments were nearly done, and we happily anticipated our first home-baked bread.[30]

We would have eaten it on the 15th, had we not been compelled to march at 5:00 A.M., chasing Bragg again, via Edgefield and Mitchellville to Kentucky, where [after about forty miles] we reached Franklin on the 16th.[31] All day we slogged through terrible rains. They submerged our camp, drenching it into our wettest yet. In Bowling Green a pleasant surprise delayed the regiment. Arriving in town, we found our departed band stopping there. At once they took post at our head. How we pranced through that place! We never marched better in any grand parade—and when speaking of The Ninth, that's a mouthful. Here (Bowling Green) and now (September 18) we renewed, and with vigor, the pursuit of Bragg. The question this time: Who would reach Louisville first, Bragg or Buell? On the 20th we were near the enemy; then face to face with him near Cave City on the 21st; but there was no engagement.[32]

We realized the ultimate in short rations here, as all our baggage had been left behind, including backpacks. Normal half-rations would have included crackers but here we had none. Instead they gave us—flour! What to do with *flour* on a forced march? Were we to concoct a cold gruel and swallow *that?* The riddle shall never be solved. Cooking without salt in a tin cup warmed the flour but it remained repulsive, a mess. We had no fats [for baking or frying] either. Thus it was up to us to forage once again, but most foraging must be done while on the move. So we owed life itself to the abundance of fruit. On the 20th we actually shared an orchard with the enemy; half of it lay within his line of pickets, and his provisions were as short as ours. During this trek, by the way, our pickets must have skirmished often with his. We found evidence of such clashes the entire way—right to the outskirts of Louisville.

On the 21st, almost all our army marched past us [of The Ninth] and we became the rear-guard again. On the 22nd we could not budge because too many troops were underway ahead of us.

When we left Nashville ten days before, about a dozen dogs joined our train, a typical feature of a march, regardless who owns the dogs or where they live. Only three remained now, the rest dead of too much heat and too little water. In view of this fact, the frequent philosophical discussions, and the often-addressed question, of which could stand more hardship, man or his best friend, were natural enough but at the same time moot. We observed, with our own eyes, proof positive of man's superiority to the dog!

At last, on the 25th [after Munfordsville, Green River, and Elizabethtown] we reached West Point on the Ohio, but the steamboats that were supposed to meet us were not there. No wonder, then, that we joined the potato harvest meanwhile. With all our might, we lessened the trouble and eased the effort that faced local farmers! Late in the afternoon a fleet of steamboats arrived with provisions. The attempt at orderly distribution failed miserably at the outset, the men were so ravenous. Finally the items were simply flung ashore, and the greedy horde snatched them up. The historian of the 35th [Ohio] described the melee in terms more elegant than drastic: "The scramble for the precious morsels thus tossed among the boys, was more than interesting. The farmer who has cut up corn in his field, and thrown it over the fence for his half starved hogs, can picture the scene enacted."[33] Not a flattering rendition but unfortunately true, all too true.

By now we knew we were a step ahead of Bragg again, and ready to meet him in Louisville, should he dare attack. Next morning our regiment and the 35th moved there by boat. Our brigade, other brigades, divisions, all the army of the Ohio, followed—thousands upon thousands. Once more, however, business called Bragg east.[34]

The Army of the Ohio had been reorganized, to consist now of three corps under Generals [Thomas L.] Crittenden, [Charles C.] Gilbert, and McDowell McCook. The 35th Ohio, the 2nd Minnesota, the 18th U.S. Infantry, the 78th Indiana, and our regiment composed a brigade in General [Albin] Schöpf's 3rd Division of Gilbert's III Corps. Here [in Louisville] we met additional new regiments, of Cincinnatians wholly or in part, and in large measure German: the 106th under our former lieutenant, now lieutenant-colonel, Gustav Tafel; as well as the 108th.

The next several days [at the end of September] saw us in and around Louisville but, unpaid for six months, we were broke and could not do the beautiful city justice. Still, how splendid everything looked and seemed at first when we marched east [i.e., south] toward Shepherdsville on October 1. But, gradually, within hours, gloom settled as word spread through the ranks: "The next campaign has begun and we have not been paid for the last." Suddenly—discipline lapsed. "Paymaster!" one regiment shouted. "Paymaster!" another answered. The cry multiplied. An ugly scene ensued. To some extent its long-unpaid, always-inadequately-fed perpetrators were to be excused—if, from a military point of view, such things are ever to be excused. Let us bear in mind of course that, in legal terms, troops who have signed up of their own accord constitute one party to a contract. Despite their oath and the obligation to unconditional obedience, they can insist that the other party honor its commitments in full; which in this case meant to pay the troops every two months, not let six elapse and incidents occur that bordered on mutiny. Yet, though we had come to such a pass, we were not paid until November 6, and then only for September and October. That affair was badly handled.

Of several changes among officers of our regiment on the 28th [of September], let us mention the promotion of Major [Karl] Joseph to lieutenant-colonel, and of Captain F[ritz] Schröder [of Company D] to major. Captain Wilhelm Stängel [of Company C], our former chaplain, was cashiered after being court-martialed on an accusation by several associates who said he had reviled the president of the United States. When Colonel Kämmerling took a sick-leave in Louisville, Lieutenant-Colonel Joseph assumed command.

Perryville was a little place between [and to the west of] Harrodsburg and Danville. Concentrated at Perryville, we had neared the enemy [and we had drawn up for battle on the 7th, after skirmishes earlier] and now we faced him here on October 8 with an army much superior to his. Every advantage and all the odds were with us.[35] A blow that would smash him seemed possible; indeed, inevitable. Heavy firing began very early [at the crack of dawn] on the left. Our division, ready to attack, waited in reserve [however], idle, until after 3:00 P.M. General McDowell McCook and his corps, under fire all day, practically fought the battle themselves. More than once we thought we would have to be moved up, to pitch in and reinforce McCook. But the order to advance failed until 4:00.

At sundown we reached the battlefield and met intense fire.[36] But, on a hillside with a strong line of skirmishers in front of us, our position was superior to the enemy's. Several other brigades were stationed along the road and waiting, idle as we had been idle, unable to attack, and without orders to attack! McCook's corps, in disarray, had suffered many casualties. And still the enemy charged, wave after wave.[37] An hour earlier we would have changed things with a bayonet-assault but it was too dark now. Besides, we had not been ordered to attack. As a last resort, in the face of a withering enemy fire hurled at our lines, we awaited the enemy on our stomachs. "Don't shoot," Steedman said, "until you see the whites of their eyes!" But the situation did not become so dire. With the onset of darkness a violent artillery duel began. Union batteries inflicted obviously severe losses while ours were slight.[38]

Skirmishers were withdrawn about midnight. The chilly nocturnal hours passed in relative quiet. An occasional noise and the rumble of vehicles in the enemy's camp led us to presume he was changing positions for tomorrow morning: to attack or at least stiffen resistance. Dawn revealed, however, that he had fled under cover of darkness, abandoning his many dead. The Battle of Perryville was over.

Not only bloody, it had also been peculiar. And to say *peculiar* is to put it mildly; many attempts have been made to describe and explain what happened.[39] The fact remained, and remains, that Bragg's army could and ought to have been destroyed. And then our unsuccessful pursuit of the enemy, with a relatively small and weak detachment of forces, did not even start until the 10th of October.

Unflattering, indeed unfavorable opinions formed of the generalship of Buell, commander of the Army of the Ohio; and no wonder, as people remembered his glaring lassitude at Shiloh, together with his equally garish torpor at Perryville. The troops, as usual "quick to talk and to judge," shouted: "Treason!" The press, throughout the country, discussed this delicate matter exhaustively. But, as is well known, even a long and tedious Court of Inquiry could not clear it up. To render a verdict on such an issue is remote from our purposes in this book. We can neither hide the facts [however] nor undo them. And certainly, [looked at] over the course of the whole war, the facts [of Shiloh and Perryville] are not isolated.[40]

Chasing Bragg zigzag, we fetched up at Lancaster. The area not only flowed with milk and honey but also overflowed with whiskey, prompting us to seize a distillery on the 14th, after the owners had been pointed out to us as Rebel sympathizers. The entire brigade participated in this operation. Rewarding. Indeed, very rewarding, given the conditions under which, from day to day, we labored. An enormous volume disappeared. Here and there, men suffering a powerful thirst that demanded satisfaction, quaffed too much of a good thing. Nevertheless, a man can drink "for any reason" [besides thirst] and any necessary reason would likely have been found here!

Then we were back in Crab Orchard and Lebanon. At Lebanon we heard the news that Buell had been relieved [because of Union ineffectiveness at Perryville and the escape of Bragg afterward].

Major-General Rosecrans, who led us in West Virginia, replaced him in command of our army [on October 24]. We welcomed the switch.

The savage onset of winter dictated the need to issue coats, blankets, tents, and more clothing. Our baggage, which we left behind in Louisville a while before, appeared on the 25th but in horrible condition. And many individuals received nothing. The snow was six inches deep; the situation, critical. In New Market our brigade commander [Steedman] had to declare: "I cannot march until my regiment is better equipped." Finally, on the 30th, we got a minimum and could set out for Bowling Green. We arrived [via Island Camp and Cave City] on November 3 and were paid, reoutfitted, and ordered to remain in camp until the completion of preparations for a new campaign in Tennessee.

In the one just finished, the chase after Bragg, we suffered many hardships that, if even necessary, produced no tangible results—hardships that we do not want to discuss further. [Suffice it to say that] as much forced by necessity as driven by desire, we lived mostly and sometimes entirely on food from the region traversed, until, at last, foraging became a daily routine. At the end [of the campaign], despite what had been beautifully said and written, and what had been issued in orders, everybody realized that, south of the Ohio, we not only faced enemy troops but were also on enemy soil. We learned [this] our [most important] lesson, not a minute too soon. Then we started, however reluctantly, to see and treat the inhabitants as enemies. Still, if we gained nothing but this knowledge on that campaign, the profit was considerable. Now the upshot was to put the knowledge effectively into practice, to turn words into deeds. We would meet that challenge.

8

November 4, 1862, to July 25, 1863[1]

The Army of the Cumberland.—South Tunnel.—John Morgan.—Pilot Knob and Galatin.—Back in Nashville [after a Hard Trek].—Concord Church.—Three Months in Camp in Triune.—Roll of Honor.—A New Regimental Band.—Hoover's Gap.—Tullahoma.—Camp Thomas.

[Relative Inactivity in Tenneessee.—Court Martials.—A Declaration of Loyalty.—Vallandigham.—Soldier Life, in Camp and on the March, in Good Weather and Bad.—Confirmation of the Excellence of German Troops and Their Method of Training.—Feinting and Parrying but No Real Fighting.—Thomas Talks but Does Not Give Much of a Speech.]

"Great deeds cast leading shadows."

The reorganized Army of the Ohio became the Army of the Cumberland [January 9, 1863] and now comprised several corps under General Rosecrans. We belonged to Steedman's Third Brigade and the 3rd Division of the XIV Corps, all led by the head of the army's right wing, General Thomas. General McD. McCook commanded the [XX Corps at the] center; and General Crittenden [the XXI Corps at] the left. Steedman's brigade consisted again of five infantry regiments—2nd Minnesota, 87th Indiana, 18th Regular U.S., 35th Ohio, and ours—as well as Battery F, 14th U.S. Artillery.[2]

At that time in the corps and in our regiment, many men were absent for long periods. Most seemed to have decided to rest from recent dangers and hardships; and some never returned. These French leaves markedly reduced our strength: at one point we were below 500 [in the regiment].

Every absence, however short, and all insubordinations, had to be dealt with by court-martial. These unpleasant tribunals therefore multiplied and a ridiculous number took place. Since most of the guilty were disciplined lightly, infractions increased, as would be expected. Stern punishments would have prevented many offenses; but, at that time, the highest echelons seemingly neither could nor would learn two lessons. (1) The right management of the so-called home service [i.e., the volunteer forces] in the field is of the highest importance.[3] (2) Therefore the administration of justice must be prompt, fast, and strict.

Also at that time [November 7], McClellan was relieved of command of the Army of the Potomac [for hesitating after Antietam] and replaced by Burnside, as is well known. We thought the case seemed like what happened with us after Perryville when Buell was removed: an energetic man taking over from a procrastinator. Of course it could not be foreseen whether or to what extent things would be different. But they certainly could not be worse.

Our next foe was John Morgan, the infamous guerrilla leader, a past master at doing great damage with few forces. Against him we had to be always vigilant; for he would strike here, then there, and vanish as fast as he appeared. First [after leaving Bowling Green and passing Franklin, Kentucky, and Mitchellville, Tennessee] we addressed the task of [cleaning out and] restoring to service the South Tunnel [north of Gallatin] on the railroad to Nashville. Trying to cut off supplies, he had nearly destroyed it. Then we heard that the Rebels had captured an entire brigade [the 39th] of [General Ebenezer] Dumont's division, stationed in Hartsville, Tennessee [under Colonel A. B. Moore]. Included, unfortunately, were Tafel's 106th Ohio and the 108th Ohio.[4]

After a month of pioneer work [hard labor day and night] on South Tunnel, [the trains could pass, and] we finally arrived at Pilot Knob on December 12 [to guard the railroad and the fords of the Cumberland]. We camped at Gallatin [on December 26]. For a month, amid skirmishes and occasional clashes between patrols, we drilled vigorously and did all sorts of meaningful and senseless jobs, keeping at them hard for a time and then dropping or completing them carelessly, as we saw fit. Indeed, in our brigade [continuing to assert ourselves], we amended a general order that every man always carry 100 rounds of ammunition. We carried forty; the other sixty followed on the supply wagon. The men found eminently sensible this departure from rules, because rations were load enough.

Meanwhile, in the Army of the Cumberland, as elsewhere, the lack of cavalry made itself felt.[5] How often we heard and even saw

Rebel mounted forces, and should have sent our own in hot pursuit, had we only had them! Too many lessons were never learned, or so it seemed.

On December 23 the 18th Regular Infantry left our brigade. In this war [by the way], as in the Mexican, comradeship between regulars and volunteers never throve, especially among junior officers.

On Christmas Day and the 26th we heard the continual thunder of distant canon and several times formed to march. To where? We did not know. Perhaps these were early signs of [the Battle of] Stones River, also called Murfreesboro.

And then a new exercise. Daily, beginning on the 27th, before dawn, everybody and everything must be and remain ready to march, until daylight, when the decision could be taken to go or not. This exercise, reproached as extreme, was soon stopped.

With joy we celebrated the last day of 1862. The sutler had supplied what was needed for a good time. In the morning, however, heavy firing broke out again. This time we knew it was General Rosecrans in close combat with the enemy at Stones River. Our side won the three-day battle but at terrible cost.[6] For example [our old drillmaster] General Willich, a brigade-commander then, was taken prisoner.[7]

Our army [the Army of the Cumberland], deployed between Louisville and Nashville [and responsible for this sector of the war], was stretched excessively thin. Nowhere strong enough, having too many important positions to hold, it could not be concentrated at one for combat. This attenuation kept it from pursuing the enemy as he should have been pursued when he retreated from the battlefield. For the same reason, Morgan could continue his mischief such a long time.

In those days it was necessary that we forage often. On January 6, in one of our most successful raids, our regiment and three companies of the 35th, with two cannon and over twenty wagons, set out for Hartsville [Tennessee] to plunder two mills that we believed supplied the Rebels regularly with flour. On the way we met farmers hauling wheat to the mills. We relieved the farmers of their burdens and sent them home with about a tenth of what they carried when we stopped them. At the mills we found enough flour and wheat to return our wagons to camp full. The raid became all the more interesting as some of us turned into first-class millers for the occasion and ground additional flour on the spot. And, in the little town [of Hartsville], we got our second drum. The first had been a gift of honor in Camp Dennison. This one, an old U.S. Army instrument, was now booty [again]: a Rebel flag had been painted over its original insignia.

In the past year the Union's forces in the West had not accomplished their mission. Yet they were now expected to occupy Tennessee and try to recapture Arkansas. Worse, President Lincoln's Emancipation Proclamation, issued New Year's Day, had ruled out compromise and complicated matters considerably.

At this time, Lieutenant [Friedrich] Bertsch of Company B took a leave to Cincinnati for his health. He was also asked to get new regimental musicians. Though enlisted as common soldiers and carried on the rolls of the several companies, in every other respect they were to be our regimental band. The regiment's officers would make up the difference in salary between a common soldier's and a musician's. This arrangement must have been as agreeable to the regiment as it was generous of the officers. The Ninth's beautiful love of music, spared the miserable fate of atrophy, continued indisputably to flourish.

A celebration of the Battle of Mill Springs was planned as a monster affair for the 19th [of January]. Several officers, from our regiment and the 2nd Minnesota, journeyed to Louisville to buy the things needed. But what happened? On the 14th we must begin the march to Nashville and in a terrible rain that alternated with bursts of snow. At our destination the snow had accumulated. How difficult to pitch even a poor camp there! The Cumberland [which flows beside Nashville] had risen about thirteen feet in twenty-four hours. In the sudden cold of the 16th the water froze so solidly that many of us went via the river's ice-and-snow-covered surface to seek lodging in the city. The 19th dawned without ingredients for the celebration of Mill Springs. Instead we were again stuck deep in a morass. The river had flooded part of the city itself.

Still our occasional duty on patrol was not hard. Gradually the weather cleared. We moved. The new location was beautifully situated, not far from the old. With the sun in our favor, patrol and fatigue were much easier.

On the 30th we broke that camp, marched to Nolensville and Concord Church, and pitched another on February 2. We had not an inkling of the reason. Was it to dispose of the many court-martials still pending? They *were* something of a fixture here. We rested most of the time.[8]

Here the occasional foraging expedition might be long or short. On the 15th [of February], a Sunday, our Company C and a company of the 2nd Minnesota set off to provision the camp. About fifteen of the Minnesotans, under a sergeant, were ordered out perpendicular to the line of march, to search for hay and other fodder. Suddenly a band of enemy cavalry, about 100 men, assailed the detachment and demanded surrender. The Minnesotans, scorning surrender, holed up nearby in a log cabin. Well-aimed volleys repulsed the Rebels. They retreated, leaving four wounded men and four injured horses. Only one of the detachment was wounded, slightly. Meanwhile the other foragers, one and a half to two miles away, heard the shots and hurried to the scene. But the skirmish was finished. Back at camp the report of it prompted dispatch of the 1st Tennessee Cavalry to capture the enemy band—in vain. After this clash our cavalry roved about daily, but their hopes of engaging the enemy were disappointed.

Here, at the end of February, word reached us of the promulgation of the "Conscription Bill" [the Enrollment Act of March 3, 1863]. From now on, every man in the country, aged 18 [i.e., 20] to 45, was obligated to military service [unless unfit or entitled to exemption]. Certainly not a sign of a speedy termination of the war![9]

More meaningful to us, immediately thereafter, was the act on suffrage. Ohio's soldiers in the field who had not had the vote, were granted it; and those who had had it, were guaranteed it.[10] The news pleased us. Now, whatever our location, we could exercise that fundamental right. Therefore, at a crucial moment, we could (so to speak) strike a blow with the ballot. As the nation's history proclaims, a blow with the ballot was no less important than a stroke of the sword.

Similarly, on Washington's Birthday a few days before, the Ohio regiments of our army felt obliged to take up the pen—to compose a belligerent address to the people of Ohio. The troops (it said) were as ready and willing to destroy the enemy from the rear as to annihilate him from the front. The army would not lay down its arms until it accomplished its mission. The slogan? Not "Compromise" but "Victory or Death!" Never would the army swerve from its course. The soldiers urged the same resolve unto all citizens and friends of the Union. Hold fast, the carefully considered document begged, hold fast to the principle of the inalienable rights of man. The patience of good and loyal people had ended; and the Union's enemies—"copperheads" and others open and secret—were exhorted to cease their machinations lest the army be forced to turn on them and punish them for their hostility to the Union. When the address appeared in Ohio's German newspapers, letters to the editor accompanied it, showing that the regiments in the field were serious and, if necessary, would be deadly serious.

That such an incident could occur while the war raged—who was to blame? Surely not the men in arms. The cause, above all, was civilian faintheartedness. Many civilians, expressing the decline of courage at home, openly derided the soldiers in the field. Daily, under the greatest trial and worst tribulation, yet without grumbling, men at war risked their lives for the preservation of the Union. They fought while having to put up with scorn, ridicule, and casuistic criticism from the likes of those who, earlier, refused to volunteer and now, as a rule, shirked conscription.[11]

The immediate provocation for the address, however, was the infamous Vallandigham affair [an aspect of the diffidence on the home front]. Clement Laird Vallandigham [of Ohio and leader of the Copperheads] had been spirited across the lines of our own corps of the Army of the Cumberland. Fetched up in Canada, he was now a candidate for governor of Ohio—to the pain of every good patriot, and to the scorn of every one of us soldiers in the field.[12]

Meanwhile, March had brought spring. Then, a few minutes after midnight on the 4th, orders came to move at daybreak, with ammunition and rations for only three days, to Nolensville and Triune [Tennessee]. The orders also went to the 35th Ohio and the 87th

Indiana, as well as half of the Tennessee Cavalry. We did not know what was in the wind, but we did see—soon—supply trains and cannon advancing.

Beyond Triune we joined the 2nd Minnesota with their two cannon, and the other half of the Tennessee Cavalry. They had begun their move the day before, and now had in custody about sixty prisoners, five of them wounded: saber cuts on the face. We had seen no other wounds inflicted by Union cavalry in two years of service. Could such cuts have been dealt sooner, events would have taken a different turn.

Our entire brigade had assembled. We advanced. We knew that General Steedman had orders to reconnoiter as far as Chaplin [or Chapel] Hill, to cross the Harpeth River [at Franklin] and then to await reinforcements out of Murfreesboro. Hearing from there all day the boom of cannon, we presumed the whole army was advancing.

But, having met no reinforcements at the appointed spot, we pitched camp for the night. Our cavalry brought in more prisoners, among them a Rebel major plucked from the marriage bed.

March 5th and still no reinforcements. Steedman decided to proceed to Chaplin Hill. Soon we encountered hostile outposts, and the enemy made it hot for us at villages he occupied, but we routed him at last. He withdrew across the river. After our long and tiring march, only our cavalry could pursue him. They were about to cut off his retreat, but he disappeared, leaving a camp full of prisoners and fodder. Our wagons pulled in and loaded up as much as possible. What remained was burned, together with the huts.

We went back to Triune. On the 6th our division pitched a big camp there. We stayed three months.[13]

Doing what? All sorts of things: drilling, sapping, reconnoitering, and foraging. Court-martials took place. And more—of which I have yet to speak.

On March 23 a general order was published, creating a mounted unit, the mobile "light battalion," to be called the "Roll of Honor" and used for important and dangerous missions. To belong would be to hold a post of credit and esteem. Its members, to be chosen company by company in the regiments, were to have preference in promotions to fill vacancies among the noncommissioned officers.[14]

We were now issued so-called shelter tents: thin, light, canvas affairs [in pieces] about four feet square, which could be folded and buttoned and carried in the backpack. A tent [consisting of two pieces] slept two men. Because when pitched they looked like gable roofs or the tops of doghouses, they were immediately nicknamed "dog tents."[15]

At this time the presidential proclamation on desertion [the proclamation of amnesty, March 10] was posted. Any deserter who returned of his own free will would not be punished, on the condition that he forfeit the pay for the time absent. Many therefore came back at once, having reconsidered their truancy.

It must also be said [in fairness] that an earlier return, which many of them had wanted, had been impossible because they could not reach their regiments without a pass. And not a few fugitives, tired of being deserters, had enlisted in other units—the genuine fear of ignominious punishment having kept them from their own.

On April 7, hardship overwhelmed Private Louis Weghorst of Company H. When time and situation permitted, troops in the field cared for fallen comrades with affection and reverence; and Weghorst was buried near camp and with military honors. To illustrate [how the living felt about the dead], an accurate depiction of Weghorst's grave is reproduced here. One of the living, visiting poor Weghorsts's simple plot, might have desired the same for himself, were his fate to be death far from home in the destiny of war. For we had then not an inkling of how magnificently the grateful nation would later care for its dead.

Meanwhile, General [John M.] Schofield replaced General Steedman as division commander. Brigade drills under Schofield were a welcome change from continual reconnaissance. Usually unproductive, reconnaissance was especially disappointing when foraging was not included. Schofield thereby soon gained everyone's trust, for he knew exactly how to treat soldiers in the field.

His [new] drills were as strange to most of the brigade's officers as to its ranks, the transmission of orders was never fast and flawless, and the problem [of communication] may have seemed more appar-

The grave of Corporal Louis Weghorst, of Company H, near Triune, Tennessee

ent with The Ninth than the other regiments. People who knew nothing about The Ninth, except that we drilled in the Prussian manner and under German officers, therefore thought our efforts would soon produce confusion. The Cincinnati *Volksfreund* had predicted trouble when we were in Camp Dennison: "The German regiment is well trained, but its leadership is German rather than American. That defect of dire importance will perhaps produce fatal results. Think what might happen in an army run in English if the German officers heading the regiment should be killed or incapacitated. The possible chaos could end in massacre."

McCook [our commanding officer] had seized the bull by the horns at once, reported the situation to the high command, and pointed out that we had enlisted for three years on the condition that we retain both the Prussian manner of training and our German officers, a condition approved by the high command and the governor of Ohio. The Colonel also said we had rendered exemplary service under German officers and would continue to do so. If we wanted to be assured of further successes, we had to keep our German staff. Were the privilege of German leadership denied us, a pack of the worst consequences could follow; and he would not for a moment hesitate to take us back to Pittsburgh Landing [Shiloh] and return with us to Cincinnati.

The ill-founded assumption [about us] was true the first day [of the new exercises]—but only to a degree; and by no means was it true of us alone. In fact, skilled and experienced in our procedures, we received orders [clearly and on time] from brigade headquarters through buglers assisted by the regimental command. Nothing else was needed for the orders to be carried out; and the Babelic confusion of tongues, awaited with malicious expectation, did not occur. Thus we avoided trouble in training; everything was fine in camp, as has been shown; and the *Volksfreund*'s "chaos" and "massacre" never happened to us in battle. In short, an excellent state of affairs obtained under German officers, not only when the perceptive and capable General Schofield was in charge, but also in McCook's time [1861–1862].

That the "Dutchmen" were in trouble, and that their pride would be laid, were therefore falsehoods. People who believed them erred gravely; they knew little of The Ninth.

Truth was, excelling as we always excelled when the chips were down, we soon earned the praise of Schofield himself, because we conducted ourselves so well in training. Schofield's tribute to us, and McCook's, had their effect in the right places. Even in Triune we heard not so much as an official whisper of removing our German officers. Instead the old joy remained in having us as we were, and in being able to keep us as we had been. We received the honor calmly, happy to ascribe it to our German character, which always gave us an advantage over other units and helped produce our important successes.

Let someone else confirm what has just been stated. In April 1896, William Vocke, a former captain in the 24th Illinois, addressed the Illinois Commandery of the Military Order of the Loyal Legion and, among other things, declared:

> It may be safely said of the great host of subordinate commanders and troops of the German part of our armies that they were as true as steel and therefore enjoyed the highest confidence of our best leaders. What though the English speech was imperfect, their fighting and their loyalty could not be more perfect than they really were. The fact is, that both the 9th Ohio and the 32nd Indiana as well as other German troops were drilled and commanded by their officers in undefiled "High-Dutch" and never learned the English drill at all. The very bugle calls, which summoned them to their brilliant and resistless attacks were German, unknown to the other troops, and the soul-stirring hurrahs with which they went into battle were unmistakable deep and sonorous Teutonic sounds. The excellent conduct of these two regiments alone shows sufficiently, that like the noble Steuben and the heroic Muehlenberg of revolutionary fame, one can be just as loyal an American citizen and just as brave an American soldier in Luther's German language as in the King's English.[16]

Then, on May 4, by order of the Secretary of War [Edwin M. Stanton], the organizing of the light battalions stopped. So soon! Thus vanished what had engendered such uncommonly high hopes. Next the Roll of Honor ended—abruptly. Fervor for it had certainly not lasted long.

On the 7th we exchanged guns, replacing the old [smoothbore musket] with the Springfield [rifled musket], the newest and best infantry weapon.[17] Now we could pride ourselves on being properly armed and suitably equipped in every respect. Even the new dog tents, in our judgment, were better than they had been described; and we liked them well enough.

When the brigade was returning from the drillfield on the 11th [of May], and The Ninth had entered its bivouac area, twenty musicians suddenly took post at the head [of The Ninth] and let go with our popular regimental march. A grand *hurrah* answered the new regimental band, for that is what they were, having just arrived in camp by carriage from Nashville.[18] They proved to be a good band; the regiment was happy with them; and Lieutenant Bertsch, who had been sent after them, earned a tribute to his good taste.

Camp life now, on the whole, was agreeable, even pleasant. We began target practice and gymnastic exercises.

Lieutenant-Colonel [Karl] Joseph resigned then. His wound, of [the Battle of] Mill Springs, had disabled him for duty in the field. He returned to Cincinnati. We did not like to see him go, and held him in fond memory.

General Schofield, also popular, left us, too, for a command in Missouri. His successor, General J[ohn] M. Brannan, did not so quickly win favor among troops in the West: he had been with the Army of the Potomac and we did not think much of them. But, in time, he did well; for, at bottom, he was an exceptionally capable officer.[19]

On June 1 the signs were clear:

- A continual readiness to march, with provisions for ten days.
- The clearing and dispatch, to storage in Nashville, of nonessential baggage and equipment.
- The arrival of troops under Major-General Gordon Granger (as a captain he had commanded us in Camp Harrison).
- A review by him, he being now camp commandant and commander of the division.
- Meanwhile, cannon thundered from the direction of Franklin.

Obviously we would soon depart and the pleasant days be over.[20]

The brigade set out for Franklin on a night that began pitch-dark. We had gone about a mile when a terrible thunderstorm struck. The floodgates of heaven seemed to open. Still we pushed on, the whole night. At dawn on June 5th we gained Franklin and learned that the Rebels, thinking we had abandoned the region, had crossed the Harpeth River, to take possession of the fortifications. With an artillery bombardment we drove the Rebels back across the river.

During the day, our regiment, escorted by cavalry, had to reconnoiter. The enemy dared not cross the river again, although his numbers remained significantly greater than ours. On the 6th we returned to Triune. The enemy's expected advance finally came on the 11th. He shelled our camp, which lay in the open and unprotected, but did not hazard a serious attack. Obviously our commanders, in turn, thought us too weak to risk battle. The encounter therefore produced nothing. Again the enemy withdrew.

General [Robert Byington] Mitchell brought up cavalry that night, increasing our mounted strength to twelve regiments [in the brigade]. We were approaching a total of 20,000 men [in the division].

On June 23 (at last) we broke camp at Triune. The brigade marched up Murfreesboro Pike. Seventeen days of rain began.

Bragg's [Confederate] army was on the south bank of Duck River and headquartered in Tullahoma, with spurs of the Cumberland Mountains between him and us. To secure the narrow passes or *gaps* was therefore uppermost. We started to advance on them.

On the 26th our brigade reached Hoover's Gap [on the way to Tullahoma]. General Thomas had already engaged the enemy there. As our infantry could advance but little, so a skirmish was possible only under cover of artillery; and it was artillery that finally drove the enemy out of the gap. We thereby secured a key position without notable losses, after stiff resistance had been expected. All of General Rosecrans's army was united again; we were part of Thomas's XIV Corps. Rosecrans himself, when he rode past our regiment, once more expressed his opinion of us: the division's strongest and best. That praise had little effect on us anymore, so often had we heard it.

Next day we were to attack. Everything was set. But Bragg—we knew him to be as slippery as an eel—was gone by then.

On July 1 the weather was terrible [but we set out for Tullahoma anyhow]. Violent thunderstorms punctuated a steady rain. Creeks we had waded, without getting wet much above the ankles, now swelled to rivers. Our baggage was swept off every which way, except to the place where needed. We had nothing but what we carried personally—and some soggy crackers. In a word the situation was abominable. *Reach Tullahoma, hit the enemy's fortifications (glorified as impregnable), drive the enemy out of there, thrash him yet another time*—those hopes sustained us. We were sure of victory, would we but be released against him.

But he had disappeared again. The much-vaunted fortifications, which we found occupied in part by our 2nd Brigade, were nothing but strong abatises and unfinished earthworks. To storm and take them, however, would possibly have cost many lives.

Still we had captured about 100 prisoners and much materiel: camp-equipage, firearms, munitions, food, wagons, and an entire railway train. Pursuit of the enemy [via Fairfield and Manchester], unfortunately, proceeded as usual: at a crawl. [To make pursuit even harder] the weather, after the long spell of thunderstorms, grew exceedingly hot.

Meanwhile the enemy traversed Elk River and burned the railway bridge behind him. Therefore we in pursuit had to ford a rushing stream swollen by the rain to a depth of five feet. The [infantry units of the] division crossed single file. Each man held in his left hand the rope stretched across the torrent, and in his right his rifle. To it was fastened a bundle of his clothes and other belongings. The calm and the agile got themselves and their possessions to the other side. The shaky and the timid lost one thing or another, and some lost everything. The cavalry and artillery went over at the same time a short way downriver. The crossing demanded a full three hours. A lively scene, sometimes comical, even ludicrous.

Next day was the glorious "Fourth." Celebrating, we fired salutes, played games, and sang patriotic songs. But there was little to eat. Our wagons loaded with food were on the opposite shore; we had brought almost nothing across; and foraging offered even less. We spent two quite inactive weeks in the place, which we named Camp Winford.

There was more action elsewhere. Vicksburg [Mississippi] surrendered [July 4], Port Hudson [Louisiana] fell [July 8], and the Rebels who still occupied fortifications along the Mississippi were the last of their kind.

We thought we could use deception to get details of the surrender at Vicksburg, about which we knew nothing. On the evening of the 9th we went with our new band to "Pap" Thomas's quarters and serenaded him, in the hope he would give a speech of thanks and include something on the day's great event. Fat chance! He did appear, to say he was pleased to see his brave unit again: back at Hoover's Gap our display of the old spirit had warmed the cockles of his heart. But then—with a deep bow and "Well, boys, good night!"—the great commander and poor orator repaired to his tent. The triple hurrah we sent after him was not a thank-you for relevant news about the Mississippi.

Our respected chaplain and spiritual leader [Joseph A.] Fuchshuber left us here and was not replaced. Henceforth we had to settle things with heaven in our own way and on our own initiative, which posed little trouble for us [as skepticism predominated in our attitude to religion].

On the 18th we camped in Decherd [Tennessee] and drew four months' pay from the paymaster. [The government's problems with inflated currency had blocked our being paid.][21] So what if we were not told everything? Getting paid was at least as important to us personally as were events on the Mississippi.

On July 25th we moved to Winchester [Tennessee], where we had camped almost a year before, after our McCook was killed [August 1862]. The XIV Corps was concentrated here now, awaiting orders. In honor of our commander we called the place Camp Thomas.

And so we were only a few days' march from the Tennessee, one of the rivers destined to carry to "the grand ocean of eternity" the blood of so many brave fighters in this accursed war.

9

Passing the Time in the Field, and Other Topics Gleaned in Reflection[1]

[Food and Cooking.—Hygiene.—A Storm in Camp.—Pleasures and Pains of the Countryside.—Ways of Amusement.—Life in Camp and on the March.—Continued Camaraderie after the War.—Lessons and Ideals for Posterity.]

We have not discussed how soldiers spent free time, nor all they did merely to kill time. Surprising topics, these, for a soldier surely cannot long be idle. Indeed, it is assumed he takes his turn at a variety of duties, in camp and out (more willingly in nice weather, somewhat hesitantly in rain and cold).

At [Camp] Harrison the initial problem was how to cook what the quartermaster-sergeants delivered: meat, beans, etc.[2] First off, fires (of the wood we were brought) did not burn properly in this or that fireplace; and here and there the hungry must wait ages until meat and vegetables were finally done. And the many complaints about salt—too much or too little—in the soup! But after just a few days, experts were called upon to supervise and teach. In time, everything ran in the best of order. "Practice makes perfect" held true even here; and by the end of enlistment, everybody could cook and wash like a true housekeeper.

In The Ninth, tidiness and cleanliness prevailed. Men still unfamiliar with such rigor, got used to it fast; their tentmates inculcated proper application of soap, water, and the brush. Keeping body and clothing clean is essential in the field, as anyone knows who saw comrades in other regiments throw away near-new uniforms and underwear, forced to do it to free themselves of what had so irritatingly quartered itself there. The situation had grown so bad that the old proverb was useless: "If it itches, scratch it."[3]

In Parkersburg, West Virginia, we had to endure our first storm in camp, a sockdolager of thunder and lightning. Many a tree crashed to the ground, many a tent collapsed. No wonder an officer, armed with nothing but a red blanket, dashed among the streets of tent city, shouting and shouting: "Hell's a-poppin'! Get out of these tents! Save yourselves!"

In West Virginia we found excellent spring water, the nicest wild flowers of all shapes and colors, and wild grapes in bunches nearly a foot long and growing on vines (as thick as a man's arm) that climbed to the crowns of giant trees. A shame that the herbariums [collected and organized there] were lost on our steamboat on the Kanawa [at the end of November, 1861], stolen together with our backpacks and their essential contents. On the march to Corinth, Mississippi, we saw dwarf irises, their fragrance splendid, like that of violets. In Alabama, near Tuscumbia, there were creepers with beautifully shaped blossoms.

Time and space—unfortunately—do not permit us to describe and discuss all the beauties of nature in the several states. Nor the many hardships, such as:

- Wading chin-deep and under full pack in all kinds of waters: cold, compulsory baths;
- Flooded camps, where transportation must be by planks and oars;
- The battle with rattlesnakes and giant hairy spiders;
- And the fiercer fray with hunger, most painful before Chattanooga and in a battalion that marched over the Greenbrier Mountains, perhaps West Virginia's poorest region.

It is well and good to enumerate and embroider on such things when they are over and done with. But "war games" and the parade-field prepare you for nothing of the sort. You will not, you cannot, learn [of such misfortunes] there.

The Ninth, probably like all regiments in our volunteer army, spent free time in camp in a variety of ways to avoid ennui. Theater going, concert attendance, and saloon visits being prohibited in the field, pastimes had to be pursued in and around the tents. Still, we did not lack entertainment in Camps Harrison and Dennison. Plenty of passes were issued for Cincinnati. Daily and especially Sunday visits by relatives and acquaintances abounded. We could get permission to take girl friends on walks in camp and into its environs. Such meetings were never tame, and many a kiss spiced the farewells.

But, in West Virginia and therefore early thrown on our own resources, each squad gradually formed itself into a family. A calm and harmonious household being the rule, each man was let do as he pleased, as long as no general disturbance resulted. [Let us glimpse a typical moment.] One squad patches clothes and knits buttons to replace ones that have deserted. A detail indulges in cards or checkers or chess. Love letters are written to sweethearts and [other letters] to wives, parents, uncles, and friends. There is drawing, watercoloring, and oil painting. Books and newspapers are read, heated arguments joined, and new—and of course foolproof—battle plans cooked up while generals are raked over the coals. The whittling of pipe bowls and walking sticks has grown especially popular (the root of the wild laurel is used and very suitable) and beautifully carved bowls circulate in commerce. Gymnastics are practiced. Swords cross in fencing matches.

And there was music, vocal and instrumental. Who does not remember yet the pleasant times in "the gunboat," a tent covered with tin, led [in song] by [three men of Company A] Ernst Koegel, Charles Klintworth, Charles Haebe [Karl Häbe], et al.? Full-voiced, jolly comrades, they provided [choral] leadership but only after always providing good libations.

The several so-called whiskey-scenters in the regiment were credited with (praised for?) sniffing out the article miles off. But nobody ever addressed the miles in a private, nocturnal expedition [to verify or disprove these claims to olfactory eminence]. There are times in the field, however, when something stronger—stiffer than water of rivers and puddles—is most welcome and even salubrious. Some of the wags dubbed whiskey "courage water." When asked, they explained that a big delivery of it at headquarters meant a battle was imminent. And—that's exactly what happened!

Perhaps here it would also be proper to recall the splendid

camp we shared with the 35th [Ohio] near Battle Creek Station [Tennessee]. The camp, with its beautiful plantings, resembled a park: small gardens, gardeners' sheds, arbored walks, and tents overlaid with boughs. The order, "Strike the tents and forget the rest," was not obeyed [when we left]. We had marched scarcely half a mile, we were still in view of the camp, when it burned to the ground. The men did not want to have troubled themselves for somebody else's comfort.

Let us also mention the amenities of marching for weeks, from Mississippi through Tennessee to Kentucky under a blistering sun [in the summer of 1862]. We were to intercept General Bragg and dog his army, and, at all events, keep him from striking and sacking Louisville or even Cincinnati. Before we had marched two hours the sun seemed a blood-red disc and our teeth grated on sand that filled our mouths. Potable water was scarce and bad at best. Louisville enjoys good water, but we tasted disappointment when we arrived at last in the suburbs. Most of the wells yielded mineral water, disgusting enough to make us forget thirst until we got better water and excellent beer in Louisville itself.

Let us not overlook the woodworking shop, set up by members of Company A, in a little rural cottage near Triune, Tennessee. They must have ranged far and wide to collect its various pieces of equipment. Chessmen were crafted—turned and finished beautifully—there. Sales were brisk. (N.B. A proprietor of the shop [F. Jacker] wrote one of the poems included in this book.[4])

Near Tuscumbia, Alabama [to mention other lucrative sidelines], Company B guarded the Bear Creek bridges and profitably caught turtles. Near Florence, Alabama, Company A was assigned to ferry people by boat [across the Tennessee River], and the waterborne transport-service paid handsomely.

Has anyone in Company A forgotten the master baker in Florence, and his excellent wine cellar and cute little daughter?

Also at Florence, where there was plenty to drink, an officer once slept the sleep of the just—on a bed of empty bottles. It being the season when clothes are unnecessary, he wore none. Nobody complained, for he was off duty, but everybody marveled that he was so difficult to wake. The soft bed must have been the reason.

All those experiences and occurrences deserve to be remembered. They are offered here as a side dish, so to speak, to the main course of this regimental history.[5]

It is to be hoped that The Ninth continue to be what they have been: one big family. May every comrade, even one absent for decades, rejoice to meet again and greet once more another veteran of The Ninth and chat with him about wartime experiences.

Finally, let us wish that The Ninth's sons and daughters never forget what their fathers had to suffer. Meanwhile, sons and grandsons should stay fit through physical training (hiking, gymnastics, etc.). Then they can be drilled into soldiers in a month, ready not only to march and to shoot, but also to bear the hardships of a military campaign—hardships that demand real men. And so, in hours of need, may sons do as fathers did, and stand up for the freedom of our Republic.

F. B.

10

August 16 to September 22, 1863[1]

From Winchester to the Tennessee.—Battle Creek.—Shell Mound.—Lookout Mountain.—Chickamauga.—Rossville.—Chattanooga.

[Union Forces in Tennessee Strike Southeast at Chattanooga and Poise for a Thrust at Confederate Vitals in the Deep South.—Problems between Rosecrans and His Superiors.—Two Days of Combat.—Thomas Earns a Nickname.—The Ninth Receives Well-Deserved Praise.—The Fate of the Wounded.—Union Forces, Mauled, Withdraw to Chattanooga.]

"A battle? It was a slaughter."

On August 16, 1863, we left Winchester and headed for the Tennessee River.[2] Our hopes were high that we would cross it and strike the decisive blow for the Union in the West. But we neither suspected what adversities would have to be overcome nor dreamed what torrents of precious blood would have to be spilled.

Our perpetual problem vexed us: how to get more and better food. Uppermost, though: how to transport this army speedily over that wide river. We had no pontoons. Lacking wagons, we could not have hauled pontoons unless we left tents, ammunition, and provisions behind. Yet we must cross the Tennessee promptly, in order to take Chattanooga as soon as possible, a crucial strategic objective. And we must cross in the face of the enemy occupying the south shore. The difficulties, [therefore] immense, exceeded the comprehension of the critics and cavilers of this war then and since. The magnitude of the difficulties justified delay and apparent inertia in the conduct [of this campaign]. And the difficulties *were* overcome.

We went [southeast in Tennessee] from Camp Thomas via Estill Springs, [University Place,] Jasper, Battle Creek, and the crest [Walden Ridge] of the northern [i.e., southern] spur of the [Cumberland] mountains. A somewhat strenuous march, because of the heat, but with rewards: [the experience of] a splendid primeval forest void of human habitation, and a marvelous view of eastern Tennessee's handsome valleys stretching away before us.

On the 21st we camped near the spot where Battle Creek empties into the Tennessee [near Stevenson, Alabama]. The enemy lost no time in announcing his presence on the south shore, even though the distance prevented his hurting us with small arms or cannon. Early on the 22nd, pickets shouted across:

"Good morning, you d——d Yankees!"

We replied with equal good-will.

"Go to hell, you d——d Rebels!"[3]

On the 24th, Rebel deserters brought us news from the enemy's camp: "Union troops have already got over the river downstream [i.e., upstream] at Bridgeport [Alabama]. The Confederates have withdrawn." The latter proved false when, on the 25th, we again exchanged chummy greetings with pickets over there; and great numbers of deserters originated there. Meanwhile we worked as hard as we could on canoes or "dugouts" and rafts. In addition, for greater cohesion of our [XIV] corps, a bridge was built over Battle Creek. On Sunday, August 30, we began to negotiate the Tennessee [at or near Caperton's Ferry], using canoes for the time being. First the 35th; then, about 10:00 A.M., our regiment; and by sundown the entire brigade was over. Baggage and provisions followed during the night. On the 31st, rafts being ready, transportation accelerated, and by evening the division was across. In the same way, at different points, other divisions were ferried to the other side. The enemy bothered us not a bit, having fled once again.

We (the XIV Corps) camped at Shellmound Station on September 1. Then we were ordered over the Sand and the Raccoon Mountains to Lookout [or Will's] Valley, which separated those mountains from Lookout Mountain Ridge. We moved slowly; the way was steep and rough, and many troops were ahead of us. On the 4th we passed Nick-a-Jack Cave, important for saltpeter. We were in Georgia and truly in the Confederacy now. We reached Trenton, Georgia, in Lookout Valley, on the 10th. Here we heard that the Rebels had abandoned Chattanooga to our forces under [General Thomas L.] Crittenden.[4] So our purposes in this operation were accomplished.

Bragg had wanted to split our army and smash the parts—not a bad plan, on the whole—but we had thwarted him.

Our mission had been most difficult and of extreme significance. For, earlier, the Rebels had lost the forts [Henry and Donelson] on the Tennessee and the Cumberland, and had also been compelled to evacuate Corinth, Nashville, and Tullahoma. As a result the Rebels needed new protection for the Confederacy east of the Cumberland Mountains and the Tennessee River; and at the least [for Rebel purposes], unbroken communication within the southeastern states had to be thus secured. So the Rebels had established a new axis, with Chattanooga as the linchpin. [But now, thanks to the success of our recent operation, *we* held Chattanooga.]

Still, General Rosecrans was subsequently forced to justify himself for years against uncalled-for criticism and envious people of evil intent.[5] In the Washington *Republic* and as late as 1883 [October 24], regarding the events [just described], he said:

> In ten weeks, hampered and embarrassed by a hostile Secretary of war and a distrustful and incompetent commander-in-chief at Washington, I crossed two high mountain ranges with my army, manoeuvered Bragg, who had an army almost as large as my own, out of his stronghold at Shelbyville and Tullahoma, either of which was as well fortified as Vicksburg, and successfully crossed the Tennessee River, doing all this at a wonderfully small cost. In military history the campaign, that began the last week in June with the advance of the army from Winchester, practically terminated with the battle of Chickamauga and the seizure of Chattanooga, will stand as one of the most memorable of the war.[6]

Rebel movements remained a mystery to Washington. There they asserted that Bragg's next objective was Rome, Georgia, and that he would accordingly disengage from Union troops and withdraw south. Rosecrans disagreed but his remonstrances fell on deaf ears.[7] Reinforcements from the east were denied him. When he argued that Bragg would be reinforced from Virginia and then try to retake Chattanooga, Washington laughed and said he was dreaming.

In fact, on September 18, [Bragg's] Rebel forces had concentrated at La Fayette [had been heavily reinforced] and were again ready to strike and smash our forces piecemeal. True, this destruction did not occur; but the reason did not lie with Bragg. His excellent plan lagged in its execution; and Rosecrans managed to foil it.[8] Without peer at outwitting Rebels, Rosecrans united the scattered Federal units and did so in the very face of his antagonist. Rapid forced-marches with utmost caution by our corps, similar action by an enemy separated from us by only a line of low mountains, the enemy's ignorance of our exact position—all signs indicated a quick end to uncertainty.[9] The Count of Paris says in his history of the Civil War: "During the night of September 18, the XIV and XVIII Corps, the largest and probably best led in the [Union] army, shifted left to block Confederates about to cut off Rosecrans's communication with Chattanooga and drive Rosecrans back to Lookout Mountain."[10] Our movement succeeded and achieved what we wanted.

But what good the Union occupation of Chattanooga if the enemy remained? So Rosecrans, army regrouped and manageable, decided to fight.

Now, despite the importance of the Battle of Chickamauga, we limit the following discussion to an overview of its chief aspects. This book, as was emphasized at the start, is intended as neither a history of the war nor a definitive account of battles. Rather, we have restricted ourselves to a straightforward, veracious report of what happened to The Ninth, and to recounting as accurately as possible The Ninth's experiences as a wartime regiment. Moreover, we agree with Senator John M. Palmer of Illinois—formerly General Palmer, who commanded the 2nd Division of the XXI Corps at Chickamauga—speaking at the dedication of the Chickamauga–Chattanooga National Military Park on September 19, 1895:

> Writers, some with historical accuracy and others in the language of romance, have told the tale of the bloody contest on the field of Chickamauga. No man can know much of the events, which did not occur in his immediate presence on a field like this. We know the names of but few of the fallen, but we can remember the courage and gallantry of all who acted with us.[11]

And we know that Ohio regiments commenced the bloody affair on the 19th and the 20th. According to Bragg's plan, the battle was to begin on the 18th of September. He would hurl the chief blow at our left and then, having been reinforced by [General James] Longstreet (quite out of keeping with belief in Washington), drive his entire force between us and Chattanooga. But, as we said above, our marches the night of the 18th, and the [consequent] shifting of fronts on the 19th, ruined the plan.[12]

Now, despite events of the 18th and 19th [which included a march through blinding smoke from fences burning on both sides of the road], our [Union] line of battle remained nearly six miles long on the 19th: stretching from the west bank of Chickamauga Creek and along La Fayette Road [i.e., the State Road to La Fayette]. One after another our corps arrived on the wooded terrain. Thomas, first, at daybreak, with his XIVth, no sooner reached the spot than he must start fighting because the enemy, gaining significantly on our left, had already captured several batteries and was about to dislodge our troops engaged there, by hurling a massive onslaught at them. Our division (Brannan's) as well as [Brigadier-General Absalom] Baird's—the left of Van Derveer's brigade—stood directly opposite the enemy; and the 35th Ohio, 2nd Minnesota, and 87th Indiana succeeded in stopping him, meanwhile exposing themselves to vicious fire.

The Ninth, though we had guarded a munitions train the night before, now moved up into the brigade's right wing, to the attack. What with the enemy already pressing again, Colonel Kämmerling ordered us to fix bayonets and charge. We saved our opponents the trouble [of advancing], hurled back the front rank, penetrated to the second and third, and [in a brash assault] captured several cannon belonging originally to [Lieutenant Howard M.] Burnham's battery of the 5th U.S. Artillery [Third Brigade] and taken from Baird's [1st] division a while before.[13] Then, returning to the brigade at exactly the right moment (the enemy was crowding the brigade severely on the left now), we stopped the enemy again and for the last time that day, and drove him back to the position he had occupied at daybreak.

Our regiment counted sixty-three dead and wounded in the large and savage engagement. Not a few of the wounded died by morning.

Both armies redisposed themselves during the night. Union lines, considerably shortened and thereby toughened, ran again along the La Fayette Road. Our brigade went into reserve at the center and there spent the frigid night.[14] The troops rose early, being cold and hungry, but not until 10:00 of the beautiful Sunday morning did the roar of cannon tell them this would be a second day of battle.

Soon our brigade, ordered alone to the left flank, met there the Rebels under [General John C.] Breckinridge. Repeatedly reinforced, they were attacking as they had attacked the day before: striking in fact at the Union rear. Thus our brigade had to wheel almost full circle (as it were) to a position at the most-threatened point on our lines. The Rebels, in a large, forest-ringed cornfield there [on the Kelly farm], kept pouring a withering fire at us. Our regiment began the day's work in the manner of the day before: we charged at once with bayonets and cleaned out a stretch of the encircling forest.[15] Then a superior force of Rebels nearly surrounded us, for we had received no support for a long while. We barely saved ourselves with well-aimed shots and a slow, orderly retreat from the forest. Two regiments relieved us then, but we still maneuvered for a time under brutal bombardment before the enemy yielded and withdrew. In the judgment of war critics, our movements were like those of the parade-field, and as precise.

At last our turn came to join General Thomas [whose corps held its ground despite the otherwise sorry defeat of Rosecrans's Union forces]. His [Thomas's] troops were at Snodgrass Hill and in control of the road to Chattanooga.[16] There the battle raged. Blood flowed. But he and his faithful neither retreated nor wavered. For us it meant total engagement at once. Colonel Van Derveer reported, with the brigade, to General Thomas and asked for instructions.

Thomas: "Glad to see you, Colonel! What condition is your brigade in?"

Van Derveer (laconically): "All in line, save our dead and wounded."[17]

The battle lasted hours because a bravely superior enemy brought up division after division. We drove them back, all of them, and inflicted heavy losses. Again and again, rashly, the Rebels stormed the hill. Sometimes the front ranks even reached the top, where they, too, lost their lives. They carried up Rebel flags to plant there, and the flags joined the casualties. Each of us fired an average of fifty to sixty rounds and often wielded cold steel besides. Then we ran out of ammunition [after having been compelled to gather it from the dead and wounded]. The eternal "somebody" had sent the ammunition wagons away from the Union's right wing—to Chattanooga and before noon—obviously without regard to consequences.[18]

The same right wing, that day, indeed, caused the Union's downfall. Mistakes, oversights, unauthorized actions, and other aberrations occurred there and remain to be explained but probably never will be. Fact is, the enemy breached our line there and promptly poured through.[19] He would have knocked our axis askew at that point forthwith, and would have outflanked us, had we not forced him to steel himself to Thomas at Snodgrass Hill. Meanwhile only fragments of our troops on the right could advance to the hill before the elimination of [Thomas's] corps ruined the likelihood of a brilliant Union victory.

Leaders of the beaten [Union] forces [such as Crittenden and A. McD. McCook] hurried to Chattanooga, believing they were more needed there than on the battlefield. In the afternoon the commander-in-chief, General Rosecrans, repaired there himself, arriving at 3:30.[20] At once he took measures for the relief of troops waiting there, and for the erection of fortifications, as well as the provisioning of Thomas's unit, which had been ordered to Rossville.

Thomas meanwhile tried for reinforcements that morning, because he could already see that the battle would be decided at his position. But, as we have said, he succeeded only—and not until later in the day—in obtaining isolated elements detached from other units. Yet he clung to his hill as if to a rock in the ocean, even after he got from Rosecrans (1) the official word that the right wing had been routed and (2) the order to assume leadership of all forces on the battlefield. The historian Cist says: "There is nothing finer in history than Thomas at Chickamauga."[21] Indeed, perhaps few positions have been held, the way Snodgrass Hill was held, against a brave and superior enemy force.

Late in the afternoon the Rebels launched a concentrated and formidable drive straight to the West and almost over our weak flank—*almost:* because we refused to yield even yet. For the last time we roundly repelled the enemy and, at evening, still commanded the hill. The enemy renounced additional attempts to dislodge us.

Only now did Thomas deem the time ripe for retreat to Rossville. Under his direction we withdrew in perfect order, despite the continual threat of attack. Thomas said in his report:

> General Garfield, chief of staff of General Rosecrans, reached this position about 4 P.M., and gave me the first reliable information that the right and center of our army had been driven, and of its condition at that time. I soon after received a dispatch from General Rosecrans, directing me to assume command of all the forces, and, with Crittenden and McCook, take a strong position and assume a threatening attitude at Rossville, sending the unorganized forces to Chattanooga for organization, stating that he would examine the ground at Chattanooga, and then join me; also that he had sent out rations and ammunition to meet me at Rossville. I determined to hold the position until nightfall, if possible.[22]

What must be the judgment [in view of subsequent controversy] as to the outcome at Chickamauga? Victory or defeat for the Union? For the answer let us turn to people greater and wiser than ourselves. (In any event [whatever anybody says] the prize of the battle, the city of Chattanooga, remained in *our* hands!)

- General Halleck:

> At nightfall the enemy fell back beyond the range of our artillery, leaving Thomas victorious on his hard fought field. . . . The enemy suffered severely in these battles, and on the night of the 20th was virtually defeated, but being permitted to gather the trophies of the field on the 21st, he is entitled to claim a victory, however barren of results.

- General Bragg:

> After two days' hard fighting, we have driven the enemy after a desperate resistance from several positions, and now hold the field; but he still confronts us. The losses are heavy on both sides, especially so in our officers.

- General Rosecrans:

> The battle of the 20th was fought with all the troops we had, and but for the extension and delay in closing in our right, we should probably have driven the enemy, whom we beat on the field.[23]

According to the latest figures, the Confederates lost 17,804 killed, wounded, and captured; the Union, 16,179; on each side, therefore, about twenty-five percent of the respective forces.[24] The Ninth: 2 officers and 46 men killed, 9 officers and 176 men wounded, and 1 officer and 15 men captured or missing—a total of 249 or half the regiment, for we began the battle at 502.[25] We know that not a few comrades, listed in official reports as missing and wounded, never returned alive; some were found on the battlefield later, outside our sector, dead of wounds. We must respect the official figures now, however. What, really, would be the point of reinflicting pain after all these years?[26]

We have discussed briefly the nature of duties assigned The Ninth in the battle. How well did we fulfill them? Let our commanders speak.

Our brigade-commander Colonel Van Derveer said on the 19th:

> As the enemy slackened his fire, Colonel Kaemmerling, chafing like a wounded tiger that he had been left behind at the opening, ordered his men to charge. Away they went, closely followed by the 87. Indiana and the 17. Ohio, the enemy falling back precipitately. The Ninth in his charge recaptured the guns of Guenther's (actually Burnham's) Fifth Artillery, and held them.
>
> Again, soon: The enemy advanced rapidly, my left giving way slowly until his flank was brought opposite my right wing, when a murderous and enfilading fire was poured into his ranks by the infantry and by Rodney's section shotted with canister. Notwithstanding this he steadily moved up his second and third lines. Having observed his great force as well as the persistency of his attack, I had sent messenger after messenger to bring up the Ninth Ohio, which had not yet returned from its charge, made from my original right. At last, however, and when it seemed impossible for my brave men longer to withstand the impetuous advance of the enemy, the Ninth came gallantly up in time to take part in the final struggle, which resulted

in his sullen withdrawal. In this last attack his loss must have been severe.

And on the afternoon of the 20th when the brigade, nearly out of ammunition, must hold its position with the bayonet:

> Here again the Ninth Ohio made a gallant charge down the hill into the midst of the enemy, scattering them like chaff, and then returning to their position on the hill.[27]

Clarity and brevity—perfectly good reasons—dictate that in reports, corps commanders discuss divisions and brigades but rarely mention regiments. "Pap" Thomas makes an exception in his on Chickamauga. Speaking of movements by Baird's division and others, he pays tribute to The Ninth [the only regiment mentioned in his report]:

> As soon as formed they advanced upon the enemy, attacking him in flank and driving him in great disorder for a mile and a half, while Brannan's troops met him in front as he was pursuing Baird's retiring brigades, driving the head of his column back and retaking the artillery, which had been temporarily lost by Baird's brigades, the Ninth Ohio recovering Battery H, Fifth U.S. Artillery, at the point of the bayonet.[28]

Later the *New York Tribune* reprinted that report but omitted the passage on The Ninth. Good old General Thomas not only complained [about the omission]—in a dispatch to General-in-Chief Halleck (Chattanooga, January 11, 1864)—but he also expressed dissatisfaction publicly, on January 19, 1864, at a serenade given him by The Ninth: "I wanted to do justice to the regiment. I cannot understand why—I feel sorry—the War Department saw fit to curtail my report so as to leave this out."[29]

General Willich [captured at Murfreesboro, exchanged after four months, and back in the Army of the Cumberland] had commanded us and the First Brigade of R[ichard] W. Johnson's [2nd] division [XX Corps]. Willich [therefore] watched us all the more on the morning of September 20th [1863] when one of his regiments, the 15th Ohio, joined us in the first bayonet assault. He says in his battle report:

> The Ninth Ohio (General Brannan's division) deployed into line under heavy fire and made, supported by the 15th Ohio, a glorious charge.[30]

As everybody knows, it is practically customary, among the American military writers [i.e., Civil War memoirists] still alive, to speak again and again of The Ninth's deeds at Mill Springs and Chickamauga as radiant examples of German courage, stamina, and perseverance. Therefore we think we are justified in repeating a few of those praises.

Captain William Vocke of the 24th Illinois, eloquent defender of much-maligned German troops, always bases his statements on the most-careful research. We have already mentioned him and his address to the Illinois Commandery of the Loyal Legion, which we quote again:

> On the field of Chickamauga there rises a substantial and enduring monument for each troop that took part in the battle on the side of the Union. A superb mass of granit [*sic*] has been planted by the state of Ohio on Snodgrass Hill, not far from the headquarters of the imperial Thomas, to commemorate the splendid deeds of the Ninth of Ohio of Mill Springs fame, and we shall presently see that this regiment constituted one of the mightiest bulwarks of the Rock of Chickamauga. At some distance from that hill, there where the bloody combat commenced on the first morning, we find another monument erected in honor of a battery which tells the tale of one of the most heroic deeds of the war. This monument bears on one of its sides the inscription: "Burnham's Battery H. 5th U.S. Artillery," and on the other the following: Fought on this ground morning September 19, 1863, was captured by Liddell's Division and recaptured by Kaemmerling's 9th Ohio Vols.[31]

And [in a related compliment to The Ninth] Vocke had already mentioned the monument in an earlier speech in German to the literary society at the university [Northwestern] at Evanston, Illinois, and added: "In November, 1895, I stood before the monument with several comrades, including my former division commander, Baird. The worthy old veteran observed: 'This is not so much a monument for that battery as it is for the 9th Ohio.' "[32]

Monument to the Ninth Ohio in the National Military Park at Chickamauga

The creator of Chickamauga National {Military} Park, General H{enry} V{an Ness} Boynton, commanded the 35th Ohio, which fought with us in the same brigade in that battle. Years ago he wrote about our regiment:

> The first day at Chickamauga, coming up from guarding the trains at a moment when the fight was furious, without waiting for orders, the Ninth Ohio swept far beyond the Union front, and charging two full brigades which had captured a regular battery, it drove off the enemy and retook the guns.
>
> The second day it charged in the morning with Van Derveer's brigade, to which it belonged, across the Kelly field full into the face of Breckinridge's advancing Division, and, outstripping the rest of the line, though all were advancing on a run, it pushed on to the guns which had been supporting the Confederate advance, disabling the whole battery.
>
> In the afternoon it charged into position on Snodgrass Hill (Horseshoe Ridge), and three times in succession it cleared the slopes in front of it with its bayonets.[33]

Enough praise! Let us think also of the less fortunate and their fate. To be wounded in such a battle, and to lie among the victims waiting for help, may be a soldier's worst experience. Yet every description of Chickamauga mocks the condition of those suffering comrades. Let us hear {instead} from our regimental physician, Dr. {Konrad} Söllheim.

> The battle of the 19th was still young, but our regiment had already suffered numerous dead and wounded. I was brigade physician. Under me were a half-dozen physicians and fifteen orderlies in a field hospital, and perhaps as many {of each} at the front, to hunt up the wounded, administer first-aid, and so forth. The hospital was about two-and-a-half miles from the battlefield, in a church, a magazine, and a cooper's shop.
>
> All day countless ambulances arrived loaded with wounded. At 11:00 P.M. those buildings were overfilled. The scene was indescribable, so touching as to stir even the physicians {who were accustomed to them} and especially so because we could see we must overcome supreme hardship in order to do a few of our duties correctly, if able to do any at all.

Monument to the Burnham Battery in the National Military Park at Chickamauga

We could not start amputating until the morning of the 20th, after initial bandages had been applied, and after bullets and bits of clothing had at last been removed from wounds—in short, only after we had done what was critical to minimal care for the many injured and their manifold needs. But by 9:30—that early—fresh fighting raged near us, scarcely three-fourths of a mile from the hospital. We were soon under artillery bombardment. Then an order arrived from the chief physician. I was to take all the severely wounded with me in ambulances to Rossville, about ten miles off. The rest of the wounded, those not badly hurt, were to walk there.

Too late! The battle already threatened the hospital. Refugees, the wounded, the dying crowded around us, enemy infantry stormed at us, and the word was: *Save yourself if you can!* Chaos. Ambulances took the lead, some empty, others loaded with patients. Physicians followed afoot and on horseback. Ghastly chaos. Then came the new wounded, willing to accept the worst rather than be captured. Why [they reasoned as they fled with us] should the enemy be at all concerned about our injuries, when he had suffered so many of his own?

The poor devils were obviously right about the enemy's regard for Union casualties. We learned two months later that the enemy, in possession of the battlefield all that time, had buried few of our dead and even let many of our wounded die a miserable death. (Perhaps the fatal neglect had been unavoidable because the enemy was not able to care for all his own wounded.) Soon we also learned of his attitude to the rules of war: he made light of them. For he threw physicians into the infernal Libby Prison [in Richmond, Virginia] and confiscated their instruments, medicines, and hospital equipment. On our side, what could be done for the wounded, was done. Our ability to relieve such wholesale distress, however, nowhere met even minimal standards.

About a week later, disabled prisoners were exchanged. Processions of ambulances, loaded with wretched cargo, went back and forth between Chattanooga and the enemy's camp. When our comrades who were hurt but still alive had been returned to us, you could in truth have said: "Chattanooga is nothing but a huge hospital." Their miserable condition was deplorable. Sorrowfully we heard from them that, in Rebel hands, very many of our officers and men, lacking care and proper treatment, had died of wounds. With us, too, far more of the injured perished than should have perished, for lack of nourishing food and so much else.

All things considered, the fate of the wounded at Chickamauga served physicians, generals, and humanitarians vivid and horrifying notice. And the conduct of subsequent wars shows that the lesson was not lost on posterity.[34]

Thus Dr. Söllheim.[35] Plenty of us can confirm his description. In no way exaggerated, it could easily be made even more shocking without harm to the truth. Equally veracious is the fact that at the time, in spite of utter self-sacrifice by physicians, suffering could not be reduced.

On September 21, Union forces under General Thomas [including The Ninth] held Rossville Gap to block a Rebel advance on Chattanooga. Despite high morale, the troops were in sad condition, and I mean those who had not been wounded. We had eaten no warm food since the 18th. Though the intense excitement of two days in battle had suppressed the inevitable inanition, it would now have exerted itself in greater savagery had we at once entered quarters or gone into camp. Such comfort was out of the question. We did [for ourselves] what we were able to do, given those circumstances. General Rosecrans had already forwarded ammunition and food from Chattanooga to Rossville the prior evening. We drew rations, cooked and ate them as well as we could, then dropped our guns and rested.

At daybreak, "Pap" Thomas arrived on horseback at our tired brigade. Men not gripped by the sleep of exhaustion crowded around and blocked him. He stopped, looked at us, and said: "Well, quite a few of you are still left. If some unauthorized individual had not sent the ammunition wagons away from the battlefield, we would be there yet." He repeated that assertion and serious indictment in his battle report (September 30, 1863).[36] Spirited hurrahs greeted the hero wherever he showed himself now. In all the Army of the Cumberland, not a man lost heart, no one believed in a defeat, as long as Thomas remained on the field.

And we thought of the dead, our dead.

Where might they lie, the valiant who had fallen? What might become of those stricken comrades? We scarcely dared contemplate such things.

Our baggage, mementoes of loved ones as well as backpacks, had been lost to the enemy. Many a man appraised a missing keepsake, not in dollars and cents, but in the number of tears the memory evoked on his tanned cheeks.

The enemy did not molest us unbearably that day, but we could not remain. As General Thomas reported later:

> From information received from citizens, I was convinced that the position was untenable in the face of the odds we had opposed to us, as the enemy could easily concentrate upon our right flank, which, if driven, would expose our center and left to be entirely cut off from our communications. I therefore advised the commanding general to concentrate the corps at Chattanooga.[37]

The order to withdraw [from Rossville] came at 6:00 P.M., withdrawal began at 9:00, and we reached Chattanooga at 7:00 A.M. the 22nd. General Rosecrans had given exact directions for disposition. Thus, as each unit arrived, it moved onto the site designated for it. There it must dig in and erect fortifications before a thought could be turned to anything else.[38]

Our [Union] line ran from the mouth of Chattanooga Creek, on the Tennessee at the foot of Lookout Mountain, northerly in a half-circle to the Tennessee again, at the mouth of Citico Creek. The Tennessee itself, widening significantly to the west, completed our ringing [with defenses] the city that must be held at all costs. A general order by our commander-in-chief, published September 23, explained the situation and thanked the troops for proven valor and "gallantry often bordering on foolhardiness." "Pap" Thomas expressed his gratitude in person and, at the same time, dubbed ours "The Iron Brigade." Rosecrans telegraphed the President that day: "We hold this point, and I can not be dislodged except by very superior numbers and after a great battle."[39]

As to the fate of our wounded, we had been quite in the dark and so we remained for now. Fortunately, many fears proved groundless. But some cases were far more serious than was first thought.

An officer was sent to Cincinnati to recruit men for the regiment, which had dwindled to less than a third of former strength.[40]

In every part of the Union, letters and newspapers teemed with admiration and praise for the regiment's conduct. We cannot deny that this appreciation pleased us. And a member of the Cincinnati clergy, Pastor C[arl] Türk, composed a spirited poem,[41] to express his enthusiasm for our deeds.

11

September 23, 1863, to February 22, 1864[1]

The Siege of Chattanooga.—Orchard Knob.—Lookout Mountain.—Missionary Ridge.—Ringgold, Georgia.—East Tennessee.

[Chattanooga to Become the Staging Area for Union Operations into Georgia.—A Wounded Man's Experiences.—Reorganization of the Division.—Thomas Replaces Rosecrans.—Grant Arrives.—Important Battles.—Union Victories.—Praise for The Ninth.—Aftermath of Battle.—Reenlistments.—Soldier Life in Winter.—Sherman's March to the Sea about to Begin.]

"After all, whatever happens is the will of God."

The enemy [under Bragg], having failed to prevent our withdrawal to Chattanooga, surrounded us there. Outside our half-moon-shaped lines he extended his own in a larger [half-]circle from Lookout Mountain [which he occupied after the Battle of Chickamauga] and across Missionary Ridge [which he also occupied after the battle] and almost to where the Tennessee receives the Chickamauga. But Bragg dared not consider a serious attack; his forces were in worse shape than ours. Indeed, when Longstreet [the commander of the Confederate left] requested reinforcements near the end of the battle [of Chickamauga] on the 20th [of September], Bragg answered that his troops were not up to it: "They had all the fight knocked out of them and are of no value to be led against the Union lines."[2] And their condition could not have improved in a few days, that's for sure. Still we could expect the ingenious Rebel general to devise a way to hurt us. And how he hurt us! He addressed himself to what meant must to us now: food.

In the Union camp the necessary fortifications were being erected, hard labor abounded, the sorest absence of food prevailed, and uncommonly cold nights exacerbated the consequent suffering. Fuel fell short, too, and the men could not keep warm after dark—especially as everything had been lost in the way of tents, blankets, and clothing. We lacked even the everyday garb for the trenches, for the building of fortifications, for picket duty, and for patrols.

Soon we were on the dreaded half-rations, so called. In fact less than half, they were significantly less than a third [of normal] because, as several of the various elements of army comestibles failed entirely, so some dishes could not be served at all. In a word, ***hunger*** stalked Chattanooga; and it raged into ***famine*** after Bragg, using [General Joseph] Wheeler's cavalry [in another of Wheeler's daring raids], captured a large, 300-wagon supply train from Stevenson, Alabama [on October 1], and killed or drove off over 1,000 mules. But the [Union] Army of the West proved its greatness in this grave hour. Probably no army did better during the entire war. Working like beavers, the men exceeded themselves at improvising expedients to build shelters above and below ground; at bringing in wood; in short, at everything that would ameliorate the exigence. Meanwhile, however, even the cleverest mind boggled at the question of food. Belts had long since been drawn so tight that their purpose appeared to be to produce wasp waists. Seemingly incredible ruses, strategems, and makeshifts, intended to procure something to eat, were the order of the day; but they cannot be enumerated here. Yet not an observable trace of demoralization occurred among us, whereas deserters reported plenty of it in the Rebel camp.

More light, now, on the fate of our disabled. A noncommissioned officer of Company C, wounded on Snodgrass Hill, arrived with one of the many ambulances to Chattanooga at that time. Badly hit at about 5:00 P.M. on September 20, he had been bandaged by companions and brought to a hospital near the battle, a field-hospital better called a warehouse for the storage of the wounded. Today he lives in Cincinnati and has this to say about those experiences:

> Toward sundown I came to. For me, as for many other wounded men, there was no room in the Snodgrass Hill [farm]house nor in the yard. So I lay outside near the fence. Troops going to Rossville marched past us until late in the cold night. Being where I was, I could identify them. The Ninth, it seemed to me, left the battlefield

last. I wanted to shout to my comrades, but I was wounded in the neck and had trouble talking. This miserable condition did not improve during the long, sleepless hours of darkness—unless [speaking of the situation in general] it be mentioned that, of the wounded who lay whining and groaning all around, many died before dawn, a desirable change in their dreadful circumstances.

We never suspected that our troops had been defeated. When they marched past us the prior evening, we did not think they were retreating from the battlefield. We were confident they would get us out of this jam. Soon we realized our mistake, however, as more and more Confederate soldiers appeared in the area, gathering weaponry and equipment—in other words, collecting booty—some of it lying scattered, some of it in the possession of the wounded. We were told that the Rebels held the battlefield, and that we were their prisoners.

Near me a Rebel and a wounded man of the 21st Ohio quarreled over the Ohioan's gun. He did not want to give it up. When advised of his status—"You are a prisoner; the gun no longer belongs to you"—he smashed it against a tree, breaking and ruining it. The Rebel flew into a rage: "Only your wound keeps me from killing you in revenge." The Ohioan calmly accepted the rebuke and answered: "I'd prefer to be shot than think that someday my gun would kill one of my comrades." I did not see the end of the scene; but the Ohioan's behavior spoke to me of sensitivity and good judgment as well as courage. In those terrible hours I comforted myself by thinking of that brave and worthy man.

Medical assistance remained negligible; physicians were few, and amputations demanded all their energy and time. We nonamputees encouraged, helped, and consoled one another as best we could.

On the morning of the 23rd, ordered to a camp on Lafayette Road, we were to go in ordinary freight wagons or on foot if anyone wanted to take it on himself to walk. The man on the sickbed beside me, a stranger until two days before, less seriously wounded than I, said to me: "You are not riding in that wagon, even if I have to carry you to the camp!" The distance was only two miles. We departed early, with the Confederate officers' approval and promise of protection. We arrived at 4:30 P.M., joined many other seriously wounded men of our regiment, and took up quarters outdoors under a tree: the sky was our tent. For two days, Confederate troops marched past incessantly, to the new Confederate disposition around Chattanooga. I saw their numbers, I thought of the Federals they were surrounding in and near there, and I was sad. Conversations with many of those passers-by

> convinced me they firmly believed in the rightness of their cause and the Confederacy's eventual victory.
>
> Then prisoners were exchanged. After an arduous six-hour ride in ambulances from Chattanooga, we reached our [Union] outposts and, soon after, the city itself. Today the grand Reed House stands where the city's largest hotel had been converted to a hospital. There my wound received needed attention at last. Although care still left much to be desired, I felt as if I had begun a new life.
>
> A few of those who had lain injured with me at Snodgrass Hill were restored to sufficient health to bear arms again. Others were discharged as medically unfit. And a good many died of wounds, right there in Chattanooga.

Yet the astonishing thing was how many were saved, what with the lack of hospital space and the acute shortage of nourishing food for wounded and healthy alike.

Of many similar incidents and scenes that occurred in hospitals then, the following will illustrate the spirit that animated our troops. In a situation become undeniably extreme, the critically wounded (those given up for lost) must be put on camp-beds in the hospital's vestibule, to make room, in the wards, for those thought still to have a chance. Accordingly, a German private of our brigade, considered beyond help and near death, had been removed and left to his fate on a bed of suffering in the vestibule. He was called the Dying Man. When a patient not seriously hurt was passing, Dying Man (who obviously spoke little English) addressed him in German: "Would you carry a message to the chief physician?" The passer-by (fortunately he knew German) said he would do what the unfortunate comrade asked. "Tell him a wounded soldier is lying in the hall," Dying Man said. "And the soldier wants to come into a ward and be bandaged. And tell him"—the poor guy added—"that in all of Rosecrans's army, there aren't enough doctors to kill me!" The chief physician was soon found and informed of what the soldier in the hall wanted. The chief remembered the case and said the care would be wasted: "He cannot be saved." The messenger replied: "But he insists. He claims there aren't enough doctors in the whole army to kill him." The chief answered: "Well, if he talks like that, there's still hope. I'll see to him." Our brave comrade did not die. At Resaca he was back in the ranks.[3]

For the present our [Union] troops remained in a thoroughly disagreeable situation with few cheerful prospects for the immediate future. Nevertheless, on October 13, the Ohio troops in and around Chattanooga took seriously their right to suffrage and cast ballots. The Ninth voted unanimously for [John] Brough, the Republican for governor of Ohio.[4]

Our division underwent total reorganization at that time. General Baird assumed command, replacing a leader very popular with us, Brannan, who was named chief of artillery. Heading the three brigades: Colonels Turchin, Van Derveer, and Phelps. Ours, the old 2nd under Van Derveer, consisted of the 2nd Minnesota; the 75th, 87th, and 101st Indiana; and us, together with the 35th and 105th Ohio; thus seven regiments in all.

Then—yes, as had been expected—Rosecrans was relieved [for slowness and defeat at Chickamauga, and for being surrounded at Chattanooga]. "Pap" Thomas took command [of the Army of the Cumberland] temporarily, before it soon passed to General U. S. Grant. He headed the entire [newly created and] so-called Mississippi Department.[5] Thomas's Army of the Cumberland, which belonged to that Department, constituted the center of Union forces now converging on Chattanooga. Troops coming from the east, under General [Joseph] Hooker, were to form the right; and the Army of the Tennessee the left, being led there by General W. T. Sherman.

Grant, on the road to Chattanooga, telegraphed Thomas: "Hold the place, no matter what." Thomas replied: "We will hold it until we starve."[6] Without hesitation we would compare his remark with MacMahon's "I am here and here I shall stay" at the beleaguered Malakov; or, like the historian of the 35th Ohio [Frederick W. Keil], with that of Martin Luther at Worms: "Here I stand, I cannot do otherwise."[7]

A deputation of Cincinnatians entered our camp, to help where they could, and especially to aid the wounded.[8] Reinforcements, they assured us, were on the way from the east. Good news for stomachs literally roaring now!

Meanwhile, as on earlier occasions, relations between the two sides' pickets had become quite tolerable. Lively barter between rival lines took place on neutral ground. Silly shooting by sentries, back and forth, had stopped by agreement between generals. Hitherto the

Rebel generals had kept up larger (though equally useless) and intermittent shows [of force], however, such as the shelling of our camp from Lookout Mountain on October 5, to our great amusement. Later, cannon still roared frequently, and small-arms fire often crackled here and there. The small-arms fire could be explained for sure as part of the ongoing attempt to block our engineers' bridging the river, and to drive off steamboats that approached ever closer. By now the Rebels were also skirmishing with Hooker's and Sheridan's troops as they neared. All signs pointed plainly to a change in our state of affairs—coming soon.

General Grant arrived on October 22 [over rugged mountain roads, after dark, and on crutches, having fallen from a horse and been hurt in New Orleans]. He approved the work on fortifications and what had been done toward opening communication on the river. Unfortunately, a short while before, the Rebels had destroyed a pontoon bridge, just finished. We could not prevent the destruction, because the long and continuing rains had swollen the river. Blissful hopes had again been shattered on the verge of realization! Most of the pontoons, however, remained relatively undamaged. Congenial relations between [the two sides'] pickets stopped with the appearance of Grant, and a similar order [to stop fraternizing] seemed to have been given on the other side. We were not to speak to each other anymore—malevolence prevailed once again.

On Friday, November 6—at long last!—the siege was broken and communication opened. Actually, General W[illiam] F[arrar] Smith [Chief Engineer, Army of the Cumberland], who directed the engineers' work, had [contrived a crude sternwheel steamboat and] gone downriver several days before, with his pontoons, past enemy outposts. Steamers landed at Brown's Ferry now. Hooker's troops neared as ground had been gained in a skirmish in Lookout Valley the night of October 24th. Thus [means were established] for sending us provisions, beginning at this time. Shipped up from Bridgeport [Alabama], they were transferred to wagons at Kelley's Landing [or Kelley's Ferry] and brought to Chattanooga. In this way we also got back our blankets and other things left earlier in Triune [Tennessee, earlier in the year, while sparring with Bragg there]. Full rations were restored on the 7th.

A week later the paymaster called—

And everything was fine once more.

We had little use for money [however], now that an improved [military] situation ensured further engagements and perhaps a battle bloodier even than Chickamauga. There was little to be bought in Chattanooga anyhow. An agent from Ohio forwarded many thousands of dollars from Ohio regiments to relatives and friends at home.

Grant's task now: drive the Rebels out of the Chattanooga area and off Lookout Mountain and Missionary Ridge.[9] Accordingly, Sherman [who arrived from Memphis on November 13, ahead of his troops from Vicksburg] was to cross the Tennessee above the city and near the mouth of the Chickamauga, outflank Bragg's right, and push Bragg's army back across Tunnel Hill and beyond the railroad, thus cutting Bragg's lines of communication. At the center, Thomas's Army of the Cumberland was merely to feint toward Missionary Ridge, to keep the Rebels occupied there until Sherman had achieved his objective. Only then were they [Thomas's army] to advance on Rebel fortifications on the face of the mountain and, if it was advisable, assault the Rebel entrenchments on the heights. Hooker's army, in Lookout Valley now, was also to feint near Lookout Mountain, to keep Rebels busy and detained there, again to serve Sherman and his thrust at the Rebels' right. This thrust was to be major; all else, ancillary [and in support of him].

The plan called for attack on November 21. Delayed by bad roads and prevented repeatedly from crossing the river, Sherman was not able properly to move into action until the 24th. Consequently, despite good leadership and brave men, he could accomplish his mission neither on time nor as directed. [Thus what might have been a unified operation broke into three parts.] Meanwhile, other things happened, likewise not quite according to plan. On the 23rd, with Sherman still not across the river and Hooker therefore not to undertake anything on the right, Thomas reconnoitered toward Missionary Ridge because deserters from there had brought word that the enemy was withdrawing. We [of Thomas's reconnaisance] then captured the outlying works at the enemy's center [in the first part of the operation, the skirmish at Orchard Knob]. Let it be mentiôned that Thomas [behaved this way because he] did not approve Grant's plan. Grant, the new commander-in-chief, expected much of his plan nonetheless, and did not want to deviate from it. The speed of our penetration of the enemy's works, and the tenacity with which we held them, must at least have shown Grant that he could rely on the officers and men of his center. But [because Thomas disapproved of the plan] we [disregarded it and] disposed ourselves as had been originally intended.

Indeed, in rigid accord with what had been specified [before Grant's plan was issued], The Ninth was in position on the road to Rossville. Nothing altered during the night. About 11:00 in the morning of the 24th, a furious cannonade began to our left [signalling the start of the operation's second part, at Lookout Mountain]. Hooker was initiating his feint. But [like Thomas] not adhering to the plan, he drove the enemy back to Chattanooga Creek Bridge and Summertown Road in the so-called "battle above the clouds." We could see it beautifully from our position. Actually, fog produced the fiction that this brief phase of Hooker's movements took place "above the clouds." The fog, so thick that it yielded only momentarily to the sun now and then, cloaked the valley while leaving Lookout Mountain's heights free to be brilliantly illuminated. The view was magnificent and, for us, inspiring because we could observe exactly how the Rebels withdrew northeast along the slopes, with Hooker's troops after them, flags flying. Our ranks cheered lustily while cannon at our Forts Negley and Wood also sounded congratulations.

At about the hour that Hooker achieved his objective, Sherman at last reached *his* destination on the enemy's right. In other words, Sherman was notably late. Enemy troops driven off Lookout Mountain, whom Hooker was only supposed to engage and detain, had thus been set free; and all of them could be used again for the immediate and emphatic reinforcement of Bragg and against Grant's lines [boding ill for the fighting tomorrow].

We [of The Ninth] passed a quiet night. Each of us, whether dreaming or awake, lucubrated a plan for the next day's battle—a plan that, without doubt, would bring us victory.

Shooting started early in the morning of November 25 [in the operation's third part, at Missionary Ridge], along Sherman's positions on our left. But Sherman would fail to force the enemy to yield. Our division (Baird's) received orders to hurry there as reinforcements. We marched along the [Union] lines and almost to the Tennessee, when a counterorder arrived and we must retrace our steps and proceed nearer and nearer to the enemy's front, until finally, west of the [Nashville & Chattanooga] railway, we formed for attack. A mile to a mile and a half of bushy terrain [here at the Union/ Confederate center] separated the opposing lines. In between, at midpoint, there were enemy trenches and breastworks; and behind them, rows of enemy pickets [and on the heights farther away, cannon]. And so [we waited and] time passed [and nothing happened].

The sun was already sinking, before the real struggle at last began for us in the center, when enemy cannon hurled an instantaneous and a savage bombardment at our entire length. Fierce rifle fire broke out on the right side of our corps. The first chorus of the famous battle-cry—*Hurrah!*—announced the glitter of bayonets being fixed. The whole [Union] line advanced at once and in full swing—brigade after brigade, storming Missionary Ridge, driving the enemy before us, penetrating his works, leaping over them, on and on, to the top. The front [as we moved forward] had gradually shifted toward the left. The enemy, falling back from our assault, had thus been herded together into a smaller and smaller area. At the top [of the first elevation, our quondam objective] the briefest of pauses was necessary, that we catch our breath. The plateau [above, and its enemy cannon] awaited. With incredible speed we were there and in possession of the enemy's batteries. Not only had we done what was required of us by prior design. We had also set an objective for ourselves and reached it largely on our own initiative and brilliantly.[10]

General Grant was on Orchard Knob with Generals Thomas and [Gordon] Granger during that spontaneous action. [They watched, fascinated] when [we] Union attackers stormed the heights.

Grant to Thomas: "Who ordered those men up the ridge?"

"I don't know," said Thomas, "I did not."

Grant to Granger: "Did you?"

"No, they started without orders. When those fellows get started, all hell can't stop them."

Grant, somewhat irritated, muttered: "If the charge fails, some one will have to pay."[11]

But it succeeded and the Rebels paid.

Whether by plan, whether by improvisation, Missionary Ridge was ours, the enemy in disarray, the battle won, and the war's most magnificent feat of arms achieved. And by whom? By the same commander, General Thomas, and the same troops who retreated only when nothing else could be done on the bloody field at Chickamauga two months before.

Military strategists [however] are notorious for dissatisfaction when their plans have not been carried out exactly, and their preconceived ideas not realized precisely, even though the battle has been won. So it was with Grant [which caused his incorrect evaluation of Thomas and the Army of the Cumberland]. As Sherman says in his memoirs, Grant delayed the action at Chattanooga until he, Sherman, arrived; mainly because he [Grant] put no trust in Thomas's corps. Earlier, Grant [according to Sherman] said: "The men of Thomas' army had been so demoralized by the battle of Chickamauga, that he [Grant] feared they could not be got out of their trenches to assume the offensive." Sherman continues: "The army of the Cumberland had so long been in the trenches that he [Grant] wanted my army [i.e., troops] to hurry up to take the offensive first, after which he had no doubt the Cumberland army would fight well."[12]

Let us be more generous than Grant; let us say he erred in his estimate of the "demoralized" Army of the Cumberland—of *us*. We shall allow him to speak again [to balance the account], from his official report concerning November 23:

> General Thomas' troops attacked the enemy's left at 2 P.M. to-day, carried the first line of rifle-pits running over the knoll, taking about 200 prisoners, besides killed and wounded. Our loss is small. The troops moved under fire with all the precision of veterans on parade.

And, after neither Sherman nor Hooker had accomplished much on the 25th, Grant said:

Thomas was directed to move forward his troops, constituting our center, and carry the rifle-pits at the foot of Missionary Ridge, and when carried to reform his lines on the rifle-pits with a view to carrying the top of the ridge. These troops moved forward, drove the enemy from the rifle-pits at the base of the ridge like bees from a hive—stopped but a moment until the whole were in line—and commenced the ascent of the mountain from right to left almost simultaneously, following closely the retreating enemy, without further orders. They encountered a fearful volley of grape and canister from nearly thirty pieces of artillery and musketry from still well filled rifle-pits on the summit of the ridge. Not a waver, however, was seen in all that long line of brave men. Their progress was steadily onward until the summit was in their possession. In this charge the casualties were remarkably few for the fire encountered. I can account for this only on the theory that the enemy's surprise at the audacity of such a charge caused confusion and purposeless aiming of their pieces.

Grant also wrote to Sherman on the 25th: "No doubt you witnessed the handsome manner in which Thomas' troops carried Missionary Ridge this afternoon."[13]

We spent the night of the 25th at the place where we defeated the Rebels. Next day we joined the pursuit of them. Sherman's and especially Hooker's forces pressed them as well. Skirmishes were still breaking out persistently and many prisoners being taken. Our corps proceeded only as far as Ringgold, Georgia, then turned back toward Chattanooga on the 28th and arrived on the 29th. There we were really able to take a well-deserved rest.

How had we of The Ninth performed at Missionary Ridge? The official reports will show what we did; we must begin at the beginning. (We have already heard General Grant's opinion of Thomas's entire Army of the Cumberland on the day of the battle.)

• On November 25, Thomas sent to our corps commander, General [John M.] Palmer:

I most cordially congratulate you and your command on the splendid manner in which your portion of the work of assaulting the enemy's position on Missionary Ridge was performed. Please convey to the officers and men of the corps my hearty thanks for their gallant conduct.

• Sturdy Van Derveer, our brigade commander, said:

My brigade moved at once with cheers and a hearty good will. The precipitous ascent, the enemy's sharpshooters in front, and the terrible enfilading artillery fire upon each flank were forgotten in their eager haste to storm the heights. My second line (75th Indiana, 105th and *9th Ohio* [*sic*]) came forward at a run, and after a few moments' rest at the foot of the ridge followed closely the advance (2d Minnesota, 87th Indiana, 101st Indiana, 35th Ohio). In fifteen minutes more our colors were upon the summit, and in twenty the rebels had been driven out of their works on the crest, and we occupied the ground in front of the brigade. . . . In this action my brigade fully sustained the reputation it had won at Chickamauga. None flinshed [*sic*] from their duty.

• Our regimental commander, Colonel Kämmerling, remarked in his calm style:

The Ninth Ohio did not take an active part in the fighting before late in the afternoon of the 25th November. At 3 P.M. it was posted on the left of the second line of the Second Brigade, Third Division, Fourteenth Corps, the brigade then being in battle line in front and along the west-side of the Missionary Ridge. About 4 o'clock I received orders to advance. As soon as the line moved forward it met with a most galling fire from the enemy's batteries posted on the ridge in front and on the left of our position; but notwithstanding this, I succeeded in gaining the ridge with a comparatively very small loss in killed and wounded. My regiment participated from this moment until dark in the struggle for the possession of the ridge.[14]

On their way up [Missionary Ridge] our comrades of the 35th Ohio captured five Rebel cannon. The deed was subsequently called trivial or denied in childish fashion. The same thing had happened to us when we took the Burnham Battery at Chickamauga. Whitelaw Reid, in his *Ohio in the War* [2:74–75] states simply and accurately the facts of this incident at Missionary Ridge. "As the National troops were resting after their labors, the Rebel forces on Tunnel Hill moved against a battery of five guns, which Van Derveer's brigade had captured. The Ninth Ohio and One Hundred and First Indiana immediately formed and, though greatly outnumbered by the Rebels, repulsed them three times, when they abandoned the attack."[15]

Thus another leaf was added to the laurels, not only of our regiment, but also of all Union forces in the battle. Assistant Adjutant-General [i.e., Assistant Secretary of War Charles A.] Dana's dispatch to Secretary of War Stanton, on the evening of the great day, expressed everyone's heartfelt thoughts: "Glory to God. The day is decisively ours. Missionary Ridge has just been carried by a magnificent charge of Thomas' troops, and the rebels routed. Hooker has got in their rear."[16]

Casualties, in the action between November 23 and 27, according to official and authentic reports: Union, 753 dead, 4,722 wounded, 349 captured or missing (total 5,824); Confederate, 361 dead, 2,180 wounded, 4,146 captured or missing (total 6,667).[17] In our regiment only two perished: Corporal Ferdinand Bortz of Company A, and Private Jakob Bauer of Company B. Thirteen were wounded.

The consequences of the Battle of Chattanooga were momentous for the cause of the Union. The Confederacy's strength was broken at the center, Kentucky and Tennessee were saved for the Union, [General Ambrose E.] Burnside [besieged by Longstreet at Knoxville] was delivered from grave danger in East Tennessee [because troops from Chattanooga relieved him], and Georgia and all the [Confederate] Southeast were threatened from the rear.

Days of rest followed [the battle]. Naturally they included inspections and reviews, full rations, and new uniforms and equipment. But those things arrived with a beautiful lethargy and not all at once. Duty was easy; and trouble from the enemy, nonexistent.

On December 10 we were part of General Thomas's escort to the Chickamauga battlefield. He wanted better intelligence on the nature of the terrain, and more-definitive information about troop movements on the day of the fighting. We can record only a few hints here, from the pen of a comrade, in memory of what we saw there. "The battlefield was a shocking sight. Putrefying corpses, detached arms and legs, and skeletons with dried skin clinging to the bones, lay scattered everywhere. Our brigade had used as a hospital a log cabin near Snodgrass Hill. The cabinside well the Rebels had obviously filled with corpses, for a foot and a skull protruded from the thin layer of earth thrown over them. At the Snodgrass [farm]house itself, where our brigade stood for hours and beat back Rebels storming the hill in assault after assault, the bushes had been cut down with bullets as if with a mowing machine; and so much small-arms fire had riddled the trees that their bark resembled a sieve. Long rows of mounds of fresh earth marked the spots where friend and foe lay buried side by side. With heavy hearts we left this piece of land that held for us so many memories both glorious and sad."[18]

On the 12th and 13th [of December] the national salute was fired in Fort Wood; and the army order, expressing the gratitude of the President and the nation, was read; to memorialize the victory at Missionary Ridge.

In subsequent days the honor was reserved to us to witness the anguish of war and the suffering of soldiers: scenes that overshadowed everything hitherto experienced. I refer to the wretchedness of the XI and XV Corps, arriving after the lifting of the siege of Knoxville and the relief of Burnside's army [December 6]. Ragged of clothing and tattered of shoe; hands and feet chilblained; half-starved; shivering—thus the poor, deserving souls came to us. We gladly helped in a situation that taxed us to the utmost.

On December 30 we [of The Ninth] also marched away to East Tennessee [in charge of a battery and a provision train for Calhoun on the Hiwassee River]. We greeted the new year in frightful cold at Harrison on the Tennessee. [Temperatures, in Cairo and Memphis, fell below zero.] A New Year's celebration had to be dispensed with. We did picket duty instead, our hardest yet, as sentries had to be relieved every ten minutes lest they freeze. We arrived at Johnston Gap on the 2nd, crossed the Hiwassee, [passed Charleston] and on the 4th were in Calhoun, our destination. We took up quarters in abandoned houses, foraged again in our old way, and captured a band of Rebels drinking in a well-stocked distillery. On the 7th and 8th we marched via Cleveland back to Harrison and then returned to Chattanooga on the 9th.

There the regiments, ours included, whose three years were nearly up, were asked to reenlist for another three. The time left in the present enlistment would be waived, a month's furlough granted, and a generous bonus paid. [Despite those seductive lures] The Ninth had no desire to reenlist; we thought it behooved others to try a hitch. After a brief discussion, we [thus] discarded the proposal [that we reenlist]. Conversely, most of our friends and comrades of the 2nd Minnesota, having been willing to reenlist, went home on their 30-day furlough. Our best wishes accompanied them, after they soberly said good-bye to us. For who could know whether they would meet us again and, if so, in what circumstances.

Work temporarily ceased on the fortification of Chattanooga. On January 14, jubilation greeted the first locomotive to arrive on the rebuilt railroad. Trains soon followed with food and freight.

We [of The Ninth] celebrated the second anniversary of Mill Springs appropriately [January 19], and in the evening serenaded our esteemed leader, Thomas. As always, he gave a short speech of thanks. This time he said: "Well boys, I thank you for the serenade you have honored me with this evening! To-day it is two years that we gave the enemy the first terrific blow, and I hope we'll give them a good many more. You will, it is true, go home soon, but it will always be a happy recollection to me, to have had the good fortune to command such brave men as the Ninth Ohio Regiment consists of. Good night!"[19]

A great national cemetery for the dead of all battles around Chattanooga was begun and we were employed on it. Meanwhile, work on the fortifications [of Chattanooga] resumed, continuing until our second march to Ringgold [where March and April were spent in camp]. Thus we entered the last segment of our military service. We could look back with the greatest satisfaction on the one just finished—a satisfaction increased by the hope of a speedy and glorious return home.

12

February 22 to June 7, 1864[1]

In Camp at Ringgold, Georgia.—Tunnel Hill.—With Sherman toward Atlanta.—Snake Creek.—Resaca.—The Etowah River: We Leave Active Duty.—Arrival in Cincinnati.—Mustering-Out at Camp Dennison.—Celebration [and a Banquet] in Turner Hall in Cincinnati.—"Order Arms!"[2]

[A Widow's Good Fortune.—Germans at Meat.—Return of the 2nd Minnesota.—Looking Forward to Mustering Out.—Atlanta the Objective Now.—The Ninth Sees a Little Fighting, Then Says Good-Bye to War and Hello to Cincinnati.]

"Happily I put aside the bloody laurels."

At the start of the year 1864, many regiments of every arm were away on furloughs granted for three-year reenlistments, leaving a weakened Army of the Cumberland encamped at Chattanooga. This signing-up for another tour was called "veteranizing." Meanwhile, accordingly, the rearming of the forces proceeded slowly.[3] The move to Ringgold, Georgia, already determined and announced, remained opportune but became impossible to execute at once.

At the same time, promotions in the regiment had occurred [on February 14], including Major F[ritz] Schröder to lieutenant-colonel, and Captain B[artolomäus] Benz to major. The plucky and dashing regimental adjutant G[eorg] H. Harries became captain of Company E—brigade-commander [Ferdinand Van Derveer] had called his bravery at Chickamauga especially praiseworthy—and Lieutenant H[ermann] Pönitz replaced him [as adjutant]. Colonel Kämmerling was named brigadier-general, in recognition of service at Chickamauga, but he remained with the regiment [as McCook had done before him].

The move to Ringgold began on February 22, our division the first [i.e., in the van] of the XIV Corps. The residents had abandoned the town, and only a few buildings remained. We bivouacked near Taylor's Gap while cannon thundered in the distance, signifying bloody work at hand. The enemy had situated himself in considerable strength about six miles south of Ringgold.

On the 24th our division advanced toward Tunnel Hill where a careful reconnaissance had been conducted [and the enemy met] the day before. The enemy had drawn his battle-line opposite us; a broad valley [Crow's Valley] lay between the two armies. On the 25th we confronted him a second time, at his fortifications along the heights of Buzzard's Roost. We soon proceeded across the valley, driving his outposts back to his main position. Our regiment, at the center of the Union lines, continued the advance. Fighting boiled on the right and simmered on the left; while our status remained one of observation. [And that situation prevailed] until we retired to the camp at Taylor's Gap at 11:00 P.M. We suffered no casualties during this reconnaissance. In another on the 29th, again toward Tunnel Hill, we did not make contact with the enemy.[4]

Our baggage and camp-equipage had now been brought from Chattanooga; and on March 1, in the bad weather of that spring, our move [to Ringgold] became an accomplished fact. Then the usual agenda of life in camp: inspections, occasional alarms, and rather easy picket duty. Baptist preachers stopped by, to sweeten—with sermons, tracts, and riverine baptisms—the lives of piously inclined soldiers. Of course The Ninth was not very receptive to such things.[5] We rather inclined to the opinion that a little more sensual gratification would not be amiss here in Ringgold. But the evangelists persisted.

Good luck can be had, and prosperity ensue [however], even under the worst circumstances of a military campaign. During the time in question, something happened to our friend L. of Company D, proving the point.[6] He says:

> Our [regimental] adjutant [Hermann Pönitz] was sick. Returning to camp from an errand I ran for him March 3, I found a five-dollar gold-piece near the railway embankment. I had not had a cent to my name for a long time, so a windfall made me feel super. I spent none of the treasure, though. My piece of gold returned with me to Cincinnati later, and I didn't touch it until the day before my birthday,

November 26, 1864. Then, to buy the things I needed to celebrate the great event right, I changed the gold to vulgar greenbacks—at the profitable rate of 271 percent. So I had $18.55 and could really indulge myself in birthday style. Unfortunately, one trouble intervened: I must stop with the proceeds of one gold-piece just when I had taken a step down Easy Street! Still, my find would produce benefits beyond my pleasure at that moment. Almost thirty years later, Pönitz's widow came to me. My errand at Ringgold had been for Pönitz [you'll recall] back then. He had just died, and she heard I kept a detailed diary throughout the war. She wanted entries that concerned his illness, to use in a request for a pension. Though entitled, he had never applied; he had been able to work all his life. I gladly gave her my notes from those days, providing the evidence she needed. She got the pension right away.

Sickness raged [in Union ranks] at that time. Dysentery struck often, especially among recent arrivals, mostly new [i.e., recently organized] regiments. Clement weather and wholesome food (good provisions *were* delivered) led to the conclusion, easily drawn and quickly confirmed, that those regiments prepared food wrong. They boned most of their meat and roasted it on spits. Now, in clean and tidy households and [hygienic] commercial establishments, this method produces delicious fare; everybody should try it there. But in our circumstances, and for any troops in the field, that method is wrong and to be spurned because the meat remains partly raw.

What to do? Commanders wracked their brains, physicians themselves were at a loss, but "Pap" Thomas advised: "See what sort of food my German regiment eats and how they fix it." Visiting us, those gentlemen discovered, not half-raw "broiled steaks," but hearty soups containing meat boiled together with the bones—and very few cases of dysentery among cheerful, healthy-looking men who relished this wholesome course.[7] Our example spread, dysentery diminished, and its pale, hollow-cheeked victims grew noteworthy by their absence. So we had been commended frequently enough for every other possible excellence, we had been held up as models equally often, and now at last we enjoyed praise as master chefs and were to be imitated accordingly!

The 2nd Minnesota returned on April 10, furlough ended and another three years begun. We gave these friends the warmest welcome. Concerned for their bodily comfort, in a Ringgold where every unoccupied house had been demolished for material to build huts [for us Union soldiers], we razed an abandoned church outside the town and put its boards, beams, and other constituents at the 2nd's immediate disposal.[8]

Nothing occurred [meanwhile] to effect significant change in camp life. Nobody did anything to make duty hard. Repeated attempts failed to persuade us to reenlist. Firm was our resolve not to do so but to return home. Accordingly, we continued to be preoccupied with calculating our legal obligation in weeks, days, and minutes, crossing them off as they passed, watching our enlistment grow beautifully short! At the same time in Cincinnati, several tries failed to raise recruits for The Ninth. The failure mattered not at all to us.[9]

Perhaps nobody will be surprised [therefore] that, on Friday, April 22, we thought back on our informal taking of the oath in Turner Hall in Cincinnati [on this day] in 1861. Thus it occurred to us that we had already served three years; in our humble opinion, our time was up. Nor will anybody wonder that we must stay for a while on a provisional basis, or that (contrary to promise) we were not credited with the month served before we changed our enlistment to three years. So we pinned our hopes on the 27th of May, the [anniversary of the] day at Camp Dennison [in 1861] when we signed up for three years.

Plans for a campaign against Atlanta, largely known by now, gradually began to be implemented. We understood that General Sherman would strike at the Georgia capital with some 100,000 men. This expedition would shape Rebel operations in the West.[10] Grant had been named commander-in-chief of all Union armies [March 10, 1864], and the consequent solidifying of purpose justified belief and hope that a unified leadership would direct the campaign [to a successful conclusion]. Even we of The Ninth believed we would see battle once more before we went home.

On April 26, four regiments of our brigade—the 35th and the 105th Ohio, the 2nd Minnesota, and ours—together with a troop of about 100 cavalry, made yet another reconnaissance toward Tunnel Hill. We drove back enemy outposts without any casualties of our own. On May 2 we repeated the maneuver. Both times with the same purpose: to discover and investigate the enemy's position.

Orders arrived that convinced us that strategic circumspection and battle readiness would prevail on the Atlanta campaign. Baggage not absolutely essential, even regimental and company records and other papers, must be left behind. A special examination found some men in less-than-perfect health, unfit for [strenuous] duty and to be designated on the spot as garrison forces and stationed in towns occupied along the line of march. By this time [over the past several weeks] Union forces had been well equipped. Every soldier was always to carry three days' rations; and forty rounds of ammunition constituted every soldier's regular load. Wagons full of the rest stood ready to roll.

On May 7 we set off: General Thomas in the center with [the Army of the Cumberland], half of Sherman's entire force; General [James B.] McPherson commanding [the Army of the Tennessee on] the right; General [John M.] Schofield [leading the Army of the Ohio on] the left; General [George] Stoneman at the head of the cavalry; and General Brannan chief of artillery; besides Generals Palmer, Jeff C. Davis, [Hugh J.] Kilpatrick, Hooker, R. W. Johnson, Anson McCook, Turchin, Baird, Willich, Van Derveer, and others—a train of proven leaders. Under them the Union troops could enter with confidence upon this campaign.

The Rebels counted 75,000 under General Johnston. In numbers they enjoyed the advantage that, in being driven toward Atlanta, they could always add [to Johnston's main force] the garrisons of the towns they surrendered, and pit them [too] against the Federals in the Armageddon of this campaign, should such a decisive battle occur.[11]

Skirmishes—every day.

On the 10th [i.e., the 9th of May] the enemy took a stand behind solid fortifications on the hills near Buzzard's Roost and Rocky Face Ridge. The plan now—and the first mission of our forces: to penetrate the funnel-shaped valley between the two positions [ours and the enemy's], while the right wing cut the enemy's communication with Atlanta. The enemy would then have to withdraw from Dalton. Our operations stalled for a while, however, because General McPherson did not do his part on the right. Yet Johnston must be driven out of his fortifications and forced to battle, lest our advance be stopped without hope of restarting, or have to be given up altogether. At last we succeeded in outflanking the enemy on the left, other than as planned, when McPherson went around Snake Creek [but failed to hit Johnston's rear and withdrew to Snake Creek Gap]. Then the bulk of the Union army pierced the gap on the night of the 12th. This action forced the Rebels to surrender Dalton and draw up for battle at Resaca.

The battle—actually a series of clashes—lasted three days.[12] A giant confrontation, if measured by the number of men involved, nearly 175,000. Result: indecisive. But the enemy had been driven from his position [in rifle-pits behind earthworks across a river-bend peninsula near the town] and must either fall back to his next fortifications at the Etowah or see his lines of communication cut. He chose to fall back. Union forces pursued him—via Adairsville, Kingston, and Cassville—to the Etowah.

Our regiment had neither played an active role in the clashes nor suffered casualties in the pursuit. But near Resaca, while we stood in reserve, our old friend General Willich suffered wounds—before our very eyes, so to speak.

On May 20 the order arrived. *Return to Cincinnati, Ninth Ohio, and be mustered out.*[13] General Thomas himself relieved us of picket duty near the Etowah and led us back to camp. On the 21st we packed quickly, took heartfelt leave of our good companions in the brigade, and headed for Chattanooga in two detachments. There, where we had suffered so much, we rested one more night and looked back upon what we had experienced.

How hard, of course, to say good-bye to dear friends in the 2nd Minnesota and 35th Ohio! But the pain ended fast—soon replaced by joyous anticipation of a happy homecoming. We stood high in the eyes of our brigade; and he who holds such an elevated position with those he must leave, need not be sad long.[14] The 2nd Minnesota held us in the esteem expressed by the words of their colonel, Judson W. Bishop:

> Here, on the 21st, our longtime comrades of the Ninth Ohio were ordered to Cincinnati for muster-out, their three years' term having expired. Our men had spent most the day in saying 'good by' to them, and when they were ready to leave[,] our regiment was formed to give them a parting 'present arms' as they marched past our front, fol-

> lowed by three rousing cheers for the heroes and comrades at Mill Springs, Chickamauga, and Missionary Ridge.[15]

The 35th Ohio likewise paid tribute, through their historian, Captain F[rederick] W. Keil:

> Here the Ninth Ohio left the brigade; their term of service had expired. That regiment had been a constant companion to the Thirty-fifth, being one of the regiments that made up the original brigade to which we belonged. It was a model regiment in every respect. No finer drilled body was found in the western armies, and it is doubtful whether it had an equal in any union army, either east or west. We had rather seen any other regiment march away and leave us than the Ninth Ohio.[16]

For our part, had we stayed in the service, we could have chosen for the future no better or braver comrades than those two regiments. The 35th soon followed us to our old Buckeye home. At this hour [in 1897], friendship and respect unite us with those of its members still alive.

We arrived in Nashville on the 24th and in Louisville early on the 26th. Despite the odd hour and [unfavorable] circumstances, the citizens of Louisville did what they could to receive and welcome us. (The Ninth was well known in Louisville.) Amid expressions of the greatest warmth by the populace, we marched to the steamboat landing at 9:00 A.M. About 1:00 P.M. we headed upstream for Cincinnati, aboard the *John J. McCooms*. From both banks of the Ohio the joyous shouts continued. We reached home on the anniversary of the day we began our three years of service: Friday, May 27. All of us left bed before daybreak. At 7:00 A.M. our boat passed the outskirts of Cincinnati. Ashore: a gigantic, happy hullabaloo. Perhaps you can imagine how we felt; words cannot express it.

Our reception in Cincinnati had been prepared in the grand manner. A citizens' committee—Messrs. V. Bechmann, W. Stängel, F. J. Meyer, B. Speyer, A. Rothert—had taken pains to make the demonstration brilliant. True, The Ninth had gone forth from the core of German Cincinnati. True, the fame of The Ninth in war was nationwide and unimpeachable. But a further reason prompted the committee [to arrange for this booming hospitality]. Ohio nativist newspapers had felt obliged to chalk up to our German discredit that we chose to come back rather than stay and fight for those who waged war here on the home front. And [those papers also charged] we would gladly have made common cause with the enemy, had such treachery been possible without endangering our valuable, our precious lives.[17] [So the committee wanted to take a stand against such nativism.]

Before 7:00 A.M., droves of our friends and relatives, and many others, crowded the steamboat-landing to greet us. At 7:30 the bells of the city's fire stations announced the departure of turners and official representatives from Turner Hall, led by the turner band. At 8:00 the procession reached the waterfront. Then some 600 sunburned men, part of them looking older and fatigued, stepped ashore onto the soil of home, amid the exultation of their people—an exultation liberally mixed with nostalgia and sadness. Many were not recognized at first glance. Often from lips of tanned warriors:

"Don't you know me anymore?"

"Why, how you've grown, child!"

"Yes, I'm really your Daddy!"

Some young wives and their children wept; they had come to hear, straight from survivors, details of how husbands and fathers died a hero's death at Chickamauga. A mother who already knew the details lauded the bravery of her son who remained on the field of honor. And fathers—old soldiers themselves, grown grey—embraced their courageous sons and praised them. Probably few eyes stayed dry at those scenes.

At 8:30 the official reception occurred when the procession [from Turner Hall] reached the landing. Behind Brand's band they came: men and wives and unmarried women, with wreaths and garlands for officers and men of The Ninth, and carriages for the disabled, and streamers of honor for the two sets of regimental colors. Soon, the march back to Turner Hall, on Race, Vine, and Twelfth, through the gaily decorated quarter. After County Commissioner F. J. Meyer's cordial speech, most of The Ninth stayed at the hall, partook of the pleasures provided, and observed the happy homecoming amid singing, dancing and conversation far into the night. Others of The Ninth, however, sought the family circle early, for a more intimate celebration. Of course, on this occasion [as on all German-related occasions], the principal festivities took place "over the Rhine" in the [German] district northwest of the canal.

Understandably, that day alone could not contain the rejoicing. When the regiment had been raised [in 1861], Turner Hall buzzed like a beehive; and now, in the days following [our return], it buzzed again. It served not only as the official headquarters of The Ninth, but also as the rendezvous for those who wanted to tell their stories [of the war] and those who gladly came to listen. Each [storyteller was now] a full-fledged general! And, sooner or later, all true Germans dropped in—to raise another glass for one reason or another.

On June 2 the following regimental order appeared in the newspapers:

> Headquarters, 9th O. Vol. Inf. Reg.
> Turner Hall, 2 June 1864
> The 9th O. V. I. R. shall report today, with weapons and baggage, at Turner Hall at 11:00, to muster out.
> By order of
> Col. G. Kämmerling
> Hermann Pönitz, Adjutant

The Ninth assembled at the appointed hour. Behind their band for the last time, under the command of the esteemed Colonel Kämmerling, they marched with precision to Camp Dennison, 674 officers and men. During the following week, Captain James Thompson, of the 2nd U.S. Artillery, routinely mustered them out. Back pay, promptly disbursed, together with the stipulated 100-dollar bounty, left everybody satisfied. Everybody, that is except those—especially the musicians enlisted in 1863—who said they had been promised discharge with men enlisted in 1861. Kept in uniform, the latecomers went, one and all, back into the field to serve their years. Such was their fate:

> Where one plucks a rose, another sifts dry sand.

Dischargees returned to Cincinnati on the 10th. Our regiment ceased to exist.

Accepting an invitation carried by the Cincinnati newspapers, most of the [former] Ninth and their families attended the banquet in their honor at Turner Hall on June 11. The city's Germans gave the banquet, Judge J. B. Stallo presided, and it was congenial and festive. Three years earlier, in this place, that skillful orator inspired his audience to take up arms for what was right. Now he spoke simply, briefly, and appropriately of how they had fought for The Good Cause and the honor of the German name. He reminded them that, if some work was done, other work remained. The veterans must prove that in "the land of the free," a man's value extends beyond the uniform. "After an honorable end to the war, he must be ready and willing to enjoy the blessings and discharge faithfully the obligations of civilian life." At this banquet dedicated to the veterans, Stallo's words helped cheer them in their enjoyment of it. Moreover, what he said made them happy not only that they had chosen to lay down their arms for the last time, but also that they laid them down with honor.

The banquet did not break up until after midnight. Yet the next morning—that soon!—many a man just out of the "first German regiment" became again a law-abiding citizen in the grand army of peace and work.

III

To Honor the Past

13
The German Soldier in America[1]

[Unfair Estimate of Germans and German-Americans as Citizens and as Civil-War Soldiers.—They Deserve the Utmost Praise.]

"When the nation is in trouble, he who thinks any thought but to save it, does not deserve to live in a nation of freedom."

On September 19, 1896, when the survivors of The Ninth celebrated the anniversary of the Battle of Chickamauga, they recalled again and again the words of Colonel Robert Latimer McCook. This patriot, who urged the need to suppress the rebellion as quickly as possible, had been as ardent when the fighting began as he would later be brave as a soldier and popular as a leader. Thus, in his dramatic style, shortly after war broke out, the regiment's future commander justified why he wanted an all-German regiment to be raised in Cincinnati: "I know the Germans will fight. Our American boys mean well enough, but they don't know how."[2] At the celebration [when McCook's words were recalled in 1896] a comrade from the old 35th Ohio laughed: "Yes, but they learned it pretty well!"[3]

He was right. History knows no men who sacrificed more happily than Americans born on these shores. Free men, impassioned for the sacred cause of the Union, and mostly men who knew nothing of soldiering, they suffered the gravest of hardships and did not complain. For a lofty ideal they cheerfully gave their all. And if we are not mistaken, Americans also fought for the Confederacy, like real men and true heroes, in behalf of a cause likewise sacred and just to them. Else the war would not have assumed the magnitude of one of the bloodiest of all time anywhere.

Now, it is unfortunate that Americans disdain immigrants and disparage whatever they do, as soon as every possible advantage has been taken of the same immigrants. This general American blunder [invites discussion in particular with reference to the war]. Often enough a palpable hatred accompanies that attitude, hatred especially for Germans, often expressed in downright and nasty calumny and lies.[4]

Germans were defamed in the Civil War, too. American officers' botches were only too gladly laid on Germans under them. Failures marked time after time against German troops, and charged again and again to German officers, could not be rightly thus assigned. The latest research [tells a different story, however], above all about the German generals [Carl] Schurz and [Franz] Sigel and their German units. Impartial experts and competent military writers have established as lies, bald *lies,* the often-malicious misstatements circulated about those Germans. The same authorities—Dodge, Boynton, Doubleday, and others—have exposed as fabrications especially the reports and rumors that falsify the behavior of German troops at Chancellorsville.[5] The assertion has never been proved [moreover] that American or Irish [i.e., Irish-American] units would have acted otherwise in those circumstances. On the contrary, those authorities have denied it.[6]

Today the undeniable and generally accepted facts contradict earlier slanders. The Germans contributed not 128,000 but 188,000 men to the [Union armies in the] war; in proportion to the total population, a good 60,000 more than their share.[7] And the Germans distinguished themselves as patriotic citizens and brave and loyal soldiers in this perilous era of American history. *Item:* Early in 1862, Charles Sumner said that Lincoln would not have been elected without the German-Americans.[8] *Item:* St. Louis and Missouri would have been lost at the beginning of hostilities, without the 4,000 German-American militia at the disposal of Francis Blair and Nathaniel Lyon, who used them to end quickly the massing of Rebels at Camp Jackson.[9] *Item:* Generals Rosecrans, Thomas, Buell, Hunt, Brannon, Johnston, Wood, Palmer, and others, in battle reports, refer often and with high praise to German regiments and brigades; many references that must be based on truth. No need therefore to search for additional details and more evidence to support the claim that German-American soldiers compared unfavorably to those of other national heritages.[10] Indeed, German-Americans exceeded them in more ways than one.

German-Americans, often accused of excessive liking for their own, allegedly prefer them emphatically over birthright Americans, the Irish, and others. If this flaw exists [among German-Americans], it missed the German soldier. Take, for example, the 1,200 Germans of The Ninth, who loved and still love their Colonel McCook, the only non-German in the regiment, a non-German who did not speak German. Those Germans also venerated and do venerate the hero of Chickamauga, "Pap" Thomas. And they zealously defend the much-maligned General Rosecrans.

Germans in the war likewise honored and admired—and for good reason still honor and admire—officers of their own national heritage, the likes of Sigel, Weitzel, Kautz, Osterhaus, Willich, Schimmelpfennig, Trebra, Steinwehr, Hecker, Laiboldt, Schurz, Kämmerling, Dilger, Erdelmeier, Moor, Wagner, Buschbeck, and others. Propelled by idealistic motives, our Germans answered Lincoln's initial call [for volunteers] because they hated slavery but loved freedom and justice. And let them also be proud, not only that a German [Pastorius] wrote the first protest against slavery, but also that Germans 200 years later joined the final movement against that abomination. Follen and Lieber and Münch, for example, joined the champions [of abolition], Phillips, Garrison, Sumner, Mann, Tappan, and others, whose agitation achieved its purpose by causing the war.

Our Germans who hurried to arms for a three-month hitch in April of 1861; who, without balking, swore themselves to three years; who fought in fierce battles and suffered acute hardships and lost half their numbers;[11] who scattered east and west when their time was up, returning home covered with honors and wounds; who took up again their peacetime occupations and devoted themselves to the duties of citizenship . . . *Stop!* The story has been told so often and the American people know it so well, that to recount it here would sound like vainglory. So let us but quote again Captain W[illiam] Vocke:

> Throughout the war, while fulfilling the most sacred of their obligations, the German-Americans competed honorably with their fellow-citizens, the birthright Americans. Side by side with the Americans, the Germans distinguished themselves brilliantly in uniform. . . . The war to save the Union is replete with shining proofs that in the grandest and most perilous epoch of our history, the Germans proved themselves good citizens: competent and patriotic. They brought esteem to our nation and to their ethnic heritage, a heritage exemplary for 2,000 years of loyalty and courage.[12]

Vocke did not exaggerate; he spoke truth founded on facts and official reports. And it would be equally right and veracious to add something.[13] That is, German-Americans return again and again to the warrior ranks, to battle on the field of arms and at the ballot box. In both places, it will be admitted, they almost always strike the blow the nation's true friends want struck: the *decisive* blow. German-Americans act [so nobly] because, in spite of the wrongs they have suffered and the ingratitude they have borne, they are idealistic; they strive to be on the side of truth and justice, and to stand for freedom and honor.

Exceptions there always are to everything, such as, during the war, the exceptions [to the Germans' sterling record]. German officers and enlisted men did include adventurers who joined the army for impure reasons. They pretended to have hurried to the colors for a [good] cause; but personal gain meant far more to them.[14] And such people as likely existed among German-Americans as they certainly existed among birthright Americans. True, when somebody wants to "get something" on German-American soldiers, you'll see proven facts brushed aside at once. Yet the irrefutable numbers substantiate the truth of the parable of the mote and the beam.[15]

[We believe, however, that] an old truth endures:

> Blameless you will not become, seeking another to blame.
> Famous you will never be, diminishing another's fame.

Therefore we allow that other nationalities helped suppress the rebellion; they deserve due credit. But the Germans rate the utmost praise for their deeds and achievements. We shall not keep mum when it comes to getting their contribution recognized. The bravery, endurance, spirit of sacrifice, and daredevilry of German-American units have been only too frequently [demonstrated] beyond doubt. In those qualities, no other units could equal and few could surpass the German-Americans.

History, rising noble and sublime from irrefutable facts, transcends the quarreling historians. Often the unbiased individual rightly deems superior, not [the results of] the most careful analysis and closest reasoning, but the conclusion based upon one fact. Therefore let us emphasize, once for all, an important fact. *German* generals [Godfrey] Weitzel and [Alexander] Schimmelpfennig led the first [Union] troops into the birthplace of the Confederacy, Charleston, as well as into the capital, Richmond.

The German soldier in America, with every right to be proud, cannot be too proud. The one who does not yet feel and act proud, let him heed the example of the German-American colonel of the all-German 2nd Missouri Infantry, Bernhard Laiboldt. After August 14, 1864, he and scarcely 1,000 men defended the little town of Dalton, [Georgia,] on the Chattanooga & Atlanta Railroad, against 6,000 cavalry under the Confederate general [Joseph] Wheeler. Several times called upon to surrender, Laiboldt refused each demand. Wheeler at last said: "I want to talk to you." Laiboldt: "Come and get me!"[16]

We, all of us (people of German heritage) in this country, should—it is to be hoped we *would*—think and speak like Laiboldt. We who are always ready to sacrifice life and property for the freedom and honor of this great land.

14[1]

The Reconstituted Ninth.—The Unveiling of the Monument to McCook.—Visits to the Battlefields and Cemeteries of Mill Springs and Chickamauga.

[The Associated Veterans of The Ninth Remember and Celebrate Their Service to the Union.—Orations.—McCook's Mother Approves the Monument to Her Son.—Battles Remembered.—Margedant, Boynton, and Vocke Honored.—The Story Ends.—Glory to Germans and The Ninth!]

"Friendship can be solid only in the ripeness of age and the wisdom of maturity."

Many trials and myriad dangers created camaraderie and friendship in The Ninth. The regiment returned home happily, mustered out honorably, and began again to ply their trades and discharge their obligations as citizens—and at once wanted not only to maintain but also to strengthen the bonds that had been sealed in blood. On January 14, 1870, therefore, most of the [Ninth's] former officers and men who lived in and around Cincinnati founded a [veterans'] organization, the [Associated Veterans of the] Ninth Regiment, O[hio] V[olunteer] I[nfantry]. Its first officials were our comrades August Witte, president; Friedrich Bertsch, secretary; and Heinrich Gunklach, treasurer. Today [1897], with youthful enthusiasm, 125 comrades devote themselves to achieving the organization's purpose. Hence the quarterly meetings, the annual commemorations of important dates in the history of the regiment and the war, the special celebrations, the excursions, and so forth. The Battle of Mill Springs (January 19), the regiment's mustering-in (May 27), the death of our colonel Robert L. McCook (August 6), and the Battle of Chickamauga (September 19) have all been regularly and solemnly observed.[2]

The monument to McCook was unveiled with a celebration in Washington Park on August 23, 1877, a grand and glorious day for The Ninth, for McCook's family, and for all of German Cincinnati. About two years earlier our old regimental bugler, Musician First Class Richard Meinhardt, had already wondered to a few [of us]: Would it be possible, as well as fitting and proper, to raise to our esteemed colonel a statue in Cincinnati? The idea quickly crystalized, and a committee of veterans of The Ninth formed to translate it into reality.[3]

Not only The Ninth but also their friends and acquaintances—in a word, the Germans of Cincinnati—greeted the proposal with enthusiasm; and implementation was pursued with vigor. The Ninth laid a financial foundation of $1,000. Cincinnati Germans and other McCook admirers added $5,000. The sculptor Leopold Fettweis, Jr., accepted the commission, completed the monument (a bust atop a simple granite column), and erected it ready for the unveiling in the center of Washington Park, north of Twelfth, between Race and Elm streets.

On the afternoon of the 22nd the colonel's mother, sister, and two brothers arrived. Cincinnati's police commission welcomed them at the Grand Hotel.

The red-letter day began with unpropitious weather. The overcast morning promised rain. Still the procession—mostly turners, militia, and veterans of the Civil War—set off at the appointed hour from the corner of Walnut and Mercer, taking various streets down to Fourth, then north to Twelfth, and then to the point of the festivities. The master of ceremonies, Comrade Friedrich Diester, Company C, headed the procession, assisted by Mr. Henry Wielert and Mr. Georg Mörlein of the Citizens' Aid Committee. Then the orators of the day: Comrade and Captain M[oritz] Pohlmann, president of [the Associated Veterans of] The Ninth; Senator [Stanley] Matthews, former lieutenant-colonel of the 23rd Ohio; and Dr. [Otto?] Lilenthal. Followed by the mayor of Cincinnati [Robert M. Moore, former colonel, 10th Ohio], and the police commission. Then a band under the direction of the former music director of The Ninth, G[unther] Seidensticker. Followed by police, the 1st Ohio Militia Regiment, veterans' organizations, Turners, and the Sons of The Ninth. Finally The Ninth themselves, numbering about 150. When the procession assembled around the monument in the park, The Ninth stood directly in front of the monument. McCook's family were beside the orator's rostrum, where McCook's successor as brigade-commander, Colonel [Ferdinand] Van Derveer of the 35th Ohio, had already taken a seat.

Captain Pohlmann, master of ceremonies, opened by describing McCook's virtues in an enthusiastic speech. In erecting the monument

> the Ninth Ohio Regiment wanted neither to reawaken hostilities between the country's reunited sections, nor to diminish the merits of other officers and men. The Ninth wanted only to express respect, devotion, and love for their brave and patriotic leader, and to convey admiration for the true and unselfish love of country that had been so nobly incarnate in him.

Thus Pohlmann ended his speech and presented the monument to the city of Cincinnati.

The covering fell from the monument amid three cheers by The Ninth.[4] With a beautiful speech, Mayor Moore accepted the monument on behalf of the city, saying in conclusion:

> And now, you courageous men of The Ninth, you soldiers who followed the man whose memory we have assembled to honor, you who fought with him on the bloody fields of Carnifex [Ferry] and Mill Springs: in the name of all the people of Cincinnati, I thank you for the grand gift you have given this city! We hope others will follow your example and see to it that the grave of every Union soldier—of high rank and low, who died that the Union might live—will soon be marked by a monument in proof that the memory of them shall not die but live in the hearts of a grateful people.

The principal speaker, Senator [Stanley] Matthews, was brilliant. He mentioned the difficulty of talking about a dead man, noted the reasons for the memorial, discussed the merits of McCook's character, and referred to the fine relationship between McCook and The Ninth. "It was tit for tat: mutual respect and

Monument to Colonel Robert L. McCook in Washington Park, Cincinnati, Ohio

admiration, trust by each in what the other could do, two parties joined in a happily completed whole—colonel and men, regiment and leader—united in thought, feeling, and action."

The senator continued:

> Years ago [1861] in Camp Harrison I saw your noble colonel submitting requisitions, giving orders, virtually attempting to make the impossible possible, which is what comes of trying to raise a military unit. I asked him why he was so obviously agitated. He said: "I am just finding out, what it is to be a colonel! I am nothing but the head-clerk of [a] thousand Dutchmen!"[5] He soon thought otherwise. If his soul can look down on us today, if he could take part in this patriotic celebration, he would feel that he and the other dead soldiers of his regiment had not died in vain, that their deaths had helped bring peace and harmony to this land; and to all, the protection of the law.

Everyone stood bravely under incipient rain to hear the German speaker of the day, Dr. Lilenthal. He cited the importance of this ceremony and the erection of the monument. "This is no day of mourning," he said,

> but a day of honor—for McCook, for the Germans in America, and above all for The Ninth. O, brave McCook, you were one of the heroes and patriots of that war. You were also a *man* in the truest sense. You gained not only the trust and obedience of warriors who accepted your words and followed your sword; you gained more: the love and esteem of them all. You were not only their commander but also their father, not only their leader but also their counselor. You called your band of heroes "my bully Dutch"; and those who remain cannot forget you, cannot stop loving you. Even today they honor your memory and dedicate to your name this monument in sincere tribute and honest veneration. . . . And as this monument originated "over the Rhine," so it shall be a "watch on the Rhine" to this nation: a testimonial to German loyalty, to German honor, to the German sense of freedom, and to the German devotion to the welfare of the new fatherland, the land of our choice.[6]

The band played nice music between speakers. And now, at the close of the official proceedings, the crowd dispersed to its notes.

The Ninth staged a postcelebration at the Washington Platform in Court Street, with drinking to the day's speakers. Their speeches were repeated, partly in jest. In the evening The Ninth serenaded the McCooks at the Grand Hotel, and members of the regiment assembled to be introduced to the [McCook] family. Major-General McDowell McCook, speaking for the family, thanked The Ninth for the honor paid [to Colonel Robert L. McCook] and said in part:

> It is a singular fact, inseparable from the history of The Ninth, that our Bob was the regiment's only Anglo-American [he was Scotch-Irish]. I welcome this spontaneous amalgamation of [the country's] German and American elements as a sign of a grand and historic tendency in the homeland we occupy together. In peace the distinction of nationalities had sometimes asserted itself; but in the hour of danger the distinction was erased. In the struggle to maintain the indivisibility of their new and freely chosen fatherland, born Teutons elected as their leader a man who traced his ancestry to the British Isles. . . . I know, gentlemen, that you are here not only as former "boys in blue" but also and mainly as Germans. Therefore the tribute you have paid me and my family is all the more valuable to us.

Our McCook's mother and sister were notably active in a brief and informal discussion that followed. Then The Ninth took leave of the guests, who had obviously been most agreeably pleased [by The Ninth's visit].

When the sculptor Fettweis asked Mrs. McCook if she would like any changes in the bust, perhaps to improve the likeness, she replied: "Certainly not! The bust represents Robert as he was in life. Nothing in it can be improved." Her opinion remains that of everyone who ever saw and knew Bob McCook.

The following year [1878], several members of The Ninth visited the battlefield at Mill Springs. At that time the Cincinnati Southern Railway went to Somerset, Kentucky, a little town eleven miles from the battlefield and the place we had buried the comrades who fell in the battle, seventeen years before. (See page 86.) But the dead no longer rested there. The exhumed bodies of Union soldiers, who died in the battle and at the hospitals in Somerset, were reinterred in the national cemetery established scarcely a mile from the battlefield only a few years after the war.

If not so splendidly as their comrades of Chickamauga, the dead of Mill Springs rest nonetheless nicely in the well-tended cemetery of about three acres enclosed by a wall and beautifully planted to trees, flowers, and shrubs. A resident caretaker keeps up the graves and grounds. A marble slab marks each grave. The inscription on each slab states the apposite data on the man who sleeps beneath. The caretaker's office maintains accurate records by which the burial sites of the various units are easily found.

The simple, quiet reverence of the visitors [The Ninth, paying its respects] was no less touching than the grand ceremonies at Chattanooga fifteen years later. Both [occasions] served to show that The Ninth, by honoring fallen comrades, remains true to flag and oath [of allegiance to the United States], a shining example of the truly Germanic idea of a large, valiant, invincible people's army.

Chickamauga [and Chattanooga] National [Military] Park and its monuments to the honor of The Ninth were dedicated on September 18, 1895.[7] [Many] of the Ninth [had died during the thirty years since the war; others could not attend], but 100 had come and most brought their families, a participation reverential and sublime. The sons of the regiment led the way to the memorable places: Horseshoe Ridge and Snodgrass Hill; a laurel wreath was to be hung on one of the tall pines bulking at the door of the old log house. From there, on the afternoon of September 20, 1863, the unforgettable hero Thomas directed the last bloody stand against the desperate assaults of an enemy numerically superior and battling bravely. It was a solemn moment [this visit to the site]. But, even yet, a cheerful enthusiasm infuses the survivors of The Ninth, as it infused until death the comrades who passed away since those glorious days [of the war]. The words of comrade and senator George M. Schneider, of Cincinnati [sergeant, Company C], who spoke at the dedication of our monument, reflected that cheerful enthusiasm. His speech concluded:

> When in April 1861 our country was threatened with civil war, and President Lincoln issued his first call for troops to defend the government, the Ninth Ohio Regiment was organized within a few days, and chose as their first commander Robert Latimer McCook. Through his influence and untiring energy the regiment was promptly accepted by the Governor of our State. . . .
>
> From the very beginning the men of the regiment learned to love and esteem their commander for his manly qualifications. For his gallantry and good management at the battle of Mill Springs, January 19th 1862, he was promptly promoted to the position of Brigadier General. He assumed the command of the brigade until he met with

> his tragic and untimely death, beloved and esteemed by all who served under him. . . .
>
> The command of the regiment was later assumed by Colonel Gustave Kaemmerling, who gallantly led the regiment over many hotly contested battle-fields. . . .
>
> I recall the circumstances almost on this identical spot, 32 years ago; the hearty hurrah we were greeted with by the boys, when we rejoined the brigade on the 20th of September made us feel that the Ninth Ohio or McCook's Dutchmen, as we were sometimes jokingly called, were well thought of by our comrades.
>
> Yes, the Germans are second to none in loyalty and patriotism, for we love this country, as we love a mother; we are ready to offer our blood and our treasures for her free and matchless institutions. . . .
>
> My friends, I have no doubt that, if our fallen comrades could look down in spirit upon this scene, they would be imbued with the same emotions and would feel, as we do, that they have not died in vain. . . .
>
> Once more hands up, and let us earnestly and sacredly promise in the name of our fallen heroes: The Union forever! No North, no South, no East, no West, nothing but the whole Union indivisible and inseparable![8]

The oath and prayer [which he requested] were sworn and offered aloud. The prayer rose to heaven. They were sworn and offered not by us [of The Ninth] alone, but also by many thousands present to honor their dead and ours, and to create from a commemoration of a grand [event of the] past an enthusiasm for future times and deeds.

For a quarter-century the anniversary of Chickamauga has been celebrated annually in Turner Hall [in Cincinnati]. On the thirty-third anniversary, September 19, 1896, a number of old comrades-in-arms from the 35th Ohio joined in. Three additional notables were there. (1) The former head of the turners in Hamilton [Ohio], W[ilhelm] Margedant, comrade and captain of our second company [Company B] during our three-month enlistment. (2) General H[enry] V[an Ness] Boynton, once commander of the 35th, an honorary member of our organization for years. (3) Captain William Vocke, formerly of the 24th Illinois Infantry Regiment. Boynton and Vocke, often mentioned in earlier chapters of this book, deserve praise from historians of our great war. On this occasion, Vocke was also named an honorary member [of The Ninth]. And The Ninth gave both [Vocke and Boynton] three powerful hurrahs because they were the only comrades-in-arms [from other regiments] to have been thus honored. They remain unique in that respect.

* * * * *

We have reached the end of our history [of The Ninth]. Of those who were our comrades in that difficult but glorious time, how many are alive to read it? We cannot say for sure, they being scattered all over this vast country and enjoying the blessings of peace. No doubt every man jack also loyally fulfills the obligations of citizenship.

The American people do not neglect to recognize those who risked their lives to save the country years ago. Accordingly, The Ninth has been remembered again and again. Recently the Cincinnati *Commercial Tribune* said: "The glory of this regiment of German Turners has become a national treasure. From Mill Springs to Atlanta [*sic*], from honor to honor, it proceeded in triumph under General Thomas. On the battlefields where it stood and fought, its German battle-cries in the bayonet-assault were as well known as the notes of our national anthem."

15[1]

After the War.—Statistical Data.—Muster Roll.

"The guns are silent; the dogs of war, calm."

The nation passed quietly and readily from the savagery and blood of war to the blessings of peace—contrary to what many had expected. The two sections, so monstrously divided, were reunited satisfactorily and relatively fast. All the world knows the story; it does not belong in this book.

We have told how The Ninth, with a true sense of being honestly done with an obligation, laid down the arms they had borne so gloriously, to resume peacetime occupations. It remains, then, to note changes in personnel during our three-year enlistment, and to observe who was present when we left the service. Therefore we enter here the muster-roll and other instructive statistics. These data are as accurate as such data can be. But, of course, errors are inevitable—as anyone appreciates who is at all familiar with the keeping of records in the field, and with wartime reports and other documents concerning events of that time. We have tried to come as near the truth as possible in each and every item.

Our sources: the "Descriptive Book" of the Ninth Regiment and the "Official Roster of the Soldiers of the State of Ohio in the War of the Rebellion 1861–1866."[2]

* * * * *

The Ninth Ohio Volunteer Infantry Regiment was mustered in by Major Robert Anderson, U.S.A., at Camp Dennison, Ohio, on May 27, 1861; and mustered out by Captain James Thompson, U.S.A., on June 7, 1864.[3]

The regiment took part in these battles and engagements:

Rich Mountain, W. Va.	July 10, 1861
Carnifex Ferry, W. Va.	September 10, 1861
Mill Springs, Ky.	January 19, 1862
Perryville, Ky.	October 8, 1862
Hoover's Gap, Tenn.	June 26, 1863
Chickamauga, Ga.	September 19 and 20, 1863
Missionary Ridge, Tenn.	November 25, 1863
Buzzard Roost, Ga.	February 25, 1864
Resaca, Ga.	May 13–16, 1864

We suffered our worst casualties in the Battle of Chickamauga: 256 dead, wounded, and missing. That is, fifty-one percent of effective strength (502 men) on the morning of September 19; a figure exceeded in no battle in modern times, and matched by almost no units at Chickamauga itself.

The total to serve during the three-year enlistment: 1,155.

Losses:

Killed by the enemy	56	
Dead later of wounds	32	
Declared missing after battles	12	
Dead of illnesses in the field	31	
Discharged as unfit due to disabilities suffered in the field	164	
Ordered discharged; presumed dead, etc.	89	
Resigned (officers)	18	
Transferred to other units	79	
		481
Mustered out, June 7, 1864		674

The total with nonfatal wounds, some of whom were discharged for reasons such as those stated above, some of whom were mustered out on June 7, 1864: 203.

Of many of the "deserters," let it be said that they had no chance to return to the regiment, because of lack of transportation, etc. Therefore they joined other units. Consequently, in official lists and the like, their earlier service [in The Ninth] was obviously not taken into account [nor recorded].

Here is a table of the nationalities:

Born:

In the United States	55
In Germany	1,014
In Switzerland	56
In France	25
In Russia	3
In Holland	1
At sea	1
	1,155

The only Anglo-American was Colonel R. L. McCook.

About 400 had been common laborers before the war; the rest: lawyers, artists, merchants, and craftsmen. About 300 were Turners. Some had been soldiers in Germany, but more had trained for the army in Turner societies and in companies of militia and sharpshooters. We hope that the ten chapters of the main part of our history have shown to [the reader's] satisfaction what manner of men they all were, those soldiers, artists, craftsmen, and farmers.

Muster Roll

[The original sequence of names has been repeated in the translation, and the original arrangements of dates has been respected, though they sometimes deviate from the strictly alphabetical and the precisely chronological. "May 27, 1861," is the date of three-year enlistment. Another date, directly after a name, may be of promotion to stated rank; otherwise it is probably of enlistment. The date

of mustering-out is June 7, 1864, unless otherwise noted. *Verabschiedet wegen Untauglichkeit* and *Abschied, untauglich,* translated as "discharged, disabled," mean service-related disability while on active and honorable duty, probably the result of illness, noncombatant injury, or wound in battle. "Invalid Corps" (*zu Invaliden*) and "Veteran Reserve Corps" (*zu Veteranen*) signify the same reassignment but at a different time. That is, on March 18, 1864, the Invalid Corps became the Veteran Reserve Corps; the name changed but the nature and purpose did not. Thus a sick or injured man went to the IC before, and the VRC after March 18, 1864, assigned in either instance to limited, noncombatant duty because of disability too serious for fighting but not serious enough for discharge. See Amann, *Personnel* 2:273. Boatner, *Dictionary,* 870.]

Regimental Headquarters

Officers

Robert Latimer McCook, *Colonel.*—May 27, 1861.—Born New Lisbon, Ohio.—Wounded at Mill Springs, June 19, 1862.—*Brigadier-General of Volunteers,* April 4, 1862.—Wounded at New Market, Alabama, August 5, 1862.—Died August 6, 1862.

Charles Sondershoff, *Lieutenant-Colonel.*—May 27, 1861.—Born Danzig, Prussia.—Resigned March 8, 1862.

August Willich, *Major.*—May 27, 1861.—Born Gorzyn, Prussia.—Resigned August 22, 1861 (Colonel, 32nd Indiana Volunteer Infantry Regiment).

Karl Joseph, *Major.*—March 8, 1862.—Born Schwerin, Mecklenburg.—*Lieutenant-Colonel,* August 6, 1862.—Resigned May 10, 1863.

Fritz Schröder, *Major.*—August 6, 1862.—Born Soldin, Prussia.—*Lieutenant-Colonel,* February 14, 1864.—Mustered out.

Konrad Söllheim, *Assistant Physician.*—October 3, 1861.—Born Bayreuth, Bavaria.—*Regimental Physician,* May 23, 1863.—Mustered out.

Joseph A. Fuchshuber, *Chaplain.*—February 18, 1862.—Resigned June 9, 1863.

James Davenport, *Assistant Physician.*—August 17, 1862.—Born Delaware, Ohio.—Died Louisville, Kentucky, March 29, 1863.

Charles C. Boyle, *Regimental Physician.*—May 27, 1861.—Born Delaware [Ohio?].—Resigned April 20, 1863.

Rudolph Wirth, *Assistant Physician.*—May 27, 1861.—Transferred to the 1st Ohio Cavalry, September 20, 1861.

Georg H. Harries, *Adjutant.*—September 6, 1861.—Born Bustorf, Silesia.—*Captain,* Company E, February 14, 1864.

Wilhelm Stängel, *Chaplain.*—August 6, 1861.—Born Reutlingen, Würtemberg.—*Captain,* Company C, October 24, 1861.

Gustav Kämmerling, *Major.*—November 1, 1861.—Born Mülheim an der Ruhr, Prussia.—*Lieutenant-Colonel,* March 8, 1862.—*Colonel,* August 6, 1862.—*Brigadier-General of Volunteers,* April 7, 1864.—Mustered out.

Adam M. Beers, *Assistant Physician.*—August 6, 1863.—Born Mauch Chunk, Pennsylvania.—Mustered out.

Bartholomäus Benz, *Major.*—February 14, 1864.—Born Donaueschingen, Baden.—Mustered out.

Hermann Pönitz, *Adjutant.*—February 14, 1864.—Born Leipzig, Saxony.—Mustered out.

Noncommissioned Officers

Raimund Herrmann, *Sergeant-Major.*—May 27, 1861.—*Second Lieutenant,* Company D, September 1, 1862.

Robert Gronau, *Sergeant-Major.*—September 1, 1862.—Mustered out.

Samuel Landauer, *Commissary-Sergeant.*—May 27, 1861.—Mustered out.

Edmund Rodde, *Quartermaster-Sergeant.*—May 27, 1861.—Discharged disabled, November, 1861 [*sic*].

Friedrich Busse, *Quartermaster-Sergeant.*—November 15, 1861.—Discharged disabled, April 11, 1863.

Gustav Brockhaus, *Quartermaster-Sergeant.*—April 11, 1863.—Mustered out.

Wilhelm Schmidt, *Hospital Steward.*—May 27, 1861.—Discharged disabled, December 12, 1862.

Louis Zahn, *Hospital Steward.*—December 13, 1862.—Mustered out.

Dominik Emminger, *Principal Musician.*—August 1, 1863.—Mustered out.

Richard Schwenzer, *Principal Musician.*—August 1, 1863.—Transferred to the Commandant, Camp Dennison, June 7, 1864.

Regimental Band

Günther Seidensticker, *Music Director.*—June 18, 1861.—Mustered out September 10, 1862, by order of the Secretary of War.
Christoph Schindler, *Principal Musician.*—June 18, 1861.—Missing after December 6, 1861.

Musicians First Class

Meinhardt, Richard.—From Company A, June 18, 1861.—Mustered out September 10, 1862.
Stecher, Albin.—July 22, 1861.—Mustered out September 10, 1862.
Präger, Leopold.—June 18, 1861.—Mustered out September 10, 1862.
Blum, Ernst.—June 18, 1861.—Mustered out September 10, 1862.

Musicians Second Class

Hofrichter, Anton.—June 18, 1861.—Mustered out September 10, 1862.
Kilian, Joseph.—June 18, 1861.—Mustered out September 10, 1862.
Strebel, Louis.—June 18, 1861.—Died September 16, 1862.
Voigt, Karl.—June 18, 1861.—Mustered out September 10, 1862.

Musicians Third Class

Köhler, John.—June 18, 1861.—Mustered out September 10, 1862.
Schenk, Adolf.—June 18, 1861.—Discharged disabled, May 27, 1862.
Wolf, Georg.—June 18, 1861.—Mustered out September 10, 1862.
Hammel, Karl.—June 18, 1861.—Mustered out September 10, 1862.
Bigeler, Anton.—July 22, 1861.—Discharged disabled, May 18, 1862.
Niemann, Theodor.—July 22, 1861.—Mustered out September 10, 1862.
Meinhardt, Ernst.—July 22, 1861.—Mustered out September 10, 1862.

Dorst, Louis.—June 18, 1861.—Mustered out September 10, 1862.

Company A

Officers

Karl Joseph, *Captain.*—May 27, 1861.—Born Schwerin, Mecklenburg.—Wounded at Mill Springs, January 19, 1862.—*Major,* March 8, 1862 (regimental headquarters).
Louis Hauser, *First Lieutenant.*—May 27, 1861.—Born Schwerin, Mecklenburg.—*Captain,* November 1, 1861 (Company F).
Charles B. Gentsch, *Second Lieutenant.*—May 27, 1861.—Born Altenburg, Saxony.—*Captain,* May 20, 1862.—Mustered out.
Adam Schuhmacher, *First Lieutenant.*—November 1, 1862 [*sic*].—Born Gailburg, Baden.—*Captain,* February 14, 1864 (Company G).
Gustav Tafel, *Second Lieutenant.*—May 30, 1862.—Born Munich, Bavaria.—Transferred to the 106th Regiment, Ohio Volunteer Infantry, and promoted to *Lieutenant-Colonel,* July 24, 1862.
Hermann Pönitz, *Second Lieutenant.*—July 24, 1862.—Born Leipzig, Saxony.—*First Lieutenant,* February 14, 1864 (regimental headquarters).

Noncommissioned Officers and Privates

Ahlers, Henry.—Missing after June 18, 1861.
Albrecht, Charles.—Mustered out.
Ambsler, Georg.—Mustered out.
Armbrecht, Louis.—Mustered out.
Bär, Henry, *Corporal.*—May 27, 1861.—Discharged disabled, May 2, 1862.
Baier, Michael.—Discharged disabled, February 13, 1862.
Bauer, Gustav.—Discharged disabled, November 17, 1861.
Becker, Gustav, *Corporal.*—May 27, 1861.—Invalid Corps, January 15, 1864.
Begemann, Adolph.—To the 108th Regular Ohio Infantry, September 1, 1862.
Bergmann, Gustav.—Discharged disabled, November 15, 1862.
Berkheimer, Charles.—Discharged disabled, November 4, 1861.
Bertsch, Julius.—Wounded at Chickamauga.—Mustered out.

Beyland, Hermann.—Mustered out.

Beyland, August.—Killed at Chickamauga, September 19, 1863.

Bocklet, Albert.—Mustered out.

Bortz, Ferdinand, *Corporal.*—September 1, 1862.—Killed at Missionary Ridge, November 25, 1863.

Bräuninger, Franz.—Mustered out.

Burgmann, Rudolph.—Missing after November 26, 1863.

Dake, William.—Killed at Chickamauga, September 19, 1863.

Daum, Franz.—Missing after June 14, 1861.

Drewe, William, *Corporal.*—May 27, 1861.—*Sergeant,* September 13, 1862.—Killed at Chickamauga, September 20, 1863.

Eigner, Ernst, *Corporal.*—January 22, 1862.—*Sergeant,* December 21, 1862.—Mustered out.

Feltau, Charles, *Sergeant.*—May 27, 1861.—Discharged disabled.—December 16, 1861.

Franke, Hermann.—Discharged disabled, May 2, 1862.

Franke, Albert.—Mustered out.

Füller, Philip.—Wounded and captured at Chickamauga, September 20, 1863.—Died December 22, 1863.

Gerhardt, Emil.—Mustered out.

Glyckherr, Henry.—Mustered out.

Gössler, Joseph.—Wounded at Missionary Ridge, November 25, 1863.—Mustered out.

Grieb, August, *Corporal.*—September 13, 1862.—Wounded at Chickamauga, September 20, 1863.—Mustered out.

Griesehop, Bernhard.—Veteran Reserve Corps, May 15, 1864.

Gronau, Robert, *Corporal.*—May 2, 1862.—*Sergeant,* July 25, 1862.—*Sergeant-Major,* September 1, 1862 (regimental headquarters).

Gunklach, Henry.—Wounded at Chickamauga, September 19, 1863.—Mustered out.

Haack, Otto.—Mustered out.

Häbe, Karl.—Invalid Corps, December 1, 1863.

Hahn, Peter.—Mustered out.

Hartleb, Louis.—Discharged disabled, June 17, 1862.

Handel, Friedrich.—Mustered out.

Hartmann, Philipp.—Mustered out.

Heck, Joseph.—Mustered out.

Hermannsdörfer, John.—Discharged disabled, April 18, 1863.
Herzog, Philip.—Killed at Chickamauga, September 19, 1863.
Heyer, Friedrich.—Wounded at Chickamauga.—Mustered out.
Hildebrandt, Ferdinand.—Killed at Chickamauga, September 19, 1863.
Himmler, John.—Mustered out.
Hohendorf, Franz.—Mustered out.
Hubert, Henry.—Discharged disabled, May 2, 1862.
Hupfauf, Max.—Discharged disabled, May 27, 1862.
Jacker, Joseph.—Mustered out.
Keller, Louis.—Mustered out.
Kiehfuss, Gottfried, *Corporal.*—August 13, 1862.—Killed at Chickamauga, September 20, 1863.
Klingel, Adam.—Mustered out.
Klintworth, Charles.—Wounded at Chickamauga.—Mustered out.
Koch, Michael.—Discharged [*sic*], September 10, 1862.
Koch, Martin.—Veteran Reserve Corps, March 14, 1864.
Kögel, Ernst.—Mustered out.
Kühne, Friedrich.—Discharged disabled, November 10, 1862.
Lisset, Louis.—Missing in action at Chickamauga, September 20, 1863.
Loge, John—Mustered out.
Ludwig, Ferdinand.—Wounded at Chickamauga; died October 1, 1863.
Lüthy, Adolph.—Mustered out.
Mages, Lorenz.—Transferred to Camp Dennison, June 7, 1864.
Mark, Louis, *Corporal.*—May 27, 1861.—*Sergeant,* September 1, 1862.—*First Sergeant,* December 21, 1863.—Mustered out.
Meinhardt, Richard.—Transferred to the regimental band, June 18, 1861 (regimental headquarters).
Matthies, August.—Wounded and captured at Chickamauga.—Mustered out.
Meyer, William.—Mustered out.
Miller, Friedrich.—Discharged disabled, March 10, 1862.
Müller, Adolph, *Corporal.*—November 20, 1861.—*Sergeant,* September 22, 1863.—Mustered out.
Nadler, Charles.—Wounded at Chickamauga, September 20 [1863], and at Tunnel Hill, February 25, 1864.—Mustered out.

Neubacher, Louis.—Discharged disabled, May 27, 1862.
Otting, Louis.—Mustered out.
Panzer, Ulrich.—Mustered out.
Peters, Nickolaus.—Discharged disabled, November 20, 1861.
Pfeffer, Franz.—Discharged disabled, November 17, 1861.
Pfaffinger, Georg.—Discharged disabled, November 17, 1861.
Pfister, Ferdinand.—Mustered out.
Pönitz, Hermann, *Corporal.*—November 1, 1861.—*Sergeant,* May 30, 1862.—*Second Lieutenant,* July 25, 1862 (added to the officer list).
Poschner, Friedrich.—Transferred to the 47th Ohio Regular Infantry, September 5, 1861, as lieutenant.
Popp, Georg.—Mustered out.
Räpple, John.—Discharged disabled, November 20, 1862.
Reintanz, Hermann, *Sergeant.*—May 27, 1861.—Transferred to the 106th Ohio Infantry, September 13, 1862, as captain.
Riedel, Ernst, *Sergeant.*—May 27, 1861.—Captured at Chickamauga.
Rieger, Henry.—Mustered out.
Riehl, Philip.—Discharged disabled, June 21, 1862.
Röhrig, George.—Discharged disabled, November 14, 1862.
Rittinger, Joseph.—Mustered out.
Rumpf, Friedrich.—Wounded at Chickamauga.—Mustered out.
Sattler, Ladislaus.—Killed at Chickamauga, September 20, 1863.
Schättgen, Charles.—Mustered out.
Schätzle, Theodor.—Mustered out.
Schmid, Andreas.—Missing after June 28, 1862.
Schmid, John.—Wounded at Chickamauga.—Mustered out.
Schmitz, Joseph.—Discharged disabled, July 2, 1861.
Schuhmacher, Adam, *Sergeant.*—May 27, 1861.—*First Lieutenant,* November 1, 1861 [*sic*] (added to the officer list).
Schultz, Gustav.—Mustered out.
Schultz, Otto.—Missing after June 1, 1862.
Schulz, Ernst.—Killed at Chickamauga, September 20, 1863.
Schraffenberger, Peter.—Wounded at Chickamauga; died October 13, 1863.
Schwenzer, Richard, *Principal Musician.*—August 1, 1863 (regimental headquarters).

Seibert, Georg.—Mustered out.

Seibert, Philip.—Mustered out.

Stremmel, Eduard.—Mustered out.

Stübe, Friedrich, *Corporal.*—May 27, 1861.—*Sergeant,* November 1, 1861.—*First Sergeant,* September 1, 1862.—Died December 20, 1863.

Tafel, Gustav, *First Sergeant.*—May 27, 1861.—*Second Lieutenant,* May 30, 1862 (added to officer list).

Tafel, Hugo, *Corporal.*—May 27, 1861.—Killed at Mill Springs, January 19, 1862.

Teichmann, Charles, *Corporal.*—May 27, 1861.—*Sergeant,* December 16, 1861.—Wounded at Chickamauga.—Mustered out.

Wachs, William.—Served in the Ninth Ohio until November 8, 1862, and finished his enlistment in a Pennsylvania regiment.

Waldemayer, Jacob.—Missing, March 20, 1862.

Wagner, Adolph.—Wounded at Chickamauga.—Mustered out.

Wendel, Friedrich.—Wounded at Chickamauga.—Mustered out.

Wittlinger, Wilhelm.—Mustered out.

Wittmann, John.—Died at Corinth, July 1, 1862.

Company B

Officers

Ferdinand Müller, *Captain.*—May 27, 1861.—Born Versmold, Prussia.—Died September 25, 1863, of wounds at Chickamauga.

Jakob Müller, *First Lieutenant.*—May 27, 1861.—Born Koblenz, Prussia.—Resigned, September 27, 1861.

Friedrich Bertsch, *Second Lieutenant.*—May 27, 1861.—Born Stuttgart, Würtemberg.—*First Lieutenant,* February 7, 1862. *Company Commander* from the morning of September 20, 1863, until mustered out June 7, 1864, by David M. Meredith, Captain, 15th U.S. Infantry.

Henry Blendowski, *Second Lieutenant.*—March 1, 1862.—Born Warsaw, Russia [i.e., Poland].—Resigned November 16, 1862.

Theodor Racek, *Second Lieutenant.*—January 1, 1863.—Born Polna, Austria.—Mustered out.

Nikolas [*sic*] Willig, *First Lieutenant.*—September 29, 1861.—Born Paris, France.—Resigned February 17, 1862.

Noncommissioned Officers and Privates

Arand, Albin, *Corporal.*—September 25, 1863.—Mustered out.
Blendowski, Henry, *First Sergeant.*—May 27, 1861.—*Second Lieutenant,* March 1, 1862 (added to the officer list).
Bauer, John.—Discharged disabled, June 19, 1863.
Bauer, Jacob.—Killed at Missionary Ridge, November 25, 1863.
Baron, Jacob.—Mustered out.
Barth, John, *Corporal.*—May 27, 1861.—*Sergeant,* May 4, 1862.—Mustered out.
Benz, Louis.—Discharged disabled, June 28, 1862.
Blattermann, Louis.—Discharged disabled, February 22, 1862.
Böhler, Jakob, *Corporal.*—March 1, 1862.—Mustered out.
Boss, John.—Discharged disabled, July 23, 1862.
Bottler, Philip.—Discharged disabled, April 20, 1862.
Buchtmann, Louis.—Mustered out.
Bühl, Gustav.—Missing after April 10, 1863.
Brucker, Michael.—Discharged disabled, January 20, 1863.
Breitenbach, Clemens.—Mustered out.
Burkhardt, Julius.—Wounded at Carnifex Ferry, September 10, 1861.—Mustered out.
Brockhaus, Gustav, *Quartermaster-Sergeant.*—April 11, 1863 (regimental headquarters).
Decher, Caspar, *Corporal.*—May 27, 1861.—*Sergeant,* August 14, 1862.—Mustered out.
Deiters, John.—Wounded at Carnifex Ferry, September 10, 1861.—Discharged disabled, August 12, 1863.
Dreifuss, Arthur.—Mustered out.
Ehrlich, Louis.—Mustered out.
Emery, Moritz.—Mustered out.
Engel, John.—Mustered out.
Engelhardt, John.—Mustered out.
Fleddermann, Christian.—Discharged disabled, February 9, 1863.
Freers, Louis.—Mustered out.

Freers, Friedrich.—Mustered out.
Gierten, Michael.—Mustered out.
Gross, Maurice.—Deserted April 10, 1863.
Günther, August.—Wounded at Mill Springs, January 19, 1862.—Mustered out.
Hauser, Gottlieb.—Wounded at Carnifex Ferry, September 10, 1861.—Mustered out.
Heine, Friedrich.—Mustered out.
Heinnemann, Fritz.—Veteran Reserve Corps, June 7, 1864.
Hössli, Jost.—Mustered out.
Honeck, Emanuel.—Discharged disabled, November 13, 1861.
Hosbach, Konrad.—Killed at Carnifex Ferry, September 10, 1861.
Howald, Otis.—Wounded at Chickamauga.—Mustered out.
Hupp, Joseph.—Killed at Chickamauga, September 20, 1863.
Hufer, Eugene, *Corporal.*—May 27, 1861.—Died at Hamburg, Tennessee, June 1, 1862.
Jend, Henry.—Mustered out.
Jungclas, August.—Wounded at Chickamauga.—Transferred to Camp Dennison, June 7, 1864.
Jutzi, Charles.—Transferred to Headquarters, Camp Dennison, June 7, 1864.
Kaulig, Robert.—Discharged disabled, June 12, 1862.
Keller, Andreas.—Killed at Chickamauga, September 20, 1863.
Kiepe, August, *Corporal.*—March 27, 1863.—Mustered out.
Klunke, Theodor.—Mustered out.
Kress, John.—Veteran Reserve Corps, June 7, 1864.
Kühnle, John.—Discharged disabled, January 16, 1863.
Kutzleb, Anton.—Wounded at Chickamauga and Missionary Ridge.—Mustered out.
Lauber, Georg.—Discharged disabled, February 22, 1862.
Lässig, Julius.—Discharged disabled, April 22, 1862.
Laufer, John A.—Killed at Chickamauga, September 20, 1863.
Männle, Charles.—Wounded at Chickamauga.—Mustered out.
Maier, Georg.—Mustered out.
Märtesheimer, Fritz, *Corporal.*—August 14, 1862.—*First Sergeant,* December 1, 1863.—Mustered out.
Maithre, Peter.—Discharged disabled, August 12, 1862.

Maurer, Jakob.—Deserted April 10, 1863.

May, William.—Wounded at Chickamauga.—Mustered out.

Menninger, Philip.—Wounded in camp.—Discharged disabled, May 2, 1862.

Müller, Caspar.—Died in Cincinnati, December 11, 1862.

Miller, Rudolph H.—Wounded at Carnifex Ferry, September 10, 1861.—*Corporal,* January 2, 1863.—Killed at Chickamauga, September 20, 1863.

Orion, John.—Wounded at Missionary Ridge.—Mustered out.

Pacher, Charles, *Corporal.*—May 27, 1861.—Died of wounds, Carnifex Ferry, September 18, 1861.

Pfeifer, John.—Captured at Chickamauga, September 19, 1863.

Piesche, Joseph.—Mustered out.

Racek, Theodor, *Sergeant.*—May 27, 1861.—*First Sergeant,* May 4, 1862.—*Second Lieutenant,* November 17, 1862 (added to the officer list).

Roos, John.—Mustered out.

Rohland, Georg.—Wounded at Perryville, October 8, 1862.—Captured at Chickamauga, September 20, 1863.—Mustered out.

Rückert, Karl.—Drummed out, May 4, 1863.

Ruof, John.—Mustered out.

Späth, Adolph, *Corporal.*—May 27, 1861.—*First Sergeant,* November 17, 1862.—Wounded at Chickamauga and died October 17, 1863.

Schmitt, John, *Corporal.*—October 2, 1861.—Mustered out.

Scharringhaus, Henry.—Mustered out.

Semler, Kasper.—Wounded at Chickamauga.—Discharged disabled, December 2, 1863.

Schwesinger, Heinrich.—Wounded and captured at Chickamauga.—Mustered out.

Schnapp, Franz.—Died February 22, 1862.

Scheurer, Eduard.—Mustered out.

Scherer, Joseph.—Discharged disabled, May 27, 1862.

Schulz, Karl, *Corporal.*—March 1, 1862.—*Sergeant,* September 25, 1863.—Mustered out.

Schenk, Henry, *Corporal.*—August 14, 1862.—Mustered out.

Seeker, Friedrich.—Killed at Chickamauga, September 20, 1863.
Schlosser, Jakob.—Mustered out.
Schwartz, Johann.—Mustered out.
Schmiegel, Peter.—Mustered out.
Schäfer, Thomas.—Mustered out.
Schmidt, Franz.—Wounded at Carnifex Ferry, September 10, 1861.—Discharged disabled, May 14, 1863.
Schäfer, John.—Mustered out.
Senn, Georg.—Mustered out.
Scheer, Georg.—Wounded at Chickamauga.—Mustered out.
Schneemann, Ferdinand.—Veteran Reserve Corps, June 7, 1864.
Schuler, Joseph.—Veteran Reserve Corps, June 7, 1864.
Stöckle, August.—Mustered out.
Theobald, Adolph.—Mustered out.
Theobald, Henry J.—Died at Tullahoma, July 23, 1863.
Trautner, Georg F., *Sergeant.*—May 27, 1861.—Mustered out.
Tröster, John.—Wounded at Chickamauga and died October 12, 1863.
Ulmer, Konrad.—Transferred to the U.S. Artillery, September 5, 1862.
Voigt, Henry, *Corporal.*—May 27, 1861.—Killed at Chickamauga, September 20, 1863.
Wahle, Henry.—Mustered out.
Wedertz, Nikolaus.—Mustered out.
Weiss, Joseph.—Died November 6, 1861.
Wieget, Melchior.—Transferred to the U.S. Artillery, December 2, 1862.
Wierzbicki, John.—Discharged disabled, October 31, 1861.
Willig, Nikolaus [*sic*].—*First Lieutenant,* September 25, 1861 (added to the officer list).
Winzler, Jakob.—Discharged disabled, April 21, 1864.
Wolpold, Georg.—Wounded and captured at Chickamauga.—Mustered out.
Wüsthoff, Johann.—Mustered out.
Wyss, Benedikt.—Transferred to the U.S. Artillery, December 27, 1862.
Zahn, Charles.—Mustered out.

Company C

Officers

Henry Brodersen, *Captain.*—May 27, 1861.—Born Eckernförde, Silesia.—Resigned October 24, 1861.

George G. Harries, *First Lieutenant.*—May 27, 1861.—Born Bustorf, Silesia.—Transferred to regimental headquarters as adjutant, June 10, 1861.

Joseph Haider, *Second Lieutenant.*—May 27, 1861.—Born Ravensburg, Würtemberg.—*First Lieutenant,* September 6, 1861.—Resigned July 18, 1862.

William Stängel, *Captain.*—October 24, 1861.—Born Reutlingen, Würtemberg.—Cashiered August 28, 1862.

Henry Liedke, *Second Lieutenant.*—September 6, 1861.—Born Oldenburg.—*First Lieutenant,* September 1, 1862.—Died of wounds at Chickamauga, September 22, 1863.

Moritz Pohlmann, *Captain.*—September 28, 1862.—Born Kulm, Prussia.—Mustered out.

Heinrich Späth, *Second Lieutenant.*—September 1, 1862.—Born Schwabach, Würtemberg.—*First Lieutenant,* February 14, 1864.—Mustered out.

Noncommissioned Officers and Privates

Abel, Karl, *Corporal.*—October 1, 1862.—*First Sergeant,* February 1, 1864.—Mustered out.

Baiersdörfer, Henry.—Discharged disabled, January 6, 1862.

Balz, Peter, *Corporal.*—July 23, 1862.—Mustered out.

Bauer, Leonhard.—Mustered out.

Bihl, Jakob.—Veteran [Reserve Corps], March 14, 1864.

Birkmann, Nikolaus.—Deserted June 21, 1862.

Bleiler, Christoph.—Wounded at Chickamauga.—Mustered out.

Böcke, Clemens.—Discharged disabled, September 17, 1862.

Boshart, Constantin.—Wounded and captured at New Market, Alabama, August 5, 1862.—Mustered out.

Brucker, Georg.—Mustered out.

Brinkmann, Wilhelm, *Sergeant.*—February 22, 1862.—Mustered out.

Brümmelkamp, John.—Mustered out.

Brüggemann, Bernhard.—Transferred to the U.S. Artillery, November 30, 1862.

Busch, August.—Mustered out.

Buse, Friedrich.—Discharged disabled, December 30, 1862.

Busam, Leopold.—Wounded at Chickamauga.—Mustered out.

Busse, Friedrich, *Quartermaster-Sergeant.*—November 10, 1861 (regimental headquarters).

Deuerlich, Albert.—Mustered out.

Dister, Friedrich.—Transferred to the Signal Corps, October 17, 1863.

Eckerle, Martin.—Wounded at Chickamauga and at Missionary Ridge.—Mustered out.

Elver, Henry, *Corporal.*—May 1, 1862.—Wounded at Chickamauga.—Mustered out.

Etz, Georg, *Corporal.*—May 27, 1861.—*Sergeant,* June 1, 1862.—Mustered out.

Fahrübel, Xaver.—Discharged disabled, January 30, 1862.

Fey, Jakob.—Died at Nashville, February, 1864 [*sic*].

Ganzmann, Heinrich.—Mustered out.

Gebhard, Wilhelm.—Mustered out.

Gerhard, Wilhelm.—Mustered out.

Gimpel, Friedrich.—Died at Corinth, June 17, 1862.

Götz, John.—Mustered out.

Gömann, Louis.—Wounded at Missionary Ridge.—Mustered out.

Grob, John.—Discharged disabled, March 10, 1862.

Groshell, Charles.—Missing at Chickamauga, September 20, 1863.

Grothe, August.—Mustered out.

Grove, Louis, *Sergeant.*—September 6, 1861.—Wounded at Fayetteville, Virginia, November 2, 1861.—*First Sergeant,* July 21, 1862.—*Second Lieutenant,* July 24, 1862 (Company K).

Günther, Louis.—Mustered out.

Gurlett, Philipp.—Mustered out.

Hartig, Wilhelm.—Died of wounds at Chickamauga, October 30, 1863.

Hegele, Georg.—Mustered out.

Henkess, Martin.—Mustered out.

Herold, Kilian, *Corporal.*—October 1, 1862.—Died of wounds at Chickamauga, October 18, 1863.

Hessberg, Isaak.—Discharged disabled, November 19, 1861.

Heyne, Wilhelm.—Mustered out.

Heyl, Magnus.—Wounded at Corinth, May 19, 1862.—Discharged disabled, December 29, 1863.

Hill, Joseph.—Discharged disabled, August 2, 1862.

Hörst, Karl.—Discharged disabled, August 13, 1863.

Haffner, Fritz.—Wounded at Chickamauga.—Mustered out.

Holzmann, Philipp.—Mustered out.

Huber, Stephan.—Mustered out.

Huett, Matthias, *Corporal.*—May 27, 1861.—*Sergeant,* July 23, 1862.—Wounded at Chickamauga.—Mustered out.

Hoffmann, Karl.—Mustered out.

Jost, Adolph.—Discharged disabled, September 8, 1861.

Kaiser, Wilhelm.—Killed at Chickamauga, September 20, 1863.

Kaiser, Frank C.—Transferred to Camp Dennison, June 7, 1864.

Kiesewetter, Joseph.—Transferred to Camp Dennison, June 7, 1864.

Kelterborn, Wilhelm.—Mustered out.

Klöffler, Friedrich.—Discharged disabled, March 10, 1862.

Krämer, Henry.—Discharged disabled, November 4, 1863.

Krite, Henry.—Mustered out.

Krüger, August.—Transferred to Camp Dennison, June 7, 1864.

Krüger, Henry.—Mustered out.

Küster, Louis, *Corporal.*—May 27, 1861.—*Sergeant,* July 4, 1861.—*Second Lieutenant,* September 28, 1862 (Company H).

Lentz, Julius.—Wounded at Chickamauga.—Mustered out.

Liedke, Henry, *First Sergeant.*—May 27, 1861.—*Second Lieutenant,* September 6, 1861 (transferred to the officer list).

Löwenstein, Nathan.—Mustered out.

Lorentz, Michael.—Mustered out.

Lotz, Henry.—Discharged disabled, July 23, 1862.

Meister, Mathias.—Transferred to Camp Dennison, June 7, 1864.

Meyer, Louis.—Mustered out.

Miller, Anton, *Corporal.*—September 6, 1861.—*Sergeant,* September 13, 1862.—Wounded at Chickamauga.—Discharged disabled, December 25, 1863.

Miller, Peter.—Mustered out.
Müller, Christian.—Wounded at Chickamauga.—Mustered out.
Müller, Joseph, *Corporal.*—May 1, 1862.—*Sergeant,* January 1, 1864.—Mustered out.
Müller, John.—Mustered out.
Nülsen, Charles, *Corporal.*—March 1, 1862.—Mustered out.
Ott, William.—Transferred to Camp Dennison, June 7, 1864.
Pape, Theodor.—Wounded at Chickamauga.—Discharged disabled, February 15, 1864.
Pope, William.—Transferred to the U.S. Artillery, November 30, 1862.
Rapp, Friedrich.—Mustered out.
Ramminger, Henry.—Mustered out.
Roselett, John.—Wounded at Chickamauga.—Died November 1, 1863.
Rosenfeld, Wilhelm.—Discharged disabled, March 10, 1862.
Schäfer, Friedrich.—Died at Nashville, January 11, 1863.
Schmidt, Anton.—Mustered out.
Schmidt, John.—Mustered out.
Schneider, George.—Mustered out.
Schneider, Nikolaus.—Mustered out.
Schneider, George A., *Corporal.*—May 1, 1862.—*First Sergeant,* July, 1862 [*sic*].—Wounded at Chickamauga, September 20, 1863.—Discharged disabled, January 27, 1864.
Schottmüller, Karl.—Discharged disabled, September 25, 1862.
Schweitzer, Jacob.—Mustered out.
Schultz, John.—Discharged disabled, June 18, 1862.
Sickemeyer, Christian.—Mustered out.
Späth, Lorenz.—Wounded at Chickamauga.—Mustered out.
Stalder, Karl.—Invalid Corps, February 2, 1864.
Steiner, Theodor.—Discharged disabled, November 10, 1862.
Steck, John.—Mustered out.
Steiner, Karl.—Mustered out.
Stiefvater, Anton.—Mustered out.
Stittelberg, William.—Wounded at Chickamauga.—Mustered out.
Thönssen, Edleff.—*Captain,* June 26, 1861 (Company K).
Thönssen, Christian.—Wounded at Chickamauga.—Mustered out.

Trost, Friedrich.—Missing at Chickamauga, September 20, 1863.
Ulrich, Philipp.—Mustered out.
Upsing, Hermann.—Mustered out.
Voll, Friedrich.—Discharged disabled, January 24, 1862.
Volmer, Stanislaus.—Transferred to Camp Dennison, June 7, 1864.
Waltenspiel, Friedrich.—Killed at Chickamauga, September 20, 1864.
Wentz, Jakob.—Mustered out.
Willenberg, Hermann.—Veteran [Reserve Corps], Camp Dennison, June 7, 1864.
Wipfler, Sebastian.—Wounded at Mill Springs and at Chickamauga.—Died December 4, 1863.
Witzell, Louis.—Discharged disabled, July 9, 1862.
Zahn, Louis, *Corporal.*—September 6, 1861.—*Sergeant,* September 28, 1862.—*Hospital Steward,* December 22, 1862 (regimental headquarters).
Zier, Michael.—Mustered out.

Company D

Officers

Fritz Schröder, *Captain.*—May 27, 1861.—Born Soldin, Prussia.—*Major,* August 6, 1862 (regimental headquarters).
Ernst Rubenow, *First Lieutenant.*—May 27, 1861.—Born Schwerin, Mecklenburg.—Resigned July 13, 1862.
Daniel Wagner, *Second Lieutenant.*—May 27, 1861.—Born Kassel, Hesse.—Resigned June 20, 1862.
Richard Schneider, *First Lieutenant.*—July 24, 1862.—Born Hildburghausen, Saxe-Meiningen.—Mustered out.
Henry Späth, *Second Lieutenant.*—July 24, 1862.—Born Schwabach, Würtemberg.—To Company C.
Raimund Herrmann [*Sergeant-Major.*—May 27, 1861].—*Second Lieutenant,* September 1, 1862.—Born Dresden, Saxony. Killed at Chickamauga, September 19, 1863.
Gustav F. Nepper, *Captain.*—September 28, 1862.—Born Bremen.—Wounded at Chickamauga.—Mustered out.

Noncommissioned Officers and Privates

Abraham, Karl.—Mustered out.

Arnold, Philipp, *Corporal.*—June 28, 1862.—Wounded at Chickamauga.—Mustered out.

Beck, John.—Discharged disabled, October 28, 1862.

Begemann, August, *Corporal.*—July 18, 1861.—Discharged disabled, December 3, 1862.

Begemann, Gustav.—Died December 3, 1861.

Begemann, Adolph.—Transferred to Company A, May 1, 1862.

Betzold, Jakob.—Missing, November 7, 1862.

Blessing, John.—Died in prison at Andersonville.

Blum, Peter.—Mustered out.

Bonträger, Georg.—Mustered out.

Bosch, Louis.—Wounded at Chickamauga.—Mustered out.

Bügler, Jakob.—Wounded at Chickamauga.—Mustered out.

Burger, Thomas.—Wounded at New Market, Alabama, and at Chickamauga.—Mustered out.

Conradi, Friedrich.—Killed at Chickamauga, September 20, 1863.

Cordes, Henry.—Mustered out.

Dolezich, Karl, *Corporal.*—May 27, 1861.—*Sergeant,* November 1, 1861.—*First Lieutenant,* July 24, 1862 (Company I).

Dorn, Bernhardt.—Mustered out.

Eberhardt, John.—Mustered out.

Eberhardt, Martin.—Mustered out.

Emminger, Dominik, *Principal Musician.*—August 1, 1863 (regimental headquarters).

Engelbrecht, August.—Died February 13, 1864.

Fath, Martin.—Mustered out.

Friedrich, Henry.—Mustered out.

Frischknecht, Rudolph.—Mustered out.

Faubel, Henry.—Wounded at Missionary Ridge.—Mustered out.

Fleitz, Valentin.—Invalid Corps, January 15, 1864.

Frohmann, Louis, *Corporal.*—April 1, 1862.—Killed at Chickamauga, September 20, 1863.

Funke, Karl.—Killed at Chickamauga, September 20, 1863.

Gruis, Gustav, *Corporal.*—May 1, 1862 [*sic*].—*First Sergeant,* May 24, 1862.—Mustered out.

Galle, Wilhelm.—Mustered out.

Gerding, Heinrich.—Mustered out.

Gerthoff, Joseph.—Mustered out.

Grundmann, Adolph, *Corporal.*—November 1, 1861.—Mustered out.

Gürtler, Peter.—Mustered out.

Hugger, Peter.—Mustered out.

Hahn, Henry.—Mustered out.

Hampe, August, *Corporal.*—May 27, 1861.—*Sergeant,* July 26, 1862.—Wounded at Chickamauga.—Mustered out.

Hellriegel, Jerome.—Discharged disabled, January 10, 1863.

Herrmann, Jakob.—Wounded at Chickamauga.—Mustered out.

Johanning, Hermann.—Mustered out.

Johanning, William.—Wounded at Chickamauga.—Mustered out.

Kniehans, William.—Discharged disabled, July 10, 1861.

Koch, Garrick.—Deserted October 1, 1862.

Koch, Michael.—Transferred to Camp Dennison, June 7, 1864.

Küchler, Ernst.—Wounded at Chickamauga.—Died September 21, 1863.

Kurz, Johann.—Deserted November 27, 1862.

Lange, Henry.—Killed at Mill Springs, January 19, 1862.

Langebohn, Andreas.—Mustered out.

Lübbert, C. W. Hermann.—Mustered out.

Lechner, Joseph.—Discharged disabled, June 16, 1863.

Lochbühler, John.—Died August 19, 1862.

Lührmann, Christian, *Corporal.*—April 1, 1862.—Wounded at Chickamauga.—Died October 7, 1863.

Malzner, Franz.—Mustered out.

Meyer, Wilhelm.—Mustered out.

Minning, Henry.—Mustered out.

Mandell, Karl.—Wounded at Chickamauga.—Mustered out.

Matt, Bartholomäus.—Wounded at Chickamauga.—Mustered out.

Meyer, Fritz.—Wounded at Chickamauga.—Mustered out.

Meyer, Heinrich.—Wounded at Chickamauga.—Mustered out.

Meyninger, Heinrich.—Missing after April 12, 1862.

Müller, Anton.—Wounded at Mill Springs, January 19 [1862].—Killed at Chickamauga, September 20, 1863.

Minning, Wilhelm, *Corporal.*—May 27, 1861.—*Sergeant,* April 1, 1862.—Mustered out.
Meyer, Gebhard.—Discharged disabled, April 10, 1863.
Neun, Wilhelm.—Mustered out.
Nordmann, Louis.—Mustered out.
Otten, Hermann.—Discharged disabled, May 16, 1862.
Pflüger, Alexander.—Deserted November 7, 1862.
Reising, Andreas.—Mustered out.
Rösch, Georg.—Mustered out.
Rössler, Louis.—Wounded at Chickamauga.—Mustered out.
Sandmann, Louis.—Mustered out.
Sandrock, Adam.—Mustered out.
Schaf, Hermann.—Mustered out.
Schlenker, Mathias.—Mustered out.
Schmidt, Christian.—Mustered out.
Schrenk, Michael.—Mustered out.
Schübel, Karl.—Mustered out.
Steinkamp, Wilhelm.—Mustered out.
Schwarztrauber, Jakob.—Mustered out.
Seeger, Friedrich.—Mustered out.
Studder, Joseph.—Mustered out.
Sauser, John.—Wounded at Chickamauga.—Mustered out.
Schaffner, Hugo.—Wounded at Chickamauga.—Mustered out.
Schmidt, Hermann.—Wounded at Chickamauga.—Mustered out.
Schmidt, Christ.—Mustered out.
Spellerberg, Henry.—Killed at Mill Springs, January 19, 1862.
Späth, Henry, *Corporal.*—May 27, 1861.—*Sergeant,* July 18, 1861.—*Second Lieutenant,* July 24, 1862 (added to the officer list).
Stagge, Wilhelm.—Mustered out.
Stratemeyer, Christian.—Mustered out.
Stratemeyer, Rudolph.—Wounded at Missionary Ridge.—Mustered out.
Strohm, Gotlieb.—Wounded November 25, 1863.—Mustered out.
Turbetz, Friedrich.—Mustered out.
Van Nida, Christoph.—Mustered out.
Vörste, Wilhelm.—Discharged disabled, November 7, 1862.
Wallon, Joseph.—Deserted November 7, 1862.

Waltenspiel, August, *Corporal.*—April 1, 1862.—Killed at Chickamauga, September 20, 1863.

Weckerle, Bernhard.—Discharged disabled, December 2, 1862.

Wegger, Casper, *Corporal.*—May 27, 1861.—*Sergeant,* July 24, 1862.—Mustered out.

Wiening, Karl.—Mustered out.

Winter, Henry.—Wounded at Mill Springs.—Discharged disabled, January, 1863 [*sic*].

Witte, August, *Sergeant.*—July 14, 1861.—*First Sergeant,* March 11, 1864.—Mustered out.

Zierer, Wilhelm.—Discharged disabled, November, 1862 [*sic*].

Zimmerer, Ferdinand, *Corporal.*—July 28, 1862.—Wounded at Missionary Ridge.—Mustered out.

Company E

Officers

Bartholomäus Benz, *Captain.*—May 27, 1861.—Born Donaueschingen, Baden.—*Major,* February 14, 1864 (regimental headquarters).

Gustav F. Nepper, *First Lieutenant.*—May 27, 1861.—Born Bremen.—Wounded at Mill Springs.—*Captain,* December 28, 1862 (Company D).

Martin Bruner, *Second Lieutenant.*—May 27, 1861.—Born Cincinnati, Ohio.—Wounded at Chickamauga, September 20 [1863].—Mustered out.

Friedrich Steimer, *Second Lieutenant.*—September 28, 1862.—Born Newport, Kentucky.—Mustered out.

Georg H. Harries, *Captain.*—February 14, 1864.—Born Hustorf, Silesia.—Mustered out.

Noncommissioned Officers and Privates

Arnold, Jakob.—Discharged disabled, July 12, 1862.

Behrens, Henry.—Mustered out.

Brandenburger, August.—Mustered out.

Busch, Theodor.—Mustered out.

Büsching, Richard.—Mustered out.

Büche, Balthasar.—Mustered out.
Barwig, Henry.—Wounded at Chickamauga.—Discharged disabled, March 29, 1864.
Bedecker, Friedrich.—Wounded at Chickamauga.—Mustered out.
Brenner, Friedrich.—Discharged disabled, November 1, 1861.
Brabender, Martin.—Wounded at Chickamauga.—Mustered out.
Bayer, Henry E., *Corporal.*—August 28, 1863.—Mustered out.
Blumenthal, Friedrich.—Discharged disabled, September 19, 1861.
Benninger, Karl.—Wounded at Chickamauga.—Mustered out.
Dorst, Dietrich.—Mustered out.
Dumbacher, Martin.—Wounded at Mill Springs.—Died January 26, 1862.
Eckelmann, Louis.—Mustered out.
Eschenbrenner, Dieboldt.—Mustered out.
Ernst, Simon.—Mustered out.
Eyser, Daniel.—Mustered out.
Ehrhardt, Friedrich.—Deserted February 10, 1862.
Edelmann, Fidel.—Killed at Chickamauga, September 20, 1863.
Eigner, John, *Sergeant.*—May 28, 1861.—Mustered out.
Finnup, Fritz.—Mustered out.
Fischer, Georg.—Mustered out.
Fortenbacher, Karl.—Mustered out.
Funke, John.—Mustered out.
Fath, Adam.—Mustered out.
Feiertag, Henry, *Corporal.*—April 14, 1864.—Mustered out.
Gross, Friedrich.—Discharged disabled, March 29, 1862.
Gfrörer, Joseph.—Mustered out.
Gaul, Georg.—Died January 29, 1864.
Guillarme, Charles.—Discharged disabled, June 2, 1862.
Hagedorn, William E.—Transferred to the U.S. Artillery, December 3, 1862.
Hellwig, John.—Discharged disabled, January 12, 1863.
Hoffacker, Karl.—Missing after November 11, 1862.
Hoffmann, Friedrich.—Mustered out.
Haegli, Joseph.—Mustered out.
Hölzer, John.—Mustered out.
Honeck, John.—Mustered out.

Halbridder, Christoph.—Discharged disabled, October 31, 1862.
Hesse, Wilhelm.—Missing after June 23, 1863.
Heurich, Sebastian.—Missing after November 30, 1862.
Hornung, Christoph.—Killed at Chickamauga, September 20, 1863.
Jäger, Hermann.—Died March 24, 1864.
Kilb, Karl.—Discharged disabled, October 22, 1862.
Kollai, Georg.—Missing after November 20, 1862.
Keller, Kaspar.—Mustered out.
Köhler, John, *Corporal.*—April 27, 1862.—*Sergeant,* April 14, 1864.—Mustered out.
Keinhardt, John.—Discharged disabled, November 14, 1863.
Kirlach, Joseph.—Discharged disabled, June 26, 1862.
Keldenich, Joseph.—Wounded at Chickamauga.—Transferred to Camp Dennison, June 7, 1864.
Koch, John.—Transferred to Camp Dennison, June 7, 1864.
Limberger, John, *Corporal.*—May 28, 1861.—*Sergeant,* November 1, 1861.—Discharged disabled, January 1, 1863.
Lippert, Georg H., *Corporal.*—October 22, 1861.—*Sergeant,* September 28, 1862.—*First Sergeant,* November 22, 1862.—Mustered out.
Lüdecke, Christian.—Mustered out.
Meyers, Friedrich.—Transferred to the U.S. Artillery, December 3, 1862.
Momberg, Henry.—Mustered out.
Mayer, Adam.—Discharged disabled, September 19, 1862.
Mayer, Andreas.—Mustered out.
Müller, John, *Corporal.*—April 30, 1862.—Wounded at Chickamauga.—Mustered out.
Müller, John (II).—Mustered out.
Massmann, Louis, *Corporal.*—February 28, 1863.—Wounded at Chickamauga.—Mustered out.
Natsch, Frank.—Discharged disabled, September 20, 1863.
Nocka, Friedrich.—Wounded at Chickamauga.—Died April 29, 1864.
Obermeyer, Georg.—Mustered out.
Passauer, Joseph.—Wounded at Chickamauga.—Mustered out.
Pfisterer, Henry.—Discharged disabled, March 28, 1862.

Rieger, Georg.—Mustered out.
Rapp, Christian.—Mustered out.
Rahe, Franz.—Mustered out.
Rost, John.—Mustered out.
Rimpler, Georg.—Wounded at Chickamauga.—Mustered out.
Rohs, David.—Transferred to the U.S. Artillery, December 3, 1862.
Ruoff, John, *Corporal.*—September 15, 1861.—Killed at Mill Springs.
Rein, Joseph.—Mustered out.
Spengler, Philipp E., *Sergeant.*—May 28, [1861].—Discharged disabled, November 1, 1861.
Sanders, Henry W., *Corporal.*—May 28, [1861].—*First Sergeant,* November 1, 1861.—Discharged disabled, November 22, 1862.
Schick, Frank.—Wounded at Chickamauga.—Mustered out.
Straub, Jakob.—Mustered out.
Schulmeyer, Wilhelm.—Mustered out.
Siemers, Heinrich, *Corporal.*—January 1, 1863.—Wounded at Chickamauga.—Died November 9, 1863.
Sturm, Georg S., *Corporal.*—November 9, 1863.—Wounded at Chickamauga.—Mustered out.
Seebach, Jakob.—Mustered out.
Schweitzer, Wilhelm.—Mustered out.
Schutte, John.—Mustered out.
Steimer, Franz.—Mustered out.
Sommer, Philip.—Mustered out.
Streiff, Thomas.—Transferred to Camp Dennison, June 7, 1864.
Schwarz, Andreas.—Missing after November 11, 1862.
Schwier, Henry S., *Corporal.*—October 24, 1861.—*Sergeant,* January 1, 1863.—Wounded at Chickamauga.—Mustered out.
Steimer, Friedrich, *Corporal.*—May 28, 1861.—*Sergeant,* May 22, 1862.—*Second Lieutenant,* September 28, 1862 (added to the officer list).
Schmitt, Frank M., *Corporal.*—October 30, 1862.—Wounded at Chickamauga.—Mustered out.
Säger, Friedrich, *Corporal.*—February 27, 1862.—*Sergeant,* November 22, 1862.—Mustered out.
Schneck, August.—Discharged disabled, January 1, 1862.

Schuler, John, *Corporal.*—February 28, 1862.—Wounded at Chickamauga.—Mustered out.
Tobergte, Frank.—Mustered out.
Trick, John.—Mustered out.
Waltz, Louis.—Mustered out.
Weber, Hermann.—Transferred to Camp Dennison, June 7, 1864.
Wiening, Hermann.—Missing after November 30, 1862.
Wipfel, Leo.—Captured at Chickamauga, September 20, 1863.
Wätterich, Franz.—Wounded at Chickamauga.—Mustered out.
Wahler, Fritz.—Wounded at Chickamauga.—Mustered out.
Wätterich, Jakob.—Wounded at Chickamauga.—Mustered out.

Company F

Officers

Gustav Kämmerling, *Captain.*—May 27, 1861.—Born Mülheim an der Ruhr, Prussia.—*Major,* November 1, 1861 (regimental headquarters).
Hermann, Lütkenhaus, *First Lieutenant.*—May 27, 1861.—Born Eppe, Prussia.—Mustered out.
John Baumgärtner, *Second Lieutenant.*—May 27, 1861.—Born Freiburg, Baden.—Wounded at Mill Springs.—Resigned July 5, 1862.
Louis Heuser, *Captain.*—November 1, 1861.—Born Schwerin, Mecklenburg.—Mustered out.
Alexis Heilbrunn, *Second Lieutenant.*—July 24, 1862.—Born Kleinfreden, Hannover.—Wounded at Chickamauga.—*First Lieutenant,* February 14, 1864 (to Company G).

Noncommissioned Officers and Privates

Appenfelder, Wilhelm.—Mustered out.
Arnolds, Henry.—Mustered out.
Altringer, Matthias.—Mustered out.
Arnold, Jakob.—Discharged disabled, November 19, 1861.
Bay, Christian.—Wounded at Chickamauga.—Mustered out.
Becker, Joseph, *Corporal.*—July 24, 1862.—Wounded at Chickamauga.—Mustered out.

Baumgärtner, Benedikt.—Wounded at Chickamauga.—Transferred to Camp Dennison, June 7, 1864.
Berger, Karl.—Discharged disabled, June 10, 1861.
Brachle, John.—Discharged disabled, April 11, 1863.
Brill, Karl.—Discharged disabled, September 13, 1862.
Braun, Nikolaus.—Transferred to the 32nd Indiana, February 28, 1862.
Bruderer, Adolph.—Missing after August, 1862 [*sic*].
Bühl, Matthias.—Died July 28, 1862.
Burgart, Prosper.—Discharged disabled, September 11, 1862.
Dahlhoff, Conrad.—Mustered out.
Deitz, Andreas.—Transferred to Camp Dennison, June 7, 1864.
Daubenmerkel, Charles, *Corporal.*—August 27, 1862.—Wounded at Chickamauga.—Mustered out.
Engelay, Fritz.—Mustered out.
Etzel, Christian, *Sergeant.*—May 27, 1861.—Wounded at Chickamauga.—Mustered out.
Feid, Georg F., *Corporal.*—May 28, 1861.—*Sergeant,* July 24, 1864.—Mustered out.
Ferber, Gerhard, *Corporal.*—May 28, 1861.—Mustered out.
Freudenreich, Karl.—Mustered out.
Gerau, Julius, *Corporal.*—May 28, 1861.—Mustered out.
Gerstätter, Christian.—Wounded at Chickamauga.—Died September 23, 1863.
Günther, John.—Wounded at Chickamauga.—Mustered out.
Heilbrunn, Alexis, *First Sergeant.*—May 26, 1862.—*Second Lieutenant,* July 24, 1862 (added to the officer list).
Habenicht, Friedrich.—Mustered out.
Haller, Karl.—Wounded at Chickamauga.—Discharged disabled, March 16, 1864.
Heinzmann, Frank, *Corporal.*—November 4, 1861.—*Sergeant,* July 24, 1862.—*First Sergeant,* July 30, 1863.—Wounded at Chickamauga, September 20, 1863.—Mustered out.
Hermann, Leonard.—Wounded at Chickamauga.—Mustered out.
Hirschmann, Georg.—Killed at Chickamauga, September 20, 1863.
Hirschbrunner, Gottlieb.—Killed at Chickamauga, September 20, 1863.

Hör, Heinrich.—Wounded at Chickamauga.—Mustered out.
Hornickel, Christian.—Discharged disabled, May 27, 1862.
Hünemann, John.—Mustered out.
Hummel, Karl, *Sergeant.*—August 27, 1862.—Mustered out.
Hunnekuhl, Wilhelm.—Mustered out.
Jessing, Paul.—Wounded at Mill Springs.—Discharged disabled, March 16, 1863.
Kaufmann, Konrad.—Discharged disabled, September 16, 1862.
Kämmerle, Wilhelm.—Mustered out.
Kramer, Konrad.—Mustered out.
Klinberg, Bernhard.—Transferred to Camp Dennison, June 7, 1864.
Knittel, Anton.—Killed at Chickamauga, September 20, 1863.
Kern, Martin.—Discharged disabled, September 19, 1861.
Kern, Karl.—Captured at Sewell Mountain.—Discharged by order of the Adjutant General, May 21, 1862.
Korn, Jakob, *Corporal.*—May 27, 1861.—Missing after April 11, 1863.
Karpp, Henry.—Wounded at Mill Springs.—Discharged disabled, August 2, 1862.
Kiliani, Wilhelm, *Sergeant.*—May 27, 1861.—Discharged disabled, August 13, 1862.
Lehnen, Joseph, *Corporal.*—February 24, 1862.—Wounded at Chickamauga.—Mustered out.
Mella, Philipp.—Wounded at Mill Springs.—Missing after April 11, 1863.
Miefert, Friedrich.—Wounded at Chickamauga.—Died September 27, 1863.
Mietsch, Georg.—Discharged disabled, November 15, 1862.
Messner, Karl.—Mustered out.
Meroth, Karl.—Missing, December 1, 1861.
Mader, Alois, *Corporal.*—May 27, 1861.—Mustered out.
May, Karl.—Wounded at Mill Springs.—Mustered out.
Moor, Henry.—Discharged disabled, September 11, 1862.
Müller, Friedrich.—Killed at Chickamauga, September 20, 1863.
Neckel, Heinrich.—Mustered out.
Nordhof, Julius.—Mustered out.
Neulmann, Heinrich.—Wounded at Chickamauga.—Mustered out.
Nolte, August.—Discharged disabled, January 4, 1862.

Oberdahn, Johann, *Sergeant.*—May 27, 1861.—Discharged disabled, November 19, 1862.

Oberkline, Friedrich, *Sergeant.*—May 27, 1861.—*Second Lieutenant,* July 24, 1862 (to Company G).

Papenberg, Henry.—Mustered out.

Prechtel, John, *Corporal.*—July 24, 1862.—Mustered out.

Roman, Karl, *Corporal.*—May 27, 1861.—Killed at Chickamauga, September 20, 1863.

Rowe, Henry.—Mustered out.

Rohr, Andreas.—Mustered out.

Rothfuss, Karl.—Mustered out.

Rung, Kasper.—Transferred to the U.S. Artillery, December 8, 1862.

Roller, Karl.—Died November 12, 1863.

Schmidt, Hermann.—Killed at Chickamauga, September 20, 1863.

Stahl, Hermann.—Discharged disabled, September 13, 1862.

Schott, Vincent.—Wounded at Chickamauga.—Mustered out.

Schönfeld, Wilhelm.—Mustered out.

Steffens, Henry.—Mustered out.

Stern, Wilhelm.—Mustered out.

Straus, Ernst.—Mustered out.

Schönfeld, August.—Mustered out.

Schmülling, Johann.—Mustered out.

Schüle, Christian.—Mustered out.

Sander, Heinrich.—Mustered out.

Steuber, Lorenz.—Mustered out.

Siebelder, Anton.—Mustered out.

Schäfer, Karl.—Mustered out.

Schröder, Friedrich.—Mustered out.

Schmidt, John.—Mustered out.

Schrör, Wilhelm.—Deserted, April 7, 1862.

Schaffner, Gottlieb.—Discharged disabled, November 19, 1861.

Schenkel, Eduard.—Invalid Corps, September 1, 1863.

Streiff, Johann B.—Died July 8, 1863.

Steuber, Philipp.—Wounded at Chickamauga.—Mustered out.

Trau, Franz.—Mustered out.

Trarbach, Johann.—Discharged disabled, November 10, 1862.

Vollet, Andreas.—Wounded at Chickamauga.—Mustered out.

Vossler, Konrad.—Mustered out.

Wahlbrink, Wilhelm.—Mustered out.
Weber, Henry L.—On special assignment, April 11, 1862.
Werth, Friedrich.—Wounded at Chickamauga.—Died September 23, 1863.
Wilke, John.—Wounded at Chickamauga.—Died November 13, 1863.
Zink, Otto.—Transferred to Camp Dennison, June 7, 1864.

Company G

Officers

Gustav Richter, *Captain.*—May 27 [1861].—Born Oels, Prussia.—Killed at Chickamauga, September 20, 1863.
Karl Jahn, *First Lieutenant.*—May 27, 1861.—Born Fulda, Hesse.—Resigned October 31, 1861.
Theodor Lammers, *Second Lieutenant.*—May 27, 1861.—Born Eppe, Prussia.—*First Lieutenant,* January 27, 1862.—Wounded at Chickamauga.—Died October 7, 1863.
Georg Hartung, *Second Lieutenant.*—June 7, 1863.—Born Mühlhausen, Prussia.—Mustered out.
Friedrich Oberkline, *Second Lieutenant.*—July 24, 1862.—Born Lotte, Prussia.—Resigned May 8, 1863.
Adam Schumacher [*sic*], *Captain.*—February 14, 1864.—Born Gaiberg, Baden.—Mustered out.
Alexis Heilbrunn, *Second Lieutenant.*—July 24, 1862.—Born Kleintreden, Hannover.—Mustered out.

Noncommissioned Officers and Privates

Adam, Wenzel.—Mustered out.
Appelmann, Georg.—Mustered out.
Arnolds, Rudolph.—Died November 30, 1863.
Bächle, Franz.—Died October 19, 1862.
Bälser, Wilhelm.—Died October 2, 1863.
Becker, Karl.—Wounded at Mill Springs and at Missionary Ridge.—Mustered out.
Biedenbender, Karl.—Wounded at Chickamauga.—Mustered out.
Blattau, Louis.—Mustered out.
Bleibel, Joseph.—Mustered out.

Brummer, Peter.—Deserted, June 18, 1862.
Bürkle, Ernst.—Wounded at Mill Springs.—Mustered out.
Büttner, Ehrhardt.—Discharged disabled, June 22, 1861.
Cramer, Friedrich.—Transferred to Camp Dennison, June 7, 1864.
Dammeier, Christoph.—Missing after November 8, 1862.
Denkinger, Franz.—Mustered out.
Deutschmann, Johann.—Mustered out.
Deutschmann, Karl.—Wounded at Chickamauga.—Mustered out.
Dietrich, John.—Mustered out.
Dodtkarte, Karl.—Wounded at Missionary Ridge.—Mustered out.
Dühlmeier, Wilhelm.—Wounded at Chickamauga.—Mustered out.
Dirksen, Heinrich.—Wounded at Chickamauga.—Mustered out.
Emmert, Friedrich, *Corporal.*—September 9, 1861.—*Sergeant,* October 4, 1862.—Mustered out.
Euler, Justus.—Mustered out.
Federlin, Wilhelm.—Killed at Chickamauga, September 19, 1863.
Fricker, John.—Discharged disabled, November 12, 1862.
Fisch, Friedrich.—Died October 20, 1863.
Gauer, John.—Missing at Chickamauga, September 20, 1863.
Gödicke, Friedrich.—Killed at Chickamauga, September 20, 1863.
Gschwind, Louis.—Mustered out.
Golde, Karl, *Sergeant.*—May 27, 1861.—*First Sergeant,* April 20, 1862.—Mustered out.
Gebhardt, August, *Corporal.*—May 27, 1861.—*Sergeant,* April 30, 1862.—Mustered out.
Grebenstein, Johann.—Missing after November 11, 1862.
Hättig, Lukas.—Discharged disabled, March 15, 1862.
Hartung, Georg, *Second Lieutenant.*—June 6, 1863.—Added to the officer list.
Heidemann, Wilhelm.—Mustered out.
Herrmann, Christian, *Corporal.*—October 4, 1861.—Mustered out.
Holl, Raymund.—Mustered out.
Hennecke, Henry.—Mustered out.
Huth, Wilhelm.—Killed at Chickamauga, September 20, 1863.
Hess, Daniel.—Wounded at Chickamauga.—Mustered out.
Hossfeld, Andreas, *Corporal.*—May 27, 1861.—Discharged disabled, April 11, 1863.
Howind, Hermann.—Wounded at Chickamauga.—Mustered out.

Honold, Georg, *Corporal.*—May 27, 1861.—*Sergeant,* November 1, 1862.—Wounded at Chickamauga.—Died October 6, 1863.

Jilke, Anton.—Deserted, August 9, 1862.

Kaschube, Karl, *Corporal.*—May 27, 1861.—*Sergeant,* November 9, 1862.—Mustered out.

Kuhne, Georg.—Killed at Chickamauga, September 19, 1863.

Kutter, Otto.—Killed at Chickamauga, September 20, 1863.

Kesting, Simon.—Discharged disabled, January 2, 1863.

Kunkel, August.—Mustered out.

Kreis, Jakob.—Mustered out.

Lämke, Friedrich.—Mustered out.

Leibnitz, Wilhelm.—Mustered out.

Löffler, John.—Mustered out.

Limberger, Georg.—Wounded at Mill Springs.—Discharged disabled, July, 1862 [*sic*].

Meiser, Michael.—Transferred to Camp Dennison, June 7, 1864.

Müller, John.—Mustered out.

Meyer, Friedrich.—Mustered out.

Meyer, Henry.—Discharged disabled, October, 1862 [*sic*].

Meyer, Wilhelm.—Discharged disabled, September, 1862 [*sic*].

Nagel, Henry, *Corporal.*—April 26, 1862.—Wounded at Corinth, May 17, 1862, and at Chickamauga.—Mustered out.

Neumann, Wilhelm.—Wounded at Chickamauga.—Died October 14, 1863.

Oberdries, Kasper.—Deserted, March 10, 1862.

Otto, Anton.—Missing after October 4, 1862.

Racke, Heinrich.—Died February 9, 1864.

Rupprecht, Heinrich.—Deserted, March 10, 1862.

Roggenbucker, Otto.—Mustered out.

Racke, Philipp.—Mustered out.

Rapp, Eduard, *Corporal.*—September 1, 1862.—Mustered out.

Rudel, John.—Missing after November 8, 1862.

Schmidt, Christian.—Mustered out.

Seppell, Ferdinand, *First Sergeant.*—May 27, 1861.—Discharged disabled, April 20, 1862.

Sutz, Hermann, *Corporal.*—May 27, 1861.—Killed at Mill Springs.

Spankuch, Otto.—Discharged disabled, September 23, 1861.

Spahn, Franz, *Corporal.*—December 1, 1862.—Mustered out.

Schweickhart, Karl, *Corporal.*—May 1, 1862.—Mustered out.
Schifferdecker, Jakob.—Missing after November 8, 1862.
Schultz, Hermann, *Corporal.*—December 1, 1862.—Mustered out.
Schneider, Joseph.—Wounded at Chickamauga.—Mustered out.
Stein, Eduard.—Missing after October 27, 1862.
Schnellmann, Wilhelm.—Discharged disabled, November, 1862 [*sic*].
Schauber, Joseph.—Wounded at Chickamauga.—Discharged disabled, June 7, 1864.
Schmidlin, Johann.—Wounded at Chickamauga.—Mustered out.
Schürbrock, Henry.—Transferred to the U.S. Artillery, December 3, 1862.
Strich, Friedrich.—Mustered out.
Schmolze, Louis.—Mustered out.
Sigmund, August.—Mustered out.
Sparenberg, Hermann.—Mustered out.
Schroppe, August.—Mustered out.
Stamm, Heinrich.—Mustered out.
Schnyder, Peter.—Mustered out.
Schetter, Christoph.—Mustered out.
Sextro, Bernhard.—Mustered out.
Stodick, Henry.—Mustered out.
Tinnemeyer, Wilhelm.—Killed at Miller's Ferry, West Virginia, October 30, 1861.
Wätterich, Peter.—Mustered out.
Wiedenroth, Georg.—Mustered out.
Willet, Joseph.—Discharged disabled, October 29, 1861.
Weinheimer, Valentin.—Discharged disabled, December 9, 1862.
Winter, Franz, *Corporal.*—May 1, 1862.—Mustered out.
Zäsky, Wilhelm.—Wounded at Chickamauga.—Mustered out.
Zerk, August.—Discharged disabled, November, 1862 [*sic*].

Company H

Officers

Jakob Gluchowski, *Captain.*—May 27, 1861.—Born Bromberg, Prussia.—Mustered out.
Moritz Pohlmann, *First Lieutenant.*—May 27, 1861.—Born Kulm,

Prussia.—*Captain,* September 28, 1862 (Company C).

Adolph Kühn, *Second Lieutenant.*—May 27, 1861.—Resigned September 29, 1861.

Hermann Groskordt, *Second Lieutenant.*—September 29, 1861.—Born Altenesch, Oldenburg.—*First Lieutenant,* September 28, 1862.

Louis Küster, *Second Lieutenant.*—September 28, 1862.—Born Betzenhausen, Baden.—Wounded at Chickamauga.—Cashiered March 21, 1864.

Noncommissioned Officers and Privates

Abel, Friedrich.—Discharged disabled, November 21, 1861.

Bachmann, John.—Wounded at Chickamauga.—Mustered out.

Brandt, Karl.—Mustered out.

Büscher, Hermann.—Mustered out.

Büscher, Wilhelm.—Mustered out.

Bütow, John.—Mustered out.

Brandt, Friedrich.—October 12, 1863.—Transferred to Camp Dennison, June 7, 1864.

Bender, Albert.—October 23, 1863.—Transferred to Camp Dennison, June 7, 1864.

Blankenheim, John.—Died December 22, 1862.

Brandt, Friedrich [*sic*], *Corporal.*—July 18, 1861.—*Sergeant,* September 15, 1862.—Mustered out.

Büscher, Louis.—Died February 1, 1864.

Beck, Georg.—Killed at Chickamauga, September 19, 1863.

Biegel, Georg.—Wounded at Mill Springs.—Discharged disabled, October 11, 1862.

Blum, Philipp.—Wounded at Chickamauga.—Mustered out.

Besecke, Wilhelm, *Corporal.*—May 27, 1861.—*Sergeant,* March 1, 1864.—Mustered out.

Bode, Louis.—Wounded at Chickamauga.—Mustered out.

Commendera, Karl, *Corporal.*—September 29, 1861.—Mustered out.

Derenkamp, Henry.—Mustered out.

Döpke, Wilhelm.—Mustered out.

Danner, Joseph.—Killed at Chickamauga, September 19, 1863.

Dietsch, Joseph.—Discharged disabled, June 25, 1862.

Dilg, Paul.—Missing after October 7, 1862.

Dixon, Lloyd.—Wounded at Mill Springs.—Discharged disabled, October 11, 1862.

Dolletscheck, Karl.—Discharged disabled, May 2, 1862.

Ehlert, Christian.—Wounded at Chickamauga.—Mustered out.

Feuerstein, Franz.—Wounded at Chickamauga.—Mustered out.

Fischer, Karl.—Mustered out.

Fischer, Hermann, *Corporal.*—September 7, 1861.—Invalid Corps, September 1, 1863.

Frommel, John.—Mustered out.

Grothen, John.—Mustered out.

Groskordt, Hermann, *Corporal.*—May 27, 1861.—*First Sergeant,* July 5, 1861.—*Second Lieutenant,* September 29, 1861 (added to the officer list).

Graf, Georg, *Corporal.*—May 27, 1861.—*Sergeant,* September 7, 1861.—Discharged disabled, May 2, 1862.

Gerberding, Wilhelm, *Corporal.*—September 15, 1862.—Wounded at Chickamauga.—Mustered out.

Gehm, Wilhelm.—Wounded at Mill Springs.—Discharged disabled, January 4, 1864.

Hagelstein, John.—Mustered out.

Hauck, Nikolas.—Mustered out.

Hebenstreit, Friedrich.—Mustered out.

Hesch, Georg.—Mustered out.

Herth, Theodor.—April 21, 1863.—Transferred to Camp Dennison, June 7, 1864.

Hirschauer, Peter, *Corporal.*—May 27, 1861.—*Sergeant,* September 29, 1861.—Wounded at Chickamauga.—Mustered out.

Höhler, Joseph, *Sergeant.*—May 27, 1861.—Mustered out.

Hiltwein, Karl.—Discharged disabled, November 20, 1861.

Hillinger, Joseph.—Wounded at Chickamauga.—Mustered out.

Haile, Robert, *Corporal.*—May 27, 1861.—*Sergeant,* December 10, 1861.—*First Sergeant,* June 1, 1862.—Mustered out.

Harty, Theodor.—Missing after November 6, 1862.

Hamm, Andreas.—Killed at Chickamauga, September 20, 1863.

Hartmann, Jakob.—Wounded at Chickamauga.—Mustered out.

Jakob, Philipp.—Transferred to Camp Dennison, June 7, 1864.

Jansen, John.—Wounded at Chickamauga.—Mustered out.
Kaiser, Gustav.—Mustered out.
Kleinschmidt, Christian.—Mustered out.
Kraus, Johann.—Mustered out.
Krumdieck, Heinrich.—Mustered out.
Kuhn, Isidor.—Mustered out.
Ketteler, August, *Corporal.*—March 1, 1864.—Mustered out.
Kiefer, Heinrich.—Killed at Chickamauga, September 20, 1863.
Köhn, Theodor.—Wounded at Chickamauga.—Mustered out.
Lindner, Johann, *Corporal.*—May 27, 1861.—*Sergeant,* May 2, 1862.—Invalid Corps, November 1, 1863.
Lübbert, Henry.—Mustered out.
Meier, Wilhelm.—Mustered out.
Meinking, Heinrich.—Mustered out.
Münzer, Friedrich.—Mustered out.
Meier, Mathias.—Deserted, January 13, 1863.
Meinking, Wilhelm.—Wounded at Chickamauga.—*Corporal,* December 31, 1863.—Mustered out.
Motz, Andreas.—Wounded at Chickamauga.—Mustered out.
Marting, Henry, *Corporal.*—May 27, 1861.—*Sergeant,* June 21, 1861.—Discharged disabled, September 14, 1862.
Müller, Christoph.—Wounded at Chickamauga.—Mustered out.
Opitz, Friedrich.—Mustered out.
Ortmann, Bernhard.—Mustered out.
Pott, Friedrich.—Mustered out.
Pfaffenbach, Heinrich.—Missing after October 8, 1862.
Präger, Leopold.—Veteran Reserve Corps, June 7, 1864.
Quinke, Lorenz.—Mustered out.
Quinke, Bernhard.—Mustered out.
Rapp, Michael.—Discharged disabled, January 19, 1863.
Riddermann, Bernhard.—Wounded at Chickamauga.—Mustered out.
Riddermann, John.—Invalid Corps, November 1, 1863.
Röse, August.—Mustered out.
Rulle, Gustav.—Mustered out.
Sabin, Theodor.—Killed at Mill Springs, January 19, 1862.
Schäfer, John.—Wounded at Chickamauga.—Mustered out.
Schaller, Mathias.—Mustered out.

Schätzlein, John.—Mustered out.
Schatzmann, Georg.—Mustered out.
Schick, John.—Mustered out.
Schmidt, Albert.—Mustered out.
Schubert, Emil.—Mustered out.
Skinner, Theodor.—Mustered out.
Strüwe, Henry.—Mustered out.
Schneider, Jakob.—Mustered out.
Stühle, Karl, *Corporal.*—December 10, 1861.—Mustered out.
Stöppel, August, *Corporal.*—May 2, 1862.—Mustered out.
Stolz, Peter, *Corporal.*—September 6, 1863.—Wounded at Mill Springs and at Chickamauga.—Mustered out.
Sieverding, Georg.—Wounded at Chickamauga.—Mustered out.
Seger, Georg.—Wounded at Chickamauga.—Mustered out.
Tolle, Christian.—Wounded at Chickamauga.—Mustered out.
Vehrenkamp, Friedrich.—Wounded at Chickamauga.—Mustered out.
Voss, Henry.—Wounded at Chickamauga.—Mustered out.
Vöckel, Christian.—Mustered out.
Weghorst, Louis, *Corporal.*—December 10, 1861.—Died April 7, 1863.
Wild, Anton.—Wounded at Mill Springs.—Discharged disabled, September 16, 1863.
Wilsbacher, August, *Corporal.*—July 4, 1861.—Invalid Corps, December 1, 1863.
Wegener, Joseph.—Deserted, June 21, 1861.
Wösner, Andreas.—Mustered out.

Company I

Officers

John Gansen, *Captain.*—May 27, 1861.—Born Cologne, Prussia.—Died October 28, 1863.
Wilhelm Heubig, *First Lieutenant.*—May 27, 1861.—Born Neu Strelitz, Mecklenburg.—Resigned July 5, 1862.
Joseph Gräff, *Second Lieutenant.*—May 27, 1861.—Born Bamberg, Bavaria.—*Regimental Quartermaster* (regimental headquarters), September 6, 1861.

Karl Dolezich, *First Lieutenant.*—July 24, 1862.—Born Neustadt, Prussia.—Mustered out.

Andreas Jenny, *Second Lieutenant.*—September 29, 1861.—Born Lahr, Baden.—Mustered out.

Hermann Lütkenhaus, *Captain.*—February 14, 1864.—Born Eppe, Prussia.—Mustered out.

Noncommissioned Officers and Privates

Balke, Christoph.—Mustered out.

Bickmeyer, Wilhelm.—Mustered out.

Bock, Wilhelm.—Mustered out.

Böhler, Jakob.—Mustered out.

Bauermeister, Fritz.—Wounded at Chickamauga.—Veteran Reserve Corps, December 21, 1863.

Becher, Emil.—Wounded at Chickamauga.—Mustered out.

Becker, Gustav.—Deserted, October 2, 1862.

Beiser, August.—Deserted, December 3, 1862.

Blattner, Jakob.—Deserted, March 7, 1862.

Blomeyer, Heinrich.—Wounded at Chickamauga.—Died October 27, 1863.

Böhler, Leo.—Killed at Chickamauga, September 19, 1863.

Burkhard, Philipp.—Wounded at Chickamauga.—Mustered out.

Boccard, John.—Wounded at Chickamauga.—Mustered out.

Bauer, Jakob.—Transferred to Camp Dennison, June 7, 1864.

Conrath, Joseph.—Mustered out.

Constanz, Christian.—Transferred to the U.S. Artillery, December 3, 1862.

Demme, Hermann.—Mustered out.

Doll, Joseph, *First Sergeant.*—July 25, 1862.—Killed [at Chickamauga] September 20, 1863.

Doller, Leopold.—Mustered out.

Ehrhardt, Theodor.—Died October 3, 1861.

Erkel, Philipp.—Mustered out.

Filian, Franz.—Mustered out.

Fitz, Philipp.—Wounded at Chickamauga.—Mustered out.

Fleischmann, Christian.—Mustered out.

Folz, Benjamin.—Mustered out.

Grau, Michael.—Missing after April 11, 1863.

Greiner, Anton, *Corporal.*—February 1, 1862.—Wounded at Chickamauga.—Mustered out.

Grimm, Daniel.—Wounded at Chickamauga.—Mustered out.

Hamann, Michael, *Corporal.*—May 27, 1861.—*Sergeant,* June 16, 1862.—Killed at Chickamauga, September 19, 1863.

Hammel, Eduard.—Mustered out.

Haack, Karl.—Deserted, October 10, 1862.

Haack, Louis.—Mustered out.

Haffner, Christian.—Mustered out.

Höndorf, Louis.—Mustered out.

Heine, John.—Mustered out.

Höller, Friedrich.—Mustered out.

Hölscher, Rudolph.—Mustered out.

Hüttenmüller, Wilhelm, *Corporal.*—August 1, 1861.—*Sergeant,* September 1, 1861.—Wounded at Chickamauga.—Mustered out.

Hoch, Ignatz.—Wounded at Chickamauga.—Mustered out.

Hoppert, Karl, *Corporal.*—June 16, 1862.—Killed [at Chickamauga] September 20, 1863.

Hobstetter, Peter.—Missing after August 14, 1863.

Hoerr, Louis.—Wounded at Chickamauga.—Mustered out.

Hölscher, Bernhard.—Discharged disabled, September 21, 1863.

Jenny, Andreas, *Corporal.*—May 27, 1861.—*Sergeant,* August 1, 1861.—*Second Lieutenant,* September 25, 1861 (added to the officer list).

Jaut, Friedrich, *Corporal.*—September 25, 1861.—Mustered out.

Kadow, Louis.—Wounded at Chickamauga.—Veteran Reserve Corps, June 7, 1864.

Keiffenheim, Urban.—Discharged disabled, September 18, 1861.

Keutel, John.—Killed at Chickamauga, September 19, 1863.

Kull, Friedrich.—Killed at Chickamauga, September 19, 1863.

Kopp, Georg.—Transferred to the U.S. Artillery, December 3, 1862.

Koffater, Fridolin.—Mustered out.

Lavo, Jakob.—Discharged disabled, June 26, 1862.

Leimann, Hermann, *Corporal.*—July 28, 1861.—Mustered out.

Leyser, Karl M.—Wounded at Chickamauga.—Mustered out.

Messemer, Caspar, *Corporal.*—May 27, 1861.—*Sergeant,* June 24, 1861.—Killed [at Chickamauga] September 20, 1863.

Mensing, Karl.—Discharged disabled, June 26, 1862.

Meyer, Anton.—Wounded at Chickamauga.—Mustered out.
Meyer, Michael.—Veteran Reserve Corps, March 15, 1864.
Mertz, Philip.—Mustered out.
Mauerer, Wilhelm.—Mustered out.
Müller, Karl.—Killed at Chickamauga, September 20, 1863.
Ney, John M.—Discharged disabled, March 15, 1862.
Neubeck, Adolph.—Wounded at Chickamauga.—Mustered out.
Opitz, Ferdinand, *Corporal.*—May 27, 1861.—*Sergeant,* September 25, 1861.—Mustered out.
Ortwein, John.—Mustered out.
Ohl, Karl.—Mustered out.
Paul, Henry.—Mustered out.
Ruf, Alexander.—Mustered out.
Rohland, Peter.—Mustered out.
Reiber, Gottlob, *Corporal.*—August 10, 1861.—Killed at Chickamauga, September 19, 1863.
Reichmann, Wilhelm.—Killed at Chickamauga, September 20, 1863.
Runk, Louis.—Wounded at Chickamauga.—Died September 21, 1863.
Schuhmann, John.—Mustered out.
Stöcker, August.—Mustered out.
Scherer, Christian.—Mustered out.
Staut, Karl.—Mustered out.
Schmidt, Friedrich.—Mustered out.
Schmidt, Robert.—Mustered out.
Siefert, John.—Mustered out.
Schneider, Richard, *Corporal.*—May 27, 1861.—*First Sergeant,* May 28, 1861.—*First Lieutenant,* July 24, 1862 (Company D).
Schäfer, Jakob.—Captured at Chickamauga.
Steffel, Johann, *Corporal.*—February 1, 1862.—Mustered out.
Springard, Konrad.—Killed at Chickamauga, September 20, 1863.
Stöcker, Wilhelm.—Wounded at Chickamauga.—Mustered out.
Stöcker, Gustav.—Killed at Rich Mountain, West Virginia, July 10, 1861.
Steenken, Georg, *Corporal.*—September 1, 1861.—*Sergeant,* September 21, 1863.—Mustered out.
Stierle, Karl.—Wounded at Chickamauga.—Mustered out.

Schmidt, Daniel.—Deserted, December 4, 1862.
Schmidt, John, *Corporal.*—December 29, 1863.—Mustered out.
Sander, Hermann.—Wounded at Chickamauga.—Mustered out.
Schröder, Leo.—Missing after February 2, 1863.
Schott, Christian.—Deserted, February 2, 1863.
Sturm, Joseph.—Wounded at Chickamauga.—Mustered out.
Schneider, Daniel—Deserted, December 6, 1861.
Tauchert, Karl, *Corporal.*—May 27, 1861.—Discharged disabled, July 14, 1862.
Uttendörfer, Eduard.—Killed at Chickamauga, September 20, 1863.
Vonau, Georg.—Wounded at Rich Mountain.—Died January 25, 1862.
Warnke, Hermann, *Corporal.*—September 21, 1863.—Mustered out.
Westmeyer, Henry.—Mustered out.
Wiemer, Fabian.—Mustered out.
Wickert, Joseph.—Deserted, November 28, 1861.
Wolf, Konrad.—Mustered out.

Company K

Officers

Georg Sommer, *Captain.*—May 27, 1861.—Resigned June 22, 1861.
Theodor Haffner, *First Lieutenant.*—May 27, 1861.—Born Munich, Bavaria.—Resigned July 5, 1862.
Louis Fricker, *Second Lieutenant.*—May 27, 1861.—Born Stuttgart, Würtemberg.—Resigned May 10, 1862.
Edleff Thönssen, *Captain.*—June 26, 1861.—Born Groven, Holstein.—Captured at Chickamauga, September 20, 1863.—Mustered out.
John Mangold, *First Lieutenant.*—July 24, 1862.—Born Buchenau, Hesse.—Cashiered, January 15, 1863.
Louis Grove, *Second Lieutenant.*—July 24, 1862.—Born Heide, Holstein.—*First Lieutenant,* February 14, 1864.—Mustered out.

Noncommissioned Officers and Privates

Angst, Jakob.—Mustered out.
Axer, Bernhard.—Mustered out.
Bäsler, Martin.—Mustered out.

Behringer, Sebastian.—Mustered out.
Buchta, Thomas.—Mustered out.
Brandner, Adolf.—Transferred to Camp Dennison, June 7, 1864.
Baldinger, Friedrich.—Wounded at Chickamauga.—Mustered out.
Bauer, Heinrich.—Wounded at Chickamauga.—Mustered out.
Berg, Wilhelm.—Wounded at Chickamauga.—Mustered out.
Beck, Jakob.—Wounded at Chickamauga.—Mustered out.
Bauer, Louis.—Discharged disabled, July 3, 1862.
Büttner, Georg.—Wounded at Rich Mountain.—Discharged disabled, June 26, 1862.
Dämon, Reinhard.—Mustered out.
Dämon, Alexander.—Mustered out.
Erbacher, Peter.—Mustered out.
Fellinger, Georg.—Mustered out.
Fischer, Julius.—Transferred to Camp Dennison, June 7, 1864.
Fuchs, Joseph, *Corporal.*—September 8, 1861.—Mustered out.
Grether, John.—Mustered out.
Gopfer, Theodor.—Mustered out.
Gschwind, Konstantin.—Mustered out.
Grösser, Gottfried.—Killed at Chickamauga, September 20, 1863.
Gerhard, Wilhelm.—Died October 14, 1861.
Geiger, John.—Wounded at Chickamauga.—Mustered out.
Greuther, Georg.—Wounded at Chickamauga.—Transferred to Camp Dennison, June 7, 1864.
Hautt, Gottfried.—Killed at Stone[s] River [Tennessee], December 31, 1862, while on duty with the Kentucky Artillery.
Hartmann, John.—Mustered out.
Hartmann, Friedrich.—Mustered out.
Homeyer, Albert.—Died in Cincinnati, March 10, 1864.
Holtz, Jakob.—Deserted, November 29, 1862.
Holthof, August.—Mustered out.
Höhn, Jakob.—Mustered out.
Haury, Karl.—Transferred to Camp Dennison, June 7, 1864.
Hauck, Wilhelm.—Transferred to Camp Dennison, June 7, 1864.
Hof, Georg.—Wounded at Chickamauga.—Mustered out.
Jetter, Jakob.—Wounded at Chickamauga.—Mustered out.
Kunzler, Peter, *Sergeant.*—May 27, 1861.—Mustered out.

Kämpf, Karl, *Sergeant.*—May 27, 1861.—Wounded at Chickamauga.—Mustered out.

Kämpfer, John, *Corporal.*—July 8, 1861.—*Sergeant,* April 17, 1863.—Wounded at Chickamauga.—Mustered out.

Krebs, Joseph, *Corporal.*—May 27, 1861.—Invalid Corps, September 1, 1863.

Kühn, Adam.—Deserted, May 1, 1862.

Kull, John.—A minor, discharged by order of the Secretary of War.

Kettenbach, Peter.—Transferred to Camp Dennison, June 7, 1864.

Kull, Christoph.—Discharged disabled, November 10, 1862.

Kühn, Johann.—Discharged disabled, August 14, 1861.

Knobel, Joseph.—Mustered out.

Kircher, Leonhard.—Mustered out.

Kirschbaum, Jakob.—Mustered out.

Kramer, Martin.—Mustered out.

Lauch, Friedrich, *Corporal.*—July 8, 1861.—Transferred to the U.S. Artillery, December 3, 1862.

Lenzer, Wilhelm.—Mustered out.

Leibold, John.—Died January 8, 1864.

Mangold, John, *First Sergeant.*—May 27, 1861.—*First Lieutenant* (added to the officer list).

Müller, Lorenz, *Sergeant.*—July 8, 1861.—Wounded at Chickamauga.—Mustered out.

Müller, Wilhelm.—Discharged disabled, November 22, 1861.

Müller, John.—Discharged disabled, February 18, 1862.

Müller, Friedrich.—Mustered out.

Mahler, Anton, *Corporal.*—May 27, 1861.—Discharged disabled, February 18, 1862.

Mandery, Jakob.—Mustered out.

Maier, Jakob.—Mustered out.

Meixner, Georg.—Mustered out.

Marrer, Leopold.—Died December 2, 1862.

Marrer, Philipp, *Corporal.*—July 25, 1862.—Mustered out.

Marthi, Emanuel.—Wounded at Chickamauga.—Mustered out.

Mathes, Jakob, *Corporal.*—May 1, 1862.—*Sergeant,* November 8, 1862.—*First Sergeant,* April 17, 1863.—Mustered out.

Mutter, Georg.—Wounded at Chickamauga.—Mustered out.

Neumann, Henry.—Transferred to the U.S. Artillery, December 3, 1862.
Nickel, John.—Discharged disabled, October 22, 1862.
Obenauer, Johann.—Mustered out.
Orth, Johann.—Transferred to Camp Dennison, June 7, 1864.
Preissel, Louis.—Transferred to the U.S. Artillery, December 3, 1862.
Rauber, Karl.—Mustered out.
Rentschler, Michael.—Mustered out.
Ruedy, Viktor.—Mustered out.
Roller, Georg.—Killed at Chickamauga, September 20, 1863.
Rehse, Theodor.—Discharged disabled, September 11, 1862.
Renner, Johann.—Discharged disabled, February 18, 1862.
Radley, Johann, *Corporal.*—February 24, 1863.—Mustered out.
Sommer, Jakob.—Mustered out.
Schenk, J. Georg.—Mustered out.
Schubert, Philipp.—Mustered out.
Seifert, Martin.—Mustered out.
Schanz, Peter.—Transferred to Camp Dennison, June 7, 1864.
Sommer, Georg.—Deserted, December 3, 1861.
Schenk, John.—Discharged disabled, December 2, 1862.
Scheuermann, John.—Wounded at Chickamauga.—Mustered out.
Schneider, Salomon.—Killed at Gauley Bridge, October 4, 1861.
Schneider, John.—Wounded at Chickamauga.—Died October 22, 1863.
Seyfried, Ferdinand.—Deserted, November 8, 1862.
Siegel, Julius, *Corporal.*—May 27, 1861.—Mustered out.
Schubert, Friedrich.—Wounded at Chickamauga.—Mustered out.
Schreyeck, Andreas.—Missing at Chickamauga, September 20, 1863.
Sauerwein, Wilhelm.—Discharged disabled, December 31, 1862.
Seyler, Martin.—Discharged disabled, November 22, 1861.
Sommerhalder, Alfons.—Mustered out.
Struppler, Jakob.—Discharged disabled, March 26, 1863.
Seidel, Johann.—Missing after August 14, 1863.
Thaler, David, *Corporal.*—April 17, 1863.—Mustered out.
Teichert, Hermann.—Missing after November 14, 1862.
Völzmann, August.—Wounded at Chickamauga.—Mustered out.

Voigt, Cyriak.—Wounded at Chickamauga.—Died October 13, 1863.

Wächter, Henry.—Mustered out.

Wittmaier, Leonhard.—Mustered out.

Wieser, Markus.—Discharged disabled, July 11, 1862.

Zellweger, Jakob.—Mustered out.

Ziegler, Konrad.—Discharged disabled, November 22, 1861.

Ziegenhart, Markus.—Wounded at Chickamauga.—Mustered out.

Poems

"Gustav Kämmerling Becomes a General" by Friedrich Bertsch.—"The Battle of Chickamauga" by C[arl] Türk.—"Death of a Warrior" by F. [or Joseph] Jacker.

["No translation of verse can get by without concoctions."[1] These poems have therefore been freely rendered into "semiprose" because the reproduction of all poetic features would distort the content, deviate thereby from accuracy and completeness of information, and thus swerve from the purpose of this book. Besides, though valuable as information, these poems do not merit attention as literature.]

Gustav Kämmerling Becomes a General[2]

by Friedrich Bertsch

Why does joy ring out in camp?
What fills the heart with delight?
And eases the pangs of homesickness?
  That which is rare has happened:
  Not fine words but proper payment
  To him who deserves it:
  Kämmerling is a general,
  Named by Abe Lincoln himself;
  And the Ninth Regiment
  Proudly calls him Leader.

Did you see him in the heat of battle?
His eyes blazing with the urge to fight,
His breast heaving like the very storm,

Bold and daring in the attack,
Protected by the free hand of God,
Then and there in those hours of war?
Kämmerling the general, I mean,
Chosen by Abe Lincoln himself;
And the Ninth Regiment
Proudly calls him Leader.

Simple, without pomp and bluster,
At work or in the field,
He was at home anywhere.
Faithfully he did his duty,
Even though life's road was rough,
Even though the path was thorny—
Kämmerling, general now,
Chosen by Abe Lincoln himself;
And the Ninth Regiment
Proudly calls him Leader.

Without a thought for honors and titles,
Impassioned for freedom and nothing else,
He took up his sword in those days,
Marched off with German comrades
To brave and daring deeds—
To destroy slavery—
Kämmerling the general,
Named by Abe Lincoln himself;
And the Ninth Regiment
Proudly calls him Leader.

But in the midst of celebration
Keep ever in your thoughts
Those days of bloody battle:
When we stood without flinching,
Though many brave ones fell,
At Chickamauga and Missionary Ridge:
And Kämmerling the general,
Abe Lincoln's very own choice,

Driving at the enemy and victorious
With his German regiment.

There on the hills of Chickamauga,
Thomas stood like a block of granite.
And his right-hand man
Leading the battle-tested ranks,
Crowding and splitting the enemy's,
On that much-contested ground:
Kämmerling, general now,
As Abe Lincoln himself would have it,
Whose German regiment
Always proudly called him Leader.

He strives for freedom, only freedom—
And freedom shall owe its salvation
To German valor known so well.
And so in the old German homeland,
And so in the new fatherland
Still stained by slavery—
Kämmerling the general,
Chosen by Abe Lincoln himself,
Leads his German regiment yet
Against the enemies of freedom.

The Battle of Chickamauga[3]

by C. Türk[4]

On the banks of the Chickamauga far away,
In Secessia, that hot and sunny land,
There the ferocious battle is joined.
There stand the host of freedom's warriors,
And, out front and foremost, cheerful and bold,
Our first German regiment.
Remember [McCook] the much-lamented hero
Who led them and was assassinated.

There the warriors are, with eyes that say:
"Today, let it be victory or death!"

The front is unshakable, those hearts courageous.
Bravery surges like the nearby creek.
Thoughts turn to home, that beloved place.
Tears wet the sunburned cheeks—
To embrace wife and child one more time,
To look again into mother's eyes—
And from trembling lips the words:
"Bless my loved ones, O Lord,
And guide them Yourself through life,
And lead them down a gentle path!"

Listen! the guns spit fire now,
A hail across mountain and valley,
Announcing death to our heroes.
"Brother, speak to my wife if I fall,
Tell my child, and give my regards to my loved ones all.
Kiss me yourself, Brother, one last time!"
So they speak, the heroes in the ranks.
A courageous pugnacity seizes them now:
No matter that they must dedicate themselves to Death.
Their hearts leap and they grow bolder.

Forward! even should our comrades yield,
Forward over blood and corpses,
Storm ahead, bayonets fixed. *Charge!*
Kämmerling leads the way to battle.
At his side, Harries, ever faithful.
The earth trembles beneath their feet.
"*Hurrah! Hurrah!*" bursts from a thousand throats.
And from their eyes, vengeance spurts and flashes.
Every man wants to measure up to holy battle.
Not a man avoids the lethal cannon.

Many a heart has broken,
Many a man has suffered the pain of death,
But with joy they give their lives for their country.
Yes, the warriors wade in blood,

But fearlessly, nobly, and in good cheer:
They look beyond to Freedom.
In behalf of Freedom they enlisted.
For Freedom they remain until the roar of victory.
They who died, died for Freedom—
Better death than slavery's vile disgrace!

On the banks of the Chickamauga far away,
There in the baking sands the heroes rest.
There where no monument preserves their names,
Hundreds fell to the arrow of Death.
So small, so small, now,
Our German regiment.
Cut down by cowardly hordes of slavers,
Many a young man bit the dust,
But he went to the grave under the dry leaves
Amid the chords of triumph.

Fellow Germans, honor the remains of heroes
Buried there in fallow meadows!
They sleep in the lap of the Earth now.
No marble proclaims their resting places.
Instead, over their crude beds, will grow
Green moss soon with the coming of spring.
In the heart they are inscribed,
In songs their names go on and on,
All those noble men who died in battle,
They who fought and died for Freedom.

Fellow Germans, honor the greatness of heroes!
Guard against the nakedness, fight the hunger,
That threaten the widows and orphans now.
Lay your mite upon the altar, the one
Your fellows in heroic battle
Built with the blood of the heart.
And the day the wounds of warriors ache no more,
Then let rise from a thousand throats:
"Fame and glory to the German regiment!"

Death of a Warrior[5]

by F. Jacker[6]

How nice and cozy the warm little room
When the storm rages through the night outside
And you sit happily beside your sweetheart
And she smiles tenderly at you.
You feel no pain, nothing hurts, now.
Happiness beams at you; you are loved,
You pass the time in lively pleasantries, and
Not a shred of cloud darkens your sky.

The father sits in his family circle
Looking joyfully at his wife
And blissfully at his little ones at play:
From his love springs his happiness.

* * *

But the soldier in the distant South
Enjoys not wife, or child, or sweetheart.
Gone is the warm and cozy little room.
Oh, how he would like to be home!
Instead he lies in winter's cold
In the open drafty tent
That God Himself has pitched,
Quietly waiting for the dawn;
And there is no sleep to refresh his limbs.
The air is cold, the ground so hard.
Again and again his blanched lips whisper,
"Oh, I wish I were home!"
He smiles, dreaming of loved ones,
Despite rain, cold, and the snowstorm's gusts,
And a sweet solace remains with him:
Perhaps there will be a reunion *here.*
Suddenly the muffled, funereal roll of the drum
Interrupts the dreams.
He leaps to his feet, he dare not dawdle,

It is the call to a bloody clash of arms.
Now, at dawn's first glow,
Cannon roar their heavy roar.
Their mouths spit lightning with a bang.
Death mows with a brazen scythe.
Muskets rattle and crackle,
Accompanying the cannonade.
Rockets fly, glaring, hissing,
Laying waste everywhere.
Louder and louder the chaos of battle,
Wilder and wilder the shouting and screaming.
Earth and sky, as if in mourning,
Wrap themselves tightly in blankets of cloud.
The noblest creation on Earth,
Man, heinous in his rage,
Must here become a wild beast,
Thirsty for nothing but the enemy's blood.
So the battle is joined in blood,
Until the sun sinks slowly,
And the moon, in glowing silver of splendid beauty,
Mounts the vault,
Leisurely rising, looking down
On the battlefield grown quiet.
The tumult of struggle has stilled
To bloody charnel house, desolate.

* * *

But listen!—a whimper, soft, painful,
Far away, at dark forest's edge,
A wail, so strange—
There it is, beside that oak!
A warrior, pale and bloody,
Who fought so bravely but hours ago,
Hewing the task courageously,
Until hit by the bullet of death.
No loving wife smiles at that poor devil
Nor with a gentle hand
Cools and soothes the bloody wound.

He lies alone in a foreign place,
Alone in the last battle,
(The dead in great numbers all around)
Alone in the last, the death, struggle,
His pain the pain of Hell.
So the warrior lies, sorely wounded,
Eyes turned gently to heaven—
There he can pin hope,
Surely *there* he can expect reunion.
The cooling dew settles
Soothing the pain of his wound—
He breathes easier again.
Morning comes. His heart stops.
A large wooden cross
Fashioned by faithful comrades
Shows you where he suffered and found eternal rest.

* * *

At home, in a little cottage,
Wife and child still wait and hope.
He who left their loving presence
Now sleeps far away, so alone.
She sits crying bitter tears.
The child rests quietly in her lap.
The husband will never come back:
The poor little one is—*fatherless!*

English Words and Phrases

This list, of English used spontaneously in the German text, does not include the English of deliberate quotation. Specialized English, quoted because it defied translation into German, is also not entered here: *Copperhead,* for instance.

acting commissary
acting quartermaster
blanket
bloody Dutch
bounty
boys in blue (Union soldiers)
broiled steaks
crackers (food; hardtack)
crack regiment
damned Dutch
dog tents
dress parade
dugouts (boats)
Dutch devils
Dutchmen
gap (in mountains)
graybacks (Confederate money)
greenbacks (Union money)
guerrillas
home guards
light battalion
mud roads
paymaster
peaches (fruit)
shelter tents
Southern brothers
speeches
tramp (a vagrant)
unconditional surrender
would-be

Notes

Introduction

1. For this episode in the senate, see Cox, "War Preparations," 84–86.
2. Lonn, *Foreigners,* 116–45. *New York Times,* 22 April 1861.
3. Margedant, "Address," 353–54.
4. Hannaford, *The Story of a Regiment,* 46, 48.
5. Keil, *Thirty-Fifth Ohio,* 245.
6. Ibid.
7. Margedant, "Address," 353. See also Reid, *Ohio in the War* 1:892.
8. Keil, *Thirty-Fifth Ohio,* 245.
9. Shaw, *Tenth Indiana,* 282.
10. Gustav Tafel is often called the author, because his name and not Grebner's appears on the title page, but Tafel wrote the Foreword only. See the Editorial Committee's Preface infra.
11. Leser, "Deutsche Dichtkunst in den Vereinigten Staaten," 389. Zimmermann, *Deutsch in Amerika,* 1 (Anhang): 12.
12. Marvine Howe, "New York's Foreign-Language Press," *New York Times,* 15 Sept. 1985, sec. 1. See also Arndt and Olsen, *German-American Newspapers.*
13. On this large and vital literature, see *passim* Heinrici, *Das Buch der Deutschen in Amerika;* Zimmermann, *Deutsch in Amerika;* Neef, *Vom Lande des Sternenbanners.* For a recent discussion in English, see Wandel, *German Dimension,* 122–25.
14. This sketch of Grebner's life and work is based on Fick, "Constantin

Grebner." The need for teachers of German in Cincinnati resulted from Cincinnati's law of March 9, 1840, which "made the teaching of German [in the primary schools] upon proper request compulsory"; and German was introduced in the secondary schools in 1853–1854. Greve, *Centennial History* 1:784–85. For examples of Grebner's anthologies, see Grebner, *Die Deutschen,* and Wieck and Grebner, *Höheres viertes Lesebuch.* Grebner's essays include "Die Deutsche Sprache." Zimmermann, *Deutsch in Amerika,* and Neef, *Vom Lande des Sternenbanners,* have examples of his poetry.

15. Infra, 141.

16. Kaufmann, *Die Deutschen im amerikanischen Bürgerkriege,* 505. Though captains supplied much information, the point of view is that of an enlisted man.

17. On the "above average" study, see Robertson, "Military Aspects," 139. On the quality of style, completeness and interest, see Ryan, *Civil War Literature of Ohio,* 415.

18. Infra, 187.

19. Faust, *German Element* 1:522–27.

20. Lonn, *Foreigners,* 666–72.

21. Chukovsky, *Art of Translation,* 6, 89.

22. That is, Grebner's statistics have been compared with those of these authorities: Amann, *Personnel of the Civil War;* Gould, *Investigations in Statistics;* Livermore, *Numbers and Losses;* Phisterer, *Statistical Record.*

23. For full citations of all three, see the Bibliography infra.

Preface

1. This Preface includes initial and terminal remarks by the committee, at the beginning and end of *"Die Neuner,"* v–vi, 291.

Foreword

1. Tafel was first a sergeant, then a lieutenant of The Ninth; and later, colonel of the 106th Ohio. These remarks of his, on the start of The Ninth, appear as the "Einleitung," 11–17, of the original.

2. Tafel, founder and head of the Cincinnati Turners, here expresses the viewpoint of German-Americans generally and especially their Turner societies, that slavery was the evil to be crushed by the Civil War. See Wittke, *Refugees,* 191, 195. Still, German-Americans understood that more than slavery was at issue. See the discussion in Chapter 2, infra, 32–34.

3. And mobilization was eager and rapid. Seeing Ohio's special need to defend itself because of location, Governor William Dennison seconded Lincoln's call for volunteers. "Great activity prevails among all the military companies of the city [such as the Zouaves, Rovers, and Lafayette Guards]. In every armory last evening the men were drilling with full ranks, and crowds of citizens were in

attendance, many of whom were seeking admission into the various companies." *Cincinnati Daily Commercial,* 16 April 1861.

4. Turner Hall, meeting place of the Turner Society or *Turnverein* (a gymnastic union or an athletic club), was a spacious building of brick, painted dark red. Writers' Program, *Cincinnati,* 218–19. Nothing better represented Germans in America than the Turners. In Cincinnati they flourished amid the large and distinctive community of Germans settled "over the Rhine," north and east of the Miami Canal. The quarter looked like one transplanted from Europe: short, narrow streets; well-swept sidewalks; neat, brick houses with whitewashed steps; and mercantile signs in German. Harlow, *Serene Cincinnatians,* 183. Ever since the Turners originated in resistance to Napoleon in Prussia in 1811, they espoused order, discipline, comradeship, and physical fitness, as well as social reform, humanitarian ideals, and honesty in government. Always semimilitary and patriotic, they had been associated with insurgent armies in 1848. In a word, when The Ninth marched in its muster-parade, it manifested the Turner and German-American spirit *incarnate.* Wittke, "Ninth Ohio," 402–408, and *Refugees,* 147–56.

5. He was "Gallant Bob," the "frank, open, laughing" member of Ohio's "Fighting McCooks." Howe, *Historical Collections* 1:767. For sketches of him and them, see Chapter 1 infra, 11–13, 27–30. See also Warner, *Generals in Blue,* 297.

6. Stallo immigrated to Cincinnati in 1839. A notable scholar and teacher, later a judge and an ambassador, he seems to have been a salient influence on McCook. See Faust, *German Element* 2:658–60.

7. This speech is in English in the original.

8. "Signed: J. C. Baum, M. Göpper, G. Tafel, L. Wielert, L. Hoffmann, F. Rathgeber, L. Eckart, H. Dilg, J. Fetzer, Ch. Nuss, W. Raine, F. Werner, H. Wolff, H. Ficke, H. Quentin, P. Theobald, M. Meyer, A. Biermann, L. Schreiber, G. Becker." In the original this list occurs in the text.

9. The *Cincinnati Daily Commercial,* of 18 April 1861, reported the meeting under this headline: "Immense Meeting Last Night at Turner Hall — Measures Inaugurated to Raise a German Regiment," and added: "The large Hall was crowded to the utmost at an early hour." Many men enlisted. "The German heart is effectually fired."

10. "J. Glaser, G. F. Kestner, F. Hassaureck, St. Molitor, G. Klotter, K. Kuhlenkamp, V. Eichenlaub, F. Meyer, F. Pfisterer, Dr. Emmert, J. C. Baum, H. Klöpfer, G. F. Eichenlaug, M. Eckart, M. Göpper, D. H. Niemeier, C. Kistner, L. Ballauf, C. Geist, A. Aupperle." In the original this list occurs in the text.

11. In a "spirited address" he "pledged his time and his means to the Cause." *Cincinnati Daily Commercial,* 18 April 1861.

12. The captains were "Karl Joseph, Ferdinand Müller, Henry Broderson, Friedrich Schröder, Ferdinand Benz, Gustav Kämmerling, Gustav Richter, Jakob Gluckowsky, John Gansen, [and] Georg Sommer." In the original this list occurs in the text.

13. "Margedant engaged Edward Scheurer as a drummer boy and visited the shops of the city [Hamilton], where he recruited a company of fifty men . . . which

marched from the Turner's Hall [in Hamilton] . . . and left for Cincinnati, and joined the Ninth Ohio. . . ." Cone, *Biographical and Historical Sketches,* 330.

14. Nine companies and "a surplus to make one or two more," 950 men in all, marched "with three bands of music" and "created an immense deal of enthusiasm." Shouts from each company brought vociferous shouts from citizens on the sidewalk. *Cincinnati Daily Commercial,* 20 April 1861. This "magnificent soldierly body of men" wore white Turner uniforms. Howe, *Historical Collections* 1:767.

1 Our Leaders and Comrades-in-Arms

1. Chapter 9, pp. 174–200 of *"Die Neuner."*

2. The younger, also known for martial exploits, was that of John McCook (1806–1865) of Steubenville. *Dictionary of American Biography,* s.vv. "McCook, Alexander McDowell," "McCook, Henry Christopher," and "McCook, John James."

3. "The Germans at once thought of him as the Colonel of their first regiment. He knew nothing of military matters, but they had plenty of experienced officers among their number who could drill them. What they wanted in their Colonel was a man in whom they could trust, and whose standing and character with the authorities would secure them from the annoyances which, as citizens of foreign birth, and mostly ignorant of the English language, they feared they would otherwise encounter. This they thought Robert L. McCook peculiarly qualified to do; and in accordance with their wishes and his own earnest desire to enter the service as soon as possible, he was commissioned Colonel of the regiment. . . ." Reid, *Ohio in the War* 1:876. "McCook was the volunteer's ideal of a general. He had a way to appear as an equal among equals; and hide the appearance of authority. It was difficult to tell him from a private soldier in his dress; for he wore no insignia of office." Indeed, he was once taken for "some infernal old secesh," a Confederate civilian who had wandered into camp. Keil, *Thirty-Fifth Ohio,* 87–88.

4. They were "McCook's Dutchmen" who used "only German language and German tactics." Bishop, "Van Derveer's Brigade," 3. At Camp Harrison he was "busily employed" at organizing them but "ill provided with office furniture, his seat being the sill of his wooden shantee, and his knee serving for his desk." *Cincinnati Daily Commercial,* 26 April 1861.

5. He "devoted himself to their comfort, saw to their supplies, the condition of their camp, and the wants of their sick. The *morale* of the regiment was thus kept up. . . ." Reid, *Ohio in the War* 1:876.

6. The remains arrived on "the mail boat at noon," August 9, 1862. "Flags throughout the city were at half-mast, and there were other demonstrations of mourning." *New York Times,* 11 August 1862.

7. See Stewart, "A Bachelor General." Warner, *Generals in Blue,* 565–66.

8. The revolutionaries lost both battles. Survivors escaped to Switzerland and France. Friedrich Karl Hecker (1811–1881) led the rebellion in Baden, fled to

Switzerland and the United States, and fought in the Civil War. *Dictionary of American Biography,* s.v. "Hecker, Friedrich Karl Franz."

9. That is, the International Workingmen's Association or First International. In point of fact, however, the IWA did not exist yet. Wilczynski, *Dictionary,* 189. Willich must have been involved with the trade unions and the socialists and communists around Marx and Engels in London, who formed the IWA in 1864.

10. Like many Forty-Eighters, he was an experienced soldier who believed in the Union's cause and therefore signed up at once. See Wittke, *Refugees,* 221, 224, and 222–42 passim.

11. Grebner also says here that "the promotion to general inspired our comrade, Lieutenant Friedrich Bertsch, to a poem." Which see infra, 243–45.

12. In the original this quotation is in English.

13. In the original this quotation is in English.

14. Nevins (*War for the Union* 3:185–86) thinks as highly of Rosecrans, though not for the same reasons. Still, to Nevins (3:197–99), Rosecrans was at fault and grievously wrong in the battles of Chattanooga. Dislike for Rosecrans in his time, mentioned by Grebner below, has persisted into ours: a "third-rate" general who had "most of McClellan's faults without his ability" and who approached "a state of imbecility." Morison and Commager, *Growth of the American Republic* 1:723–24. Yet Rosecrans "might have become" the North's "greatest and most famous commander," being "abler than Joseph Hooker or George G. Meade." Lamers, *Edge of Glory,* 3. For the divided opinion of Rosecrans after Chattanooga, see ibid., 400–405. Rosecrans's "campaign of maneuver" before Chattanooga, "as brilliant as any in American military annals," ended in "a crushing defeat" for Rosecrans, ruining his military career. Warner, *Generals in Blue,* 411.

15. Relieved of command of the Army of the Cumberland, he assumed it of the Department of the Missouri in 1863. Relieved again in 1864, he awaited orders in Cincinnati until he resigned on March 28th, 1867. *Dictionary of American Biography,* s.v. "Rosecrans, William Starke." Warner, ibid.

16. Not to be confused with other "iron brigades," especially the best-known one, of Wisconsin and Indiana troops. See Nolan, *The Iron Brigade.*

17. *Official Records,* Ser. 1, Vol. 30, Pt. 1, 402. Brannan here (pp. 400–405) discusses his units' parts in the Battle of Chickamauga, but does not use the term "Iron Brigade."

18. See Bishop, *Story of a Regiment.*

19. "Attached to each other by the strongest friendship, perfect harmony of feeling existed between them, and each was always watchful for the honor of the other." Reid, *Ohio in the War* 2:73.

20. See Keil, *Thirty-Fifth Ohio.*

21. The 87th was "regarded as a somewhat soft regiment" because, not used to hard marches, it grew footsore and weary on the pursuit of Bragg out of Louisville in September, 1862, "and many a joke passed at its expense." The 87th clustered under walnut trees in bluegrass pastures, hulled and cracked nuts, and were called the "Walnut Crackers." Ibid., 245–46.

22. The elements of the caption repeated in the text of the original have been eliminated in the translation.

23. This sentence is probably a hyperbole to make the point; but the McCooks did serve many generals, in many places, and with merit.

24. Grebner quotes the lines in English. Horatius (sixth century B.C.), legendary Roman hero, defended a bridge across the Tiber, perhaps by himself, perhaps with two comrades, against the entire Etruscan army—described in Macaulay's poem in *The Lays of Ancient Rome* (1842), from which these lines are taken.

25. In the original the quotation is in English.

2 North against South

1. Anhang, "Der Krieg," pp. 261–72 of *"Die Neuner."*

2. This phrase does not occur, nor this idea exactly, in Pastorius's best-known document, "Protest against Negro Slavery" (1688), but the phrase and the idea agree with the "Protest" and could occur elsewhere in Pastorius's voluminous and largely unpublished writings. See Learned, *Pastorius,* 260–62.

3. In point of fact, the Virginia convention voted secession on April 17 and scheduled a referendum on it for May 23. Long, *Civil War Day by Day,* 60.

4. After May of 1861, and through the *Trent* affair of December-January, 1861–1862, the Lincoln administration made clear that if Great Britain (and any lesser power *a fortiori*) "became the active friend of the rebellion, she must become the enemy of the United States," and that the United States would view relations in London between rebel commissioners and the British government "as hostile," requiring "some corresponding action accordingly." Nicolay and Hay, *Lincoln* 4:276–77. See also 5:21–41. But the diplomatic record fails to show a December 1 announcement of the sort mentioned by Grebner. Cf. Basler, *Collected Works of Lincoln* 5:33–35.

5. In point of fact, the proclamation only "opened the door to the end of slavery in the United States." Long, *Civil War Day by Day,* 306. True and complete abolition, at least according to law, would not occur until the war was over.

6. Grant to J. C. Pemberton, commander of Confederate forces at Vicksburg, 3 July 1863, *Papers of Grant* 8:455. "Unconditional surrender," however, is usually associated with Grant's terms at Fort Donelson: "No terms except an unconditional and complete surrender can be accepted." Grant to Simon B. Buckner, commander of Confederate forces at Donelson, 16 Feb. 1862, ibid., 4:218.

7. To Henry W. Halleck, 11 May 1864, ibid., 10:422.

8. Hood, whose forces were not 40,000 but fewer than 30,000, did suffer heavy losses, especially by comparison with Thomas's; and Hood's army was driven from the field and rendered ineffective after "a complete and disasterous failure." But Grebner is wrong to say that Hood's forces were "annihilated" (*total vernichtet*). See McMurry, *John Bell Hood,* 179–80. See also Long, *Civil War Day by Day,* 611.

9. "From the beginning of the campaign, Grant had been explicit . . . [that] he would shatter Lee's army in battle if he could. . . ." Catton, *Grant Takes Command,* 274.

10. Fires of diverse origin burned in Charleston, "a city of ashes," during and after its evacuation by Hardee; but he seems not to have put the city to the torch. Burton, *Siege of Charleston,* 317–25.

11. Ewell, in command of Richmond's defenses and under orders to destroy stores, had marked warehouses, bridges, and ammunition to that end; but a mob carried out much of the destruction that devastated the city the night of April 2. Stern, *End to Valor,* 177–78.

12. To be precise, Colonel John S. Ford "led the main Southern drive" in this "skirmish known as Palmito Ranch." Long, *Civil War Day by Day,* 688.

13. This quotation, source unknown, does not correspond to the address in Basler, *Collected Works of Lincoln* 8:333. The ellipses are Grebner's.

14. These sentiments occur, but not exactly in these words, in the House Divided speech of August 21, 1858; in the First Inaugural; and in the Annual Message to Congress on December 1, 1862. See Basler, *Lincoln Speeches and Writings,* 372, 586, 677.

15. The end of Reconstruction is usually put at 1877. See, for example, Randall and Donald, *Civil War and Reconstruction,* 535, 700–701.

3 April 17 to June 16, 1861

1. Chapter 1, pp. 18–34 of *"Die Neuner."*

2. Cincinnati's population was over 250,000 in 1860 and two-thirds German, with the Irish next in number, and British elements "nine-tenths of the residue." Cist, *Sketches and Statistics,* 164–65. "The type of organization . . . most prevalent and . . . [with] the deepest influence on the composition of the [Union] army was that based on racial groups," the foreign-born who enthusiastically formed "companies, regiments, and even divisions among their fellow countrymen": "brigades of Irish and divisions of Germans" and units of many other nationalities. Lonn, *Foreigners,* 92–93. See also 94–145 and passim. Later "our colored regiments" assembled and went to war: the Negro units, later called Black. See Cornish, *The Sable Arm,* vii–xii and passim. McPherson, *The Negro's Civil War,* 161–239. Quarles, *The Negro in the Civil War,* passim.

3. The regiment's companies were originally numbered from one to ten. Later they were designated in the more typical fashion, by letters. Since Grebner's initial company reference is to Company A, subsequent references have been regularized by changing numbers to letters; e.g., "first company" to "Company A."

4. Such trouble, or at least suspicion of it, could be expected in Cincinnati, "the Copperhead center of the Northwest," where "bombs made here were used to blow up Federal gunboats on the river, and arms and munitions were shipped from here to Indiana Copperheads trying to foment revolution farther west." Writers' Program, *Ohio Guide,* 200. Klement, *Copperheads in the Middle West,* a later and more authoritative source, does not single out Cincinnati or any city as so notably Copperhead.

5. "This is the list of those elected: *Headquarters:* Colonel Robert L. McCook, Lieutenant-Colonel Karl Sondershoff, Major Frank Link, Regimental Physician

Charles Krause, Assistant Regimental Physician Rudolph Wirth, Adjutant August Willich, Quartermaster Joseph Gräff; *Company A:* Captain Karl Joseph, First Lieutenant Louis Heuser, Second Lieutenant Ferdinand Müller; *Company B:* Captain Wilhelm C. Margedant, First Lieutenant Gerhard Krug, Second Lieutenant Jakob Müller; *Company C:* Captain Henry Broderson, First Lieutenant Georg H. Harries, Second Lieutenant Joseph Haider; *Company D:* Captain Fritz Schröder, First Lieutenant Ernst Rubenow, Second Lieutenant Charles Lauenstein; *Company E:* Captain Louis C. Frintz, First Lieutenant Gustav Nepper, Second Lieutenant Martin Brunner; *Company F:* Captain Gustav Kämmerling, First Lieutenant Bartholomäus Benz, Second Lieutenant Charles Munn; *Company G:* Captain Theodor Lammers, First Lieutenant Karl Jahn, Second Lieutenant Henry Hunger; *Company H:* Captain Frank Coquelin, First Lieutenant Moritz Pohlmann, Second Lieutenant Adolf Kühn; *Company I:* Captain John Gansen, First Lieutenant Nathan Levy, Second Lieutenant Jakob Gluchowsky; *Company J* [or, probably, K, as J was usually avoided, to prevent the likely confusion, in German, between I and J]: Captain Georg Sommer, First Lieutenant Lukas Schwank, Second Lieutenant Theodor Haffner." In the original the list occurs in the text. According to the state constitution and by the authority granted in the federal constitution (probably under the tenth amendment), all officers in the state militia, from subaltern to major-general, "shall be elected by the persons subject to military duty in their respective districts" and the governor "shall appoint the Adjutant-General, Quartermaster-General and such other staff officers as may be provided for by State law." Commanders of regiments and battalions were to appoint their staffs; and captains, their noncommissioned officers and musicians. *Cincinnati Enquirer,* 24 May 1861.

6. Cincinnati's Irish 10th Ohio, for example, called itself the "Bloody Tinth." Cox, "War Preparations," 98. Other units mobilized, by wards, as Home Guards. *Cincinnati Enquirer,* 15–30 April 1861.

7. "Several thousand persons" had also watched The Ninth take shape in front of Turner Hall earlier, for a long and circuitous march through Cincinnati to the station. *Cincinnati Enquirer,* 25 April 1861. "The war was yet in its gala period of cheers, music, exciting new scenes, and exalted patriotism. . . ." Nevins, *War for the Union* 1:178. Lacking uniforms, The Ninth wore their white Turner outfits with the short, round, linen jacket. McCook, in his civilian clothes and stovepipe hat, looked military in but one respect: the sword buckled to his side. Greve, *Centennial History* 1:820. Troops were to "load and unload [a train] by platoons, one to a car. A train can load in ten minutes." Carrington, *Ohio Militia,* 25.

8. Indeed, The Ninth was "in high glee" at Camp Harrison. "The Band, prior to dress parade, were playing waltzes and polkas, while the men, with an occasional frow [*sic*] or sweetheart, whirled around in complete Teutonic abandon to the musical inspiration. When it is remembered that most of these recruits slept upon the sward the night before, with no covering but an occasional blanket, their animated feelings under depressing influences, can be appreciated." *Cincinnati Daily Commercial,* 26 April 1861.

9. On May 3, after a night awash in the rain, "wet, soggy, wheezy, coughing,

half-sick soldiers" looked "like sick roosters." Some, wrapped in blankets, wandered about in the mud, while others plugged holes in their "cantonments," and all suffered short rations and the lack of straw. Often at night it was perforce three men to a blanket. *Cincinnati Daily Commercial,* 4 May 1861. "The soldiers constructed the frame shacks known as Camp Harrison," after they "were compelled to lie down and sleep in the water and mud of the drill ground, which had been rented by the state for $20 an acre." The "inadequate supplies, poor equipment, and the failure to provide proper shelter, blankets, shoes, and dry straw" provoked "vigorous criticism" and "ugly charges of corruption and graft." Wittke, "Ninth Ohio," 413.

10. Turner Hall, The German Republic, Workers Hall, and Music (specifically Singers) Hall, respectively.

11. Another Cincinnati newspaper called the reports of shortages "a canard" caused by thoughtless letters to "several daily papers" and "without foundation in fact." Indeed, there are "more than enough [provisions] to supply the most exorbitant demand of the volunteers." *Cincinnati Enquirer,* 7 May 1861. Instead the *Enquirer* (25 May 1861) wondered about the cost to the government of Camp Dennison's 550 acres leased for three years at $60 an acre, and the $1,200 paid every month to the supplier of wood and water. Better, the *Enquirer* exclaimed, that the army be maintained on enemy soil!

12. An allusion to Schiller's *William Tell,* act 4, sc. 3: "The milk of human kindness thou hast turn'd / to rankling poison in my breast."

13. Literally "shooting sticks" or "cows' feet": probably the "brown-barreled muskets, altered from flint to percussion locks," called by the men "Old Brown Bess"—pieces so bad that some troops refused to accept them until threatened with expulsion for mutiny. Bates, "Ohio's Preparations," 132. Similarly the 10th Indiana, in the late summer of 1861, got "old muskets" with "neither 'lock[,] stock or barrel' and about the only thing dangerous about them was the 'bayonet,' which some fool was liable to use accidentally or otherwise." Shaw, *Tenth Regiment,* 53.

14. Five trains a day ran between here and Cincinnati, bringing visitors. *Cincinnati Enquirer,* 27 April 1861.

15. McClellan chose the site as "healthy and well watered" and Rosecrans laid it out as a camp. *Cincinnati Daily Commercial,* 29 April 1861. When Jacob Cox, a new brigadier-general of Ohio volunteers, arrived on April 29, he found fields of wheat and corn. Rosecrans, then a captain of engineers, came with lumber and surveying equipment. Cox made headquarters of "a little brick school-house," slept between the pupils' desks and the teacher's pulpit, and next day "resumed the duty of organizing and instructing the camp." Rains turned the fields to mud. For the time being, shelter remained inadequate at best, faulty camp-kitchens ruined many a meal, and measles struck down half the men. Cox, "War Preparations," 94–96. Indeed, since many of the men had never had the childhood diseases, these were rife. The camp hospital, a big barn, was filled with men with measles. Greve, *Centennial History* 1:821. In time, however, the troops at the camp appreciated "the beautiful Little Miami River." Soon, good weather dried the mud, the camp was

cheerful, and discipline sufficed between the rigidity of the regular army and the laxness of citizen soldiers. Lacking other sources of meat, notably chickens, the troops were "powerful upon the pig." *Cincinnati Enquirer,* 25 May 1861.

16. Dennison's request was a response to the Secretary of War's request for longer enlistments, of three years or the duration, to provide continuity and prevent lapses in Northern strength that might have left the Union defenseless in the middle of a war. Shannon, *Organization and Administration of the Union Army* 1:36.

17. Anderson "read the oath in English, and Judge [Johann B.] Stallo repeated it in German." Wittke, "Ninth Ohio," 414. Hats were removed, right hands help up, and the men solemnly swore to support the Constitution, defend the country against all enemies, obey orders, and perform all duties strictly and promptly. Shaw, *Tenth Indiana,* 54. The Ninth "was the first three years' organization from the State of Ohio." Reid, *Ohio in the War* 2:72. "Springfields" probably refers to the rifle-musket, M1861, one of the better infantry arms, widely used by Union forces. See Coggins, *Arms and Equipment,* 32. Or, perhaps, the "old '69–100 caliber Springfield," a "smooth bore altered to a rifle." Keil, *Thirty-Fifth Ohio,* 109.

18. In the original this speech is in English.

19. The work referred to is the Ohio Roster Commission's *Official Roster.* See Bibliography infra.

20. Probably here as in the 46th New York (also entirely German), "there was the savor of German cooking in their mess, the sound of German songs in their camp; all the commands were given in German at drill, and the various calls, such as reveille and tattoo, were the same as those used in the German army." Porter, "Letter to Editors," 8. No record was left of what the "Prussian method of training," the *preussische Exerzitium,* meant exactly. It seems to have differed from the American more in language than drill or tactics. For the German units were integrated smoothly enough into the Union army, where their actions were not idiosyncratic or peculiar as long as English-language commands had been understood.

21. The "incumbents" described in this sentence were probably those three-month officers not reelected for three years. Cf. the list of three-month officers supra with this one of three-year officers: "*Headquarters:* Colonel Robert L. McCook, Lieutenant-Colonel Karl Sondershoff, Major August Willich, Regimental Physician Charles C. Boyle, Assistant Physician Adolph Wirth, Adjutant Georg H. Harries, Quartermaster Joseph Gräff; *Company A:* Captain Karl Joseph, First Lieutenant Louis Heuser, Second Lieutenant Karl Gentsch; *Company B:* Captain Ferdinand Müller, First Lieutenant Jakob Müller, Second Lieutenant Friedrich Bertsch; *Company C:* Captain Henry Broderson, First Lieutenant Georg H. Harries, Second Lieutenant Joseph Haider; *Company D:* Captain Fritz Schröder, First Lieutenant Ernst Rubenow, Second Lieutenant Daniel Wagner; *Company E:* Captain Bartholomäus Benz, First Lieutenant Gustav Nepper, Second Lieutenant Martin Bruner; *Company F:* Captain Gustav Kämmerling, First Lieutenant Herman Lütkehaus, Second Lieutenant John Baumgartner; *Company G:* Captain Gustav Richter, First Lieutenant Karl Jahn, Second Lieutenant Theodor Lammers; *Company H:* Captain Jakob Gluchowsky, First Lieutenant Moritz Pohlmann, Second Lieutenant Adolph Kühn;

Company I: Captain John Gansen, First Lieutenant Joseph Gräff, Second Lieutenant Wilhelm Heubig; *Company K* [J being skipped to avoid confusion with I]: Captain Georg Sommer, First Lieutenant Theodor Haffner, Second Lieutenant Louis Fricke." In the original this list is in the text.

22. The band played "Hail Columbia" and "The Star-Spangled Banner" and Willich called for the "Marseillaise." Lonn, *Foreigners,* 357.

23. Krause, about 30, single, a native of Germany and "a prominent physician," died of poison, an extract of belladonna, "administered by his own hand" the night of May 18, 1861, "while laboring under insanity," according to the jury of inquest. "Those who knew him well, say he had manifested symptoms of insanity for some time." *Cincinnati Daily Commercial,* 22 May 1861. The *Commercial* agreed on May 6 that he would have been a good physician for The Ninth.

24. The Ninth was at full strength and part of the 1st Brigade, "uniformed and equipped with ambulances, tents, knapsacks, haversacks, ammunition, etc." And, "peculiar" tactics on the Prussian model notwithstanding, The Ninth was "the best drilled regiment in the camp." *Cincinnati Enquirer,* 9 June 1861.

25. The Lincoln administration and especially Governor Dennison of Ohio wanted to save it for the Union, as it was Union in sympathy and would shield Ohio and Pennsylvania. Moreover, Confederate forces in West Virginia had cut the railroad between Washington and the West; the threat to the Union was clear and present. Thus, Dennison dispatched McClellan and Ohio troops, including The Ninth. See Cox, "McClellan in West Virginia," 126–27.

4 June 16 to November 26, 1861

1. Chapter 2, pp. 35–62 of *"Die Neuner."*

2. The Ninth was "well drilled, perfectly equipped, and in the best of spirits." Reid, *Ohio in the War* 1:876.

3. "Morgenrot," from Wilhelm Hauff's "Reiters Morgengesang" (Cavalryman's Matitutinal Hymn) in Hauff's *Kriegs- und Volkslieder* (Martial and Popular Songs) of 1824.

4. If this flag had four stars, it must have been special, perhaps one created ad hoc. Neither official Confederate flag had but four stars. See Eggenberger, *Flags,* 138, 142.

5. McClellan was then commander of Ohio's forces, having not yet been promoted to a department head and major-general of regulars. Leaders of Virginia's western counties, loyal to the Union, had appealed for help should the rest of Virginia secede. It seceded and Ohio's Governor Dennison ordered McClellan into western Virginia. Nevins, *War for the Union* 1:142, 152.

6. The "troops already there" were Union regiments organized in West Virginia, and others from Indiana and Ohio, under Brigadier-General Thomas A. Morris of Indiana, the initial commander of Union troops in West Virginia. The Ninth arrived among other reinforcements, and McClellan took over from Morris. Cox, "McClellan in West Virginia," 126–27, 130.

7. Perhaps Cyrus O. Loomis's First Michigan Artillery. Ibid., 130.

8. For the life and character of Letcher, see Boney, *John Letcher.* Letcher's exhortation, despite the allusion to the Declaration of Independence, failed. Western Virginia continued to adhere to the Union, as it had since the bombardment of Fort Sumter. In 1863 it became West Virginia, a Union state. For Letcher's position on West Virginia, see ibid., 178.

9. And their commander, McCook, "rose rapidly in the confidence first of McClellan and then of Rosecrans." Reid, *Ohio in the War* 1:877.

10. This action was part of the continuing Federal campaign in western Virginia to save that part (and perhaps all) of Virginia for the Union. The action was also preparation for the imminent Battle of Rich Mountain. The phrase, "in the middle of a war," did not exaggerate: Union advances against Confederates now were "the first real field action of the war." Nevins, *War for the Union* 1:142.

11. This was the Union victory in the Battle of Rich Mountain, July 11, 1861.

12. While Rosecrans engaged Pegram at Rich Mountain, Brigadier-General Thomas A. Morris's Federals attacked the main Confederate force under Garnett at Laurel Hill, and the Confederates retreated from there and the Cheat River Valley, toward Staunton, Virginia, opening the way for McClellan to occupy Beverly and consolidate Union gains, leaving the Confederates beaten and in disarray. See Cox, "McClellan in West Virginia," 133–35. Lamers, *Edge of Glory,* 33–35. Nevins, *War for the Union* 1:225.

13. Grebner seems confused about *countersign* and *parole.* Both were watchwords. The parole was communicated by officers of the guard and was usually a personal name, typically that of a distinguished officer. The countersign, conversely, went to all the guard and was a place name, such as that of a battlefield. *Password,* more general than *parole* or *countersign* and including them both, has usually meant any identifying answer to a sentry's challenge. See Boatner, *Dictionary,* 619–20. Cf. Scott, *Military Dictionary,* 202, 453. Gaynor, *New Military Dictionary,* 69, 190.

14. In point of fact, Scott did not resign until October 31, 1861, and McClellan replaced him then. Here McClellan is being called to the Army of the Potomac, to replace General Irvin McDowell, commander in the Union defeat at Bull Run, July 21, 1861. The West Virginia campaign occasioned "McClellan's promotion to the command of the Potomac army," because McClellan in West Virginia had become "the hero of the moment" and "the young Napoleon." Cox, "McClellan in West Virginia," 135.

15. This copy of the order is substantially the same as that in *Official Records* (Ser. 1, Vol. 2, 236–37), the most significant difference being that *OR* has the date as July 16, 1861.

16. In the only major battle of the war in Missouri, Brigadier-General Sigel and his German-American troops, under Brigadier-General Nathaniel Lyon, were badly beaten at Wilson's Creek on August 10, 1861. Long, *Civil War Day by Day,* 107. Their being German probably made the news doubly bad for The Ninth.

17. The Ninth, many members of which were Forty-Eighters, seems to have represented the important liberal element, the "intellectual radicals," of the Forty-

Eighters in religion: free-thinking, materialist, and rationalist. See Wittke, *Refugees,* 122. Thus The Ninth was unlike the heavily German but traditionally pious 107th Ohio: "We never omitted entreating God's blessing upon us and our labors for the speedy overthrow of the rebellion, and for the salvation of all mankind." Smith, *107th Ohio,* 155.

18. Friedrich Ludwig Jahn founded the Turners, in Berlin, in 1811. The Ninth comprised many Turners. Turner regiments typically celebrated his birthday "by putting up lanterns and floral decorations, singing Turner lyrics, and listening to speeches and declamations." Wittke, *Refugees,* 226. Queen's Rock may have been Queen's Point. See *Official Atlas,* Plate CXXXV-C, 2.

19. Rosecrans's forces were operating as an army of occupation and defense in West Virginia now. "By the middle of August, Rosecrans had established a chain of posts, with a regiment or two at each . . . from Weston, by way of Bulltown, Sutton, and Summersville, to Gauley Bridge." Cox, "McClellan in West Virginia," 143.

20. This sentence is problematical. McClellan had left in July, to head the Army of the Potomac; and the *Official Records* for this time contain no order by him on how Sundays were to be observed.

21. In due course, recognized for "activity, zeal, and military capacity," he was commissioned a brigadier-general of volunteers but he kept The Ninth always in his brigade. Reid, *Ohio in the War* 1:877.

22. "A woods" was in fact dense timber in which Confederate works could not be seen at long range, a fact that probably contributed to subsequent Union confusion. See *The Union Army* 5:223–24.

23. In the original this sentence is in English.

24. Cf. Lonn: "A part of the Ninth . . . charged almost up to the enemy's works" but "the attack was never made." *Foreigners,* 500.

25. There was good reason to fear the Confederates after dark, and to shoot first and ask questions later, for the Confederates had been neither defeated nor driven off but, for tactical reasons, withdrew during the night. See *The Union Army* 5:223–24.

26. "Ruined the master plan" perhaps refers to the failure to break Confederate lines. See Long, *Civil War Day by Day,* 116. In point of fact as to Floyd's strength, the Confederates withdrew toward Dogwood Gap and Sewell Mountain because, however ferociously they may have fought and whatever their strength, they were badly situated and outnumbered. See ibid.

27. The camp was probably on Spy Rock, which overlooked a broad valley toward Big Sewell Mountain, whither this part of Rosecrans's forces had moved on the 24th. Cox, "McClellan in West Virginia," 147.

28. Autumn rains had started and did not stop. "Animals of the wagon trains," useless on obstinate roads, "were being destroyed in the effort to supply the command." Ibid.

29. Unfortunately this report of the strife is disappointingly vague because names are not named and actions not specified.

30. This concern for his troops meant that "supplies, clothing, pay, transportation, everything was to be found in prompt abundance where Colonel McCook commanded. Where his wagons came from he never explained, but he generally had twice as many as any other Colonel in the department." Reid, *Ohio in the War* 1:877.

31. "Of course, all regiments resorted to foraging." Lonn, *Foreigners,* 363. McCook "suffered them [The Ninth] to act on the theory that they were entitled to anything they could find in the country that would help them make camp-life more comfortable." Reid, *Ohio in the War* 1:876.

5 November 28, 1861, to March 4, 1862

1. Chapter 3, pp. 63–81 of *"Die Neuner."*

2. Indeed, the regiment refused to pass the city without a visit, and to depart until paid. They had not got a cent since enlistment. *Cincinnati Enquirer,* 29 Nov. 1861.

3. Smith calls French leaves "French furloughs." *107th Ohio,* 22. The *Jakob Strader* was "the largest boat on the Ohio River." Keil, *Thirty-Fifth Ohio,* 52. The men practically forced McCook to grant this furlough. They even stopped the building of fires for steam in the boat's boilers—until paid. *Cincinnati Enquirer,* 29 Nov. 1861.

4. The bad behavior continued downriver. "I regret to inform you," the *Enquirer* received by telegraph on December 6, "of the disgraceful conduct of a portion of the Ninth Ohio Regiment at Jeffersonville. They fill the saloons and coffee-houses, and in their revellings and riot have greatly disturbed the quiet of that normally peaceful town. Colonel McCook is doing all that human man can do to bring together his men, after which he will apply the corrective in an unmistakable way."

5. Grebner does not identify this quotation.

6. This conical shelter, eighteen feet in diameter and thirteen high (invented by Major H. H. Sibley), accommodated twelve men and their accoutrements. All occupants could sleep with their feet to the fire in the center. It was light and easily pitched, and looked like a tepee, having, like a tepee, a hole for ventilation at the apex. Scott, *Military Dictionary,* 142. Dodge called it "incomparably superior to the other kinds in common use." *Old Second Division,* 110.

7. Many Germans had come to Louisville in the 1840s and remained loyal to the Union. Federal Writers' Project, *Kentucky,* 182. Indeed, the city tended to be a loyalist bastion surrounded by a secessionist countryside. Ibid. See also Coulter, *Civil War and Kentucky,* 125–26. Cf. Eidson, "Louisville," 224–26.

8. The 35th Ohio and 2nd Minnesota were not exclusively German but counted many Germans in their ranks, hence the unusual camaraderie between those regiments and The Ninth.

9. No such promise has been made in these pages.

10. Thomas had been ordered in November to concentrate against Confeder-

ates at Mill Springs on the Cumberland, and to attack if necessary. Cist, *Army of the Cumberland,* 11. Obeying the order, he was moving on the 18th of January to unite with Albin Schoepf's column. George Bibb Crittenden, the Confederate commander, seeking to prevent their meeting, had by now directed Felix Zollicoffer to the attack that began on the 19th. Connelly, *Army of the Heartland,* 96–97.

11. This was the small battle but important Union victory at Mill Springs, Kentucky, also called, variously, Logan's Cross Roads, Fishing Creek, Somerset, and Beech Grove, on the Cumberland River about fifteen miles south of Somerset. In the Union strategy to secure Kentucky and advance in the Mississippi Valley, Union general George H. Thomas engaged and defeated Zollicoffer and Brigadier-General George B. Crittenden. Zollicoffer, who lacked military training and battlefield experience, wearing a white raincoat and therefore a good target despite darkness and rain, was shot and killed. A Confederate rally failed and they retreated across the river, leaving camps and supplies. Long, *Civil War Day by Day,* 162. *The Union Army* 6:599–601. Connelly, *Army of the Heartland,* 97–99.

12. "Both of McCook's regiments," that is, the Second Minnesota and Ninth Ohio of McCook's brigade, "were admirably drilled and disciplined, and moved to the attack with the order and steadiness of veterans." They advanced slowly until the Ninth changed direction slightly and charged with bayonets. Kelly, "Holding Kentucky," 389. Its thrust of "cold steel . . . soon broke the rebel rank" and "a panic flight ensued." *Cincinnati Enquirer,* 24 Jan. 1862. This "bayonet charge was the most striking incident of the conflict." Lonn, *Foreigners,* 493. Perhaps what made the charge so notable was the fact that the bayonet served the infantry of both sides as a tool for digging and cutting "but seldom as a weapon." In the Wilderness (May, 1864), bayonet and sword accounted for only six of the 7,302 wounded. Coggins, *Arms and Equipment,* 29. See Also Buechler, " 'Give 'em the Bayonet,' " 128–32.

13. This statement is quoted in McCook's English and follows generally a part of McCook's report to Thomas. *Official Records,* Ser. 1, Vol. 7, 93–94.

14. This is from Thomas's report and quoted in Thomas's English. Ibid., 80. If Grebner and Thomas were right about the bayonet as used by The Ninth at Mill Springs, it was one of the few successful uses of it in battle in the war. Wounds were seldom inflicted with it. The times it made any difference—Mill Springs seems to have been one of the few—"the defending line simply broke." Buechler, " 'Give 'em the Bayonet,' " 130.

15. "Among the wounded, Colonel McCook and Captain Joseph. Our dead: Hugo Tafel, sergeant, Company A; Heinrich Lange, private, and Heinrich Spellberg, sergeant, Company D; John Ruoff, corporal, Company E; Hermann Sutz, corporal, Company H; Theodor Sabin, private, Company I." In the original this list is in the text.

16. According to Cist, 12 cannon, over 150 wagons, and more than 1,000 horses and mules. *Army of the Cumberland,* 18–19.

17. This comment on the Confederate defeat, confused and vague, refers to the Confederate muddle at Mill Springs. That is, Zollicoffer knew of the Union

advance but did nothing about it. Nor did he obey Crittenden's order to cross to the south side of the river. Thus the "main force," under Crittenden, was south of the river while Union troops were defeating Zollicoffer's to the north of it. Grebner seems to think Zollicoffer could have called on Crittenden but did not. See Long, *Civil War Day by Day,* 162.

18. "To the services of this regiment," The Ninth, Zollicoffer's defeat "is justly placed." *Cincinnati Enquirer,* 8 Aug. 1862.

19. Although in point of fact not "nearly destroyed," Lieutenant-Colonel Edward Cary Walthall's 15th Mississippi did suffer the Confederates' heaviest losses here. Kelly, "Holding Kentucky," 391.

20. He was "constantly drunk." Shaw, *Tenth Indiana,* 138. Crittenden, "arrested for drunkenness" after Mill Springs, was relieved of command. Connelly, *Army of the Heartland,* 146.

21. That is, the victory at Mill Springs aided Grant's capture of Donelson, which exposed all of Tennessee and enabled Buell to occupy Nashville without bloodshed on February 25, 1862.

22. Gen. Orders. No. 5. } Headquarters of the Army, Adjutant General's Office.

Washington, D. C., January 22nd, 1862.

The following orders received from the War Department are published to the Army:

War Department, January 22nd, 1862.

The President, Commander-in-Chief of the Army and Navy, has received information of a brilliant victory achieved by the United States forces over a large body of armed traitors at Mill Springs in the State of Kentucky. He returns thanks to the gallant officers and soldiers, who won this victory, and when the official report shall be received, the military skill and personal valor displayed in battle will be acknowledged and rewarded in fitting manner. The courage that encountered and vanquished the greatly superior number of the rebel force, pursued and attacked them in their intrenchments and paused not until the enemy was completely routed, merits and receives commendation. The purpose of this war is to attack, pursue and destroy a rebellious enemy and deliver the country from danger, menaced by traitors. A daring courageous spirit, and patriotic zeal on all occasions and under every circumstance is expected from the Army of the United States. In the prompt and spirited movements and daring battle of Mill Springs the nation will realize its hopes, and the people of the United States will rejoice to honor every officer and soldier, who proved his courage by charging with the bayonet and storming intrenchments in the blaze of the enemy's fire.

By Order of the President,

EDWIN M. STANTON, Secretary of War.

By command of Maj. Gen. McClellan,

L. THOMAS, Adjutant-General.

Official Records, Ser. 1, Vol. 7, 102. In the original this order is in the text. Grebner's quotation is not exact.

23. In the original, Boynton's statement is in English.

24. That is, literally, "the camp from which we can go no farther": Camp *Kann-nicht-weiter.*

25. *Louisville, February* 11, 1862.

COLONEL MCCOOK.

Sir!—As a testimonial of our appreciation of the gallant conduct of your regiment in the battle of Mill Springs, January 19th, I transmit with this note a flag to be presented in the name of the Loyal Ladies of Louisville. I cannot express the grateful feelings of our hearts in appropriate words, but must cordially thank the officers and men under your command.

For yourself accept my acknowledgement of your distinguished services.

Very respectfully,

NANETTE B. SMITH,
President of the Loyal Ladies' Society.

26. On this change in the North, from apathy, faintheartedness, and torpidity, to energy and rigor, see Nevins, *War for the Union* 1:395, 2:2–3.

6 Life under Arms in Europe and Here in America

1. From the Appendix, pp. 278–82 of *"Die Neuner."*

2. Bad though the American roads may have appeared, in an absolute sense as well as by comparison with Europe's, they were not as bad as Grebner alleges. A post road ran from Boston to Savannah in colonial times, three main routes went west in 1812, and the country boasted at least eight more major ones by 1850. Kagan *Pictorial Atlas,* 150–51. In 1872 the post office claimed 174,627 miles of postal-route roads. Gray, *Atlas,* 175. See also Dunbar, *History of Travel* 3:749. MacGill, *History of Transportation,* 299–305. Still the motto of Civil War forces, North and South, might have been: "We wait until the roads mend." Smith, *107th Ohio,* 59. On bad roads and their military consequences, see for example Cox, "McClellan in West Virginia," 147. Grant, "Battle of Shiloh," 478. Sherman, "Grand Strategy," 252.

3. "If a soldier can get a cup of good, strong, hot coffee, sweetened with regular army sugar, he is in good tune, and ready for any duty." Keil, *Thirty-Fifth Ohio,* 142.

7 March 25 to November 3, 1862

1. Chapter 4, pp. 82–105 of *"Die Neuner."*

2. The Ninth was already near the Cumberland, whereas the destination, Corinth, lay close to the Tennessee, so perhaps it and not the Cumberland is meant.

3. The Union forces' purpose: to join Grant in the conquest of the Mississippi Valley. Nevins, *War for the Union* 2:65. For operations between Shiloh and Vicksburg, see Catton, *Grant Moves South,* 223–449.

4. The 49th Ohio was also engaged against the Rangers and Hinman's Arkansas Brigade. Willich may thus be claiming too much for his 32nd Indiana. See Reid, *Ohio in the War* 2:301. In any event, "will be remembered forever" is an extravagant claim. But see Buell's praise, *Official Records,* Ser. 1, Vol. 7, 15–16. Still, extravagant claims and effusive praise were common among Civil War officers.

5. In point of fact the two armies were about equal in size. Grant, though surprised, did well enough to force the battle into a second day; much of Buell's army arrived to reinforce him then, and Johnston lay mortally wounded. The Ninth, among the last of Buell's force to arrive, did not join the fighting. On Shiloh (or Pittsburgh Landing), besides sources cited below, see Catton, *Grant Moves South,* 218–49.

6. Actually, what with equal numbers on each side when Johnston attacked, Grant's being unprepared seems to have been the worst Union error. "The want of organization, plan, vigilance, and discipline" hurt both sides. Nevins, *War for the Union* 2:79.

7. The number of wounded was 8,408 (Long, *Civil War Day by Day,* 195) thus a total of 13,047.

8. "Caissons, dismounted cannon, and dead artillery horses and their dead riders were piled up in heaps, and the warm sun caused a stench. . . ." Wounded men "had been pinned . . . by a fallen limb . . . and the shells setting fire to the dry leaves, the poor fellows had been burned to a crisp. . . . Squads all over the field digging trenches, rolling the dead in and covering them up . . . to be washed off by the first rain, leaving the bones to be picked by buzzards and crows." Bircher, *Drummer Boy,* 33–34.

9. Grant was second to Halleck now, who had just arrived and taken charge of field operations. On March 3, Halleck had accused Grant of misconduct at Fort Donelson but had exonerated him and restored him to command on March 15. Long, *Civil War Day by Day,* 178, 185.

10. That is, Halleck, pursuing the Confederates who withdrew from Shiloh under Beauregard, began moving from there toward Corinth on April 28 and soon occupied positions mostly north of Corinth. Skirmishes followed until Beauregard evacuated on May 30. The "siege" was not strict, for he departed south without

Halleck's knowing it. Long, *Civil War Day by Day*, 204, 218. Hence "the siege of Corinth" is not to be confused with the Battle of Corinth, the failed Confederate attack on the Corinth held by Union forces, October 2, 1862. The Ninth did not take part in the battle, being then in Tennessee as part of Buell's forces opposing Bragg.

11. Known as "the other General Sherman," Thomas West Sherman (1813–1879) was relieved at this time, for acting the way he did. Boatner, *Dictionary*, 750. On Sherman, see also *Dictionary of American Biography*, s.v. "Sherman, Thomas West." Warner, *Generals in Blue*, 440–41. Grebner quotes McCook's declaration in English.

12. Sherman's question, which Grebner has in English, is similarly reported in Keil, *Thirty-Fifth Ohio*, 72.

13. This vague reference is probably to Halleck.

14. That is, the inspectors probably lacked authority because of excessive familiarity with the troops.

15. That is, Sherman seemed to want to reinforce the penitence associated with the Christian observance of Pentecost.

16. Keil, *Thirty-Fifth Ohio*, 76. Grebner's quotation of Keil's English deviates but unimportantly from being exact.

17. Grebner's quotation of Thomas's English is exactly that of ibid., 78.

18. Union and Confederate forces alike visited pillage, plunder, destruction, and insult upon hostile civilians at this time. Nevins, *War for the Union* 2:294–97. Throughout the war, German-American units were notably guilty of plunder and destruction. Lonn, *Foreigners*, 644.

19. Nevins, *War for the Union* (2:293–94), relates this incident with more objectivity than does Grebner. See also Lonn, *Foreigners*, 212–13. Turchin (1822–1901), "Russia's only contribution to the ranks of the Civil War general officers," was "a thorough soldier" who "advocated the Continental theory that to the victor belong the spoils." Hence rape and pillage by his forces, and court martial for him. Madam Turchin got Lincoln to set aside the verdict and promote Turchin. He "fully justified" the confidence, "earning the nickname 'The Russian Thunderbolt.' " Warner, *Generals in Blue*, 511–12.

20. McCook, with dysentery, had been commanding his brigade from a cot in an ambulance. Separated by mistake from them and then his escort, he was alone with an unarmed attendant near New Market, Alabama, when mounted guerrillas, "partisan rangers," and some of the Fourth Alabama Cavalry—perhaps as many as 200 Confederates—attacked him. Though it was obvious he was alone, sick, and willing to cooperate, three shots were fired at him, two by Captain Frank Gurley, and one struck him in the side. The assailants dragged away the man trying to treat the wound, leaving the dying McCook abandoned in a neighboring house. Reid, *Ohio in the War* 1:878–79.

21. Keil, *Thirty-Fifth Ohio*, 83–85. In the original this quotation is in German, translated from Keil's English. The quotation here has not been translated back into English. Keil's English itself has been supplied.

22. "We heard today of the assassination of General Robert L. McCook, and take sweet comfort from the thought that our old friends of the Ninth will assuredly avenge his death as it deserves." Hannaford, *Story of a Regiment,* 336. Keil, *Thirty-Fifth Ohio,* tells the story of the assassination in detail; see especially pp. 86–87.

23. "A gentleman of more than ordinary intellect, of sound judgment and determined will. Of his bravery and gallantry it is needless to speak. He seemed by nature to be cut out for a soldier." *Cincinnati Enquirer,* 8 Aug. 1862.

24. The division concentrated and organized here, and awaited orders. *Constitution des neunten Regiments,* 17.

25. This statement is in the German subjunctive in the original, and that mood in German is a way to signal direct discourse, so the translation is given as a direct quotation.

26. In the original, "Let well enough alone" is in English.

27. Cincinnati itself, fearing invasion by Bragg, declared martial law, fortified the Kentucky hills across the Ohio, and mobilized a home guard under Lew Wallace. Nevins, *War for the Union* 2:280–81.

28. Guerrilla warfare racked the Confederate southwest now, harrowing civilians even more than troops. Ibid., 292–93.

29. Bragg may have intended to take Nashville but by now had decided on the bolder plan to capture Louisville. Ibid., 280.

30. Germans, unaccustomed and antagonistic to the white of army issue, wanted their black bread and would erect bakeries to bake it for themselves. See Lonn, *Foreigners,* 362.

31. Dates in this paragraph are two or three days behind those usually given for the main action in this operation, because The Ninth was at the rear.

32. "The fact was that neither general had stomach for a battle." Buell hesitated to advance until Bragg, lacking grit, withdrew. Nevins, *War for the Union* 2:283.

33. Keil, *Thirty-Fifth Ohio,* 94. Grebner's quotation of Keil's English is exact.

34. In point of fact, Bragg was vacillating now and not called anywhere on business or anything else. In a few days, accordingly, he and Buell "stumbled on each other at Perryville." Nevins, *War for the Union* 2:286.

35. In point of fact, Bragg's Confederates, if otherwise inferior were superior in numbers: 68,000 to Buell's 60,000. *The Union Army* 6:672. For events leading to Perryville, see McWhinney, *Bragg,* 293–312. Connelly, *Army of the Heartland,* 221–56.

36. "The field of Perryville was an open and beautiful rolling country, and the battle presented a grand panorama. There was desperate fighting on both sides." Urquhart, "Bragg's Advance," 602.

37. "The roar of cannon and musketry was deafening; the earth trembled under their shock. For two hours a lurid sheet of fire blazed between the opposing lines, hurling destruction into each other's ranks. Fiercer and wilder grew the contest . . . almost hand to hand" and at times "with fixed bayonets." Dodge, *Waif of the War,* 44–45.

38. Cf. Confederate General Joseph Wheeler: "Our artillery, handled with great skill, told fearfully on the enemy, who sought, when practicable, to take shelter behind stone walls and fences." Wheeler, "Bragg's Invasion," 16. Then again, "Rebel batteries" were "badly managed and did not have the correct range, [and] the [Union] loss was small." Reid, *Ohio in the War* 2:73.

39. The participants seem to have chanced upon each other, without adequate preparation, informed leadership, or even proper organization. Ibid., 286–87. Buell heard the cannonading at about 2:00 P.M. but did not believe a battle was in progress. "A great waste of powder over there," he said. "*Stop that* useless waste of *powder*." Shaw, *Tenth Indiana*, 179. "Buell was deprived of his command for not having defeated Bragg, who, in turn, was censured by the Southern people for his failure to destroy the Federal army commanded by Buell." Wheeler, "Bragg's Invasion," 19. Bragg, in this pivotal battle, "neglected to strike at the opportune moment, and from that point final victory clearly rested with our [Union] arms." Dodge, *Waif of the War*, 52.

40. Grebner does not "render a verdict" on this distinguished soldier who fell upon hard times at Perryville. Grebner thus sits on the fence with (a) the military commission that investigated Buell's alleged "dilatory tactics" at Perryville but made no recommendation and (b) the authorities who let him wait a year for orders, then mustered him out, and did not follow Grant's advice to restore him to service. See Warner, *Generals in Blue*, 51–52.

8 November 4, 1862, to July 25, 1863

1. Chapter 5, pp. 106–122 of *"Die Neuner."*

2. Cf. *The Union Army* 5:275 on this makeup.

3. Grebner's *innerer Dienst* has been translated "home service" in the apparent absence of any existing equivalent.

4. On July 24, 1862, Tafel had left The Ninth, as second-lieutenant of Company A, and become lieutenant-colonel of the 106th Ohio. At Hartsville, his regiment held out longer than the rest of its brigade even though separated from it, surrendering eventually, after being overpowered. Cist, *Army of the Cumberland*, 82–83.

5. Rosecrans too felt the lack of cavalry now, and determined to increase this arm, "so that he could meet the ten or twelve thousand cavalry of the enemy in their detached raids on more of an equal footing." Ibid., 138. See also Lamers, *Edge of Glory*, 187, 192, 194, 198, 210.

6. "In chill, rainy weather, over rough and partially wooded terrain, some 75,000 effectives, in fairly equal numbers, grappled in grim charges and hand-to-hand fighting" in "one of the stubbornest battles of the war." The armies were "terribly mangled" and Murfreesboro in effect "a drawn battle." Nevins, *War for the Union* 2:375–76. In this "big, bloody struggle" the armies "fought to a tactical draw." McDonough, *Stones River*, xi.

7. According to Cist, Willich was negligently absent from his command, and

the absence contributed to the bad showing by Union forces and led to his being captured. *Army of the Cumberland,* 105–6. Cf. Stewart: Willich, horse shot from under him, "fell into the hands of the enemy" while "hurrying from division headquarters to take charge of his brigade." "A Bachelor General," 139.

8. These movements were to counter the genuine Confederate threat in this region, one of the chief dangers to the Union at this time. Long, *Civil War Day by Day,* 317.

9. For the National Enrollment Act of March 3, 1863, see Shannon, *Union Army* 2:282. Grebner may also be speaking of the Ohio Volunteer Militia Act, which required every Ohio male, 18 to 45 years of age, to serve five years. State "drafts," under various names, coincided with or followed closely upon Federal ones as the national government drafted by calling for quotas from the states and the states filled them by various means, such as drafts and militia acts. See ibid., 1:296–97. Porter, *Ohio Politics,* 104–5. Roseboom, *Civil War Era,* 405.

10. In the first legislation of its kind in Ohio, "absentee soldier voting was provided for in an act prescribing the method and machinery whereby soldiers in the field could cast their ballots." Roseboom, *Civil War Era,* 405. See also Porter, *Ohio Politics,* 111, 113.

11. Probably the Copperheads and their Knights of the Golden Circle are meant in these paragraphs. According to Shaw they "flooded the [Union army] camp with letters urging desertion and promising protection from arrest." *Tenth Indiana,* 198. On resolutions against the "Peace Democracy," sent home by Ohio regiments in the field, see Porter, ibid., 115.

12. In May of 1863, Lincoln banished Vallandigham to the Confederacy for his treasonous, pro-Confederate ideas. A closed carriage under heavy guard carried him across Union lines near Ohio troops around Murfreesboro. He went via blockade-runner to Canada that summer and did run for office from there, through friends and by correspondence. Shaw, *Tenth Indiana,* 198–99. *Dictionary of American Biography,* s.v. "Vallandigham, Clement Laird." Klement, *Limits of Dissent,* 190–256.

13. Rosecrans began nearly six months of inactivity now, to the irritation of Grant and many others, including the War Department, who wanted him to neutralize Bragg and advance on Chattanooga. Nevins, *War for the Union* 3:189–92. Washington (Stanton and Halleck) nagged "the life out of Rosecrans . . . for him *to get busy*" but, in Rosecrans's defense, "the whole army as well as General Rosecrans knew we could make no headway" on impassable roads in a country that two armies had stripped of forage. For supplies, Rosecrans depended on one railroad; and it was short of rolling stock. Shaw, *Tenth Indiana,* 203–4.

14. That is, the Roll of Honor, established by Rosecrans, was to distinguish and record—and thus reward—the best soldiers of all ranks in an army corps; and "to promote the efficiency of the service." Each brigade was to form a Light Battalion from its Roll of Honor, which would be armed with rifles and mounted, and "looked upon as the *elite* of the army" and expected to perform "deeds of daring and enterprise." Dodge, *Old Second Division,* 454–55.

15. Also called "pup tents" and "the small shelter," they were of light canvas

(the weight of sturdy muslin), about five feet square at the base and four feet high, designed for two men and to be buttoned together before being pitched. "In sleeping in them we would have to draw up our legs into an abrupt angle, then spoon up close to each other or our feet and part of our legs would have to remain outside." Smith, *107th Ohio,* 34.

16. Vocke, "Our German Soldiers," 369. Grebner's quotation of Vocke's English differs but unimportantly from the original. On language difficulties and pros and cons of native tongues' being spoken in the Union army, see Lonn, *Foreigners,* 162–63.

17. It "greatly increased" The Ninth's efficiency, an "improvement" due mainly "to the efforts of Governor [David] Tod and [Ohio's] Quartermaster-General Wright." Reid, *Ohio in the War* 2:74.

18. "Comfortable huts had been erected" for the band. Its arrival brought "gratification to the boys of the Ninth." Ibid.

19. "We [the 10th Indiana] had not yet seen General Brannan and from reports . . . were not favorably impressed with him. We soon made his acquaintance [he instituted comprehensive brigade drills that brought respect from the men] and [we] became warm admirers. . . ." Shaw, *Tenth Indiana,* 202.

20. This was the start of Rosecrans's Tullahoma or Middle Tennessee campaign against Bragg, amounting to skirmishes but no major fighting, which lasted until early July; purpose: to aid Grant at Vicksburg "by preventing Confederate reinforcements." Long, *Civil War Day by Day,* 370.

21. A private's pay was $13 a month ($16 after June 20, 1864), payable every two months but likelier to come after four and sometimes not until six or eight months elapsed since the last visit by the paymaster. Boatner, *Dictionary,* 624–25.

9 Passing the Time in the Field, and Other Topics Gleaned in Reflection

1. From the Appendix, pp. 283–88 of *"Die Neuner."* This chapter, signed "F. B.," was probably by Friedrich Bertsch.

2. "Etc." probably meant "salt pork, fresh beef, salt beef, rarely ham or bacon, hard bread [hardtack or crackers], soft bread, potatoes, an occasional onion, flour, beans, split pease, rice, dried apples, dried peaches, desiccated vegetables, coffee, tea, sugar, molasses, vinegar, candles, soap, pepper, and salt." Billings, *Hardtack and Coffee,* 110–111.

3. "Wen's juckt, der kratze sich," usually translated: "If the shoe fits, wear it." The reference is to lice, often called *graybacks* by Union soldiers and frequently mentioned in their accounts of life in the field.

4. "Death of a Warrior," signed F. Jacker. The only Jacker on The Ninth's muster roll, however, is Joseph Jacker of Company A. See "Death of a Warrior," infra, 248–50.

5. Grebner says "dessert" (*Nachtisch*) rather than "side dish." The latter has been substituted because, as a dessert comes at the end of a meal, so the figure, to

retain its essential nature, must be altered to correspond to the movement of the chapter forward from the end of the original.

10 August 16 to September 22, 1863

1. Chapter 6, pp. 123–42 of *"Die Neuner."*

2. This was the Army of the Cumberland's advance on Chattanooga, which would become part of the Chickamauga campaign. Long, *Civil War Day by Day,* 397–98.

3. In the original, both parts of this exchange are in English.

4. From the 10th to the 18th the movement continued via Lookout Mountain Ridge, Stevens Gap, and McLemore's Cove, to Lafayette Road, with reconnaissances to Dry Gap and Pigeon Mountain, and then forced marches along the Chickamauga River, toward Gordon Mills and Rossville. *Constitution des neunten Regiments,* 19–20.

5. On October 17, 1863, Grant relieved Rosecrans from command of the Department of the Cumberland. "Rosecrans, badly beaten at Chickamauga, had been criticized for slowness, for the defeat, and now for being surrounded at Chattanooga." Long, *Civil Way Day by Day,* 423.

6. Grebner's English-language quotation has been reproduced exactly here.

7. In point of fact, Rosecrans's front had passed Lookout Mountain and entered Georgia near Ringgold and Dalton. Guided by reports from there, Rosecrans himself, at least at first, believed what Washington believed about Bragg. Nevins, *War for the Union* 3:194. See also Lamers, *Edge of Glory,* 308–11. Cleaves, *Rock of Chickamauga,* 153–55.

8. Bragg's plan "was the best arranged of [that for] any battle during the war." Bragg failed "through the intervention of Divine Providence." Shaw, *Tenth Indiana,* 265. In point of fact the plan probably "lagged" because Bragg vacillated and gave confusing orders. Connelly, *Autumn of Glory,* 192–95.

9. Indeed, Bragg was criticized for failing against Rosecrans here—failing, critics said, because he lacked knowledge of the situation and did not personally supervise the execution of his orders. "No general ever won a permanent fame who was wanting in these grand elements of success. . . ." Hill, "Chickamauga," 641–42. See also Connelly, ibid., 195–97.

10. The reference seems to be to the Comte de Paris, *History of the Civil War* 4:95, but the quotation, in German, differs from the Comte's text.

11. This is an extract (p. 36) exactly from Palmer's oration in Boynton, *Dedication,* 28–37.

12. Thus, southeast of Chattanooga, the sides faced each other in rough parallel on a three-mile front along Chickamauga Creek in underbrush and woods. Long, *Civil War Day by Day,* 411. Grebner says the front was of six miles. Otherwise his account corresponds, as a localized version, to the battle in its global dimensions. Cf. Nevins, *War for the Union* 3:196–200. To appreciate fully Grebner's discussion, consult concurrently Hill's "Chickamauga," 638–62, an appropriately detailed ac-

count of this complex event, and Opdycke, "Notes," 668–71. See also Connelly, *Autumn of Glory,* 201–34.

13. The Ninth seized this artillery, also known as Guenther's Battery, after "a sharp fight" and the loss of "a good many men"; but they had to leave it behind "for want of horses." Bishop, "Van Derveer's Brigade," 3.

14. Meanwhile, at the "Widow Glenn's log house," Rosecrans (in full uniform with sword) held a council of war. Light from the only fire in fifteen square miles flickered over the map, illuminated the officers' faces, and flashed on their swords. "Address of Capt. W. C. Margedant," in Boynton, *Dedication,* 352–53.

15. Van Derveer's brigade, "melting away" in enfilading fire, changed front and took the fire straight on and lying down. Then a volley "checked the Rebel line" when the "Thirty-Fifth and Ninth Ohio regiments rose, and with a cheer to which they had been trained, [with bayonets and] without firing a shot, charged on a full run directly into the whole Rebel division, which turned and fled. . . ." Reid, *Ohio in the War* 1:892.

16. Thomas won his nickname "The Rock of Chickamauga" here. Rosecrans, thinking the battle lost and his forces smashed, ordered those remaining to evacuate the Lookout Mountain area and withdraw to Chattanooga. Thomas refused. He held out, repelling attacks until, late in the day, Rosecrans ordered him to fall back to Rossville, and he complied because he feared being flanked. Nevins, *War for the Union* 3:199.

17. Also quoted in Keil, *Thirty-Fifth Ohio,* 146.

18. "Some unauthorized person had ordered Thomas's ammunition train back . . . ," ammunition brought up by Granger "was soon exhausted," cartridge boxes of the dead were searched, and then the enemy's final charges were repulsed with "cold steel." Cist, *Army of the Cumberland,* 211.

19. Longstreet found that "by a blunder of orders," Thomas J. Wood's division had been pulled out of the Union's center, leaving a gap. Longstreet accordingly scattered the Union forces remaining—all except Thomas on Snodgrass Hill. Long, *Civil War Day by Day,* 411–12.

20. Actually, Rosecrans and "a half-dozen generals" tried "to stay the rout" but "were carried along with it." Nevins, *War for the Union* 3:197.

21. Cist, *Army of the Cumberland,* 227.

22. Grebner's quotation deviates from the report as printed in *Official Records,* Ser. 1, Vol. 30, Pt. 1, 253.

23. Grebner's quotation of Halleck differs from ibid., 39. The quotation of Bragg coincides with ibid., Pt. 2, 23; of Rosecrans, with ibid., Pt. 1, 62. Cf. General Grant: "Rosecrans was badly defeated, with a heavy loss in artillery, and some sixteen thousand men killed, wounded, and captured." Grant, "Chattanooga," 681. But the Confederates won "a brilliant victory" without beneficial consequences (Nevins, *War for the Union* 3:200), "that 'barren victory' [which] sealed the fate of the Southern Confederacy." Hill, "Chickamauga," 662.

24. In point of fact the percentage was over twenty-five and maybe nearer fifty. Cf. Long, *Civil War Day by Day,* 412. Nevins, *War for the Union* 3:200.

25. "Our fallen comrades: *Company A:* Sergeant Wilhelm Drewe, Corporal Gottfried Kiefuss, Privates August Beyland, Wilhelm Dake, Ferdinand Hildebrand, Philip Herzog, and Ladislaw Sattler; *Company B:* Corporal Rudolf Müller, Privates Joseph Hupp, Andreas Keller, John Laufer, Heinrich Voigt, and Friedrich Seeger; *Company C:* Privates Wilhelm Kaiser and Friedrich Waltenspiel; *Company D:* Second Lieutenant Raimund Herrmann, Corporal August Waltenspiel, Privates Friedrich Conradi, Karl Funke, Louis Frohmann, and Anton Müller; *Company E:* Privates Christoph Hornung and Fidel Edelmann; *Company F:* Corporal Karl Roman, Privates Georg Hirschmann, Gottlieb Hirschbrunner, Anton Knittel, Friedrich Müller, and Herrmann Schmidt; *Company G:* Captain Gustav Richter, Privates Wilhelm Federlin, Friedrich Gödicke, Wilhelm Huth, Otto Kutter, Georg Kühne; *Company H:* Privates Joseph Danner, Andreas Hamm, Heinrich Kiefer, and Georg Beck; *Company I:* Sergeant Michael Hamann, Corporal Gottlieb Reiber, Privates Leo Böhler, John Keutel, Friedrich Kull, Karl Müller, Wilhelm Reichmann, and Konrad Springard; *Company K:* Private Gottfried Grösser." In the original this list occurs in the text. The Ninth suffered the heaviest losses of any regiment in this battle. Lonn, *Foreigners,* 531–32.

26. "I have never seen the Federal dead lie so thickly on the ground, save in front of the sunken wall at Fredericksburg." Hill, "Chickamauga," 658.

27. *Official Records,* Ser. 1, Vol. 30, Pt. 1, 428–30. Grebner's quotation is in English.

28. Ibid., 250. Grebner's quotation is in English.

29. Grebner's quotation of Thomas is in English.

30. *Official Records,* Ser. 1, Vol. 30, Pt. 1, 540. Grebner's quotation is in English.

31. Vocke, "Our German Soldiers," 357–58. Grebner's quotation of Vocke's English deviates unimportantly from the original.

32. Grebner's quotation of Baird is in English.

33. Grebner's quotation of Boynton is in English.

34. "Not lost on posterity" probably refers to the setting up of the Geneva Convention, its creation of the Red Cross in 1864, and the framing of a program for reducing the horrors of warfare, including the international protection of the wounded and of prisoners, which most Western powers ratified by 1866, with the United States following in 1882. See Nussbaum, *Concise History,* 224–26.

35. Grebner does not indicate the source of Söllheim's words and it remains undetermined.

36. *Official Records,* Ser. 1, Vol. 30, Pt. 1, 253.

37. Ibid., 254. Grebner's quotation of Thomas is in English.

38. Chattanooga was to be held because as "the center of almost the entire system of Southern railroads, it could not fail to derive importance from that fact," besides being "the great *entrepôt* of vast mines of coal and nitre." Dodge, *Waif of the War,* 99. See also McDonough, *Chattanooga,* 74.

39. *Official Records,* Ser. 1, Vol. 30, Pt. 1, 168.

40. "You went into battle [at Chickamauga] 502 strong [i.e., at half-strength]

"Address of Capt. W. C. Margedant" to veterans of The Ninth, in Boynton, *Dedication,* 353.

41. See "The Battle of Chickamauga," infra, 245–50.

11 September 23, 1863, to February 22, 1864

1. Chapter 7, pp. 145–62 of *"Die Neuner."*

2. In the original this sentence is in English. Grebner does not identify the source.

3. Grebner does not identify him. Keil (*Thirty-Fifth Ohio,* 158–59) also tells this story without naming the soldier, concluding: "On the field [at Resaca] the following day, no musket spoke louder and oftener, than did that in the hands of our German. When the contest opened[,] the barrel of his gun was bright and glistened like a newly coined silver dollar; when he came out, that glistening barrel was bluish brown and black, caused by rapid firing."

"Nothing, save his unbounded will power, or as we say 'grit and pluck' saved the life of this brave German—No, not German—but genuine American!"

4. Brough was a War Democrat on the Republican or Union ticket in this election of national significance. He defeated Vallandigham, the Copperhead, who ran from Canada by mail. Had *he* won, Northern sympathy for the Confederacy would also have won, boding ill for Lincoln's candidacy in 1864. See Long, *Civil War Day by Day,* 421. Near unanimity for Brough was true throughout Ohio troops. Clark, *Opdycke Tigers,* 142.

5. That is, strictly speaking, Grant headed the new Military Division of the Mississippi, and Thomas retained command of the Army of the Cumberland, under Grant. Long, *Civil War Day by Day,* 423.

6. "We will hold out till we starve." Clark, *Opdycke Tigers,* 140. See Grant, "Chattanooga," 683. Thomas's words became proverbial in this part of the Union army. Dodge, *Waif of the War,* 103. The words vary from author to author. Cf., for example, Catton, *Grant Takes Command,* 35.

7. Marie Edmé Patrice de MacMahon (1808–1893) military officer and president of France, fought in the Crimean War (1853–1856) and, according to tradition, said or wrote his famous *"J'y suis, j'y reste"* when asked in the Battle of the Malakov (9 Sept. 1855) whether he could hold his position in light of the fact that the Russians seemed about to blow it up. Alexandre, *Musée de la Conversation,* 436–38. The earliest printed version of Luther's *"Hier stehe ich, ich kann nicht anders"* may not have been spoken at the Diet of Worms (1521), but the seven words have come ringing down the centuries, as influential and as famous as any seven in the history of the western world. See Bainton, *Luther,* 185. Friedenthal, *Luther,* 269.

8. The Confederate siege of Chattanooga, strong enough to block an army and its supplies, was really a semisiege not tight enough to seal the city; petty traffic leaked out and dribbled in. Grant himself entered, shortly hereafter. See Long, *Civil War Day by Day,* 425.

9. To illuminate the discussion, which treats of complicated action and three

battles—Orchard Knob, Lookout Mountain, and Missionary Ridge—near Chattanooga, November 23–25, see *The Union Army* 5:264–70 and Grant, "Chattanooga"; Byers, "Sherman's Attack"; Smith and Cist, "Comments"; and Fullerton, "Army of the Cumberland" and "Bragg's Comments." See also the concise modern accounts, from the northern and southern point of view respectively: Cleaves, *Rock of Chickamauga,* 187–89; Connelly, *Autumn of Glory,* 253–76.

10. That is, "we had been instructed to carry the line of intrenchments [*sic*] at the base of the Ridge, *and then halt.*" But the troops, enthusiastic and impetuous, "bounded over them" and pressed on "without orders from any commander." Wood, "Battle of Missionary Ridge," 36. Hence it was a "soldiers' battle," one determined not by generalship but by wherewithal in the ranks.

11. This colloquy, quoted in English by Grebner, deviates but slightly from that in Fullerton, "Army of the Cumberland," 725.

12. Sherman, *Memoirs* 1:390. Grebner's quotation of Sherman's English deviates but slightly from the original.

13. Cf. Grant to Sherman, 23 Nov. 1863, in *Official Records,* Ser. 1, Vol. 31, Pt. 2, 41–42. See ibid., 34–35, 45. Grebner's quotations of Grant's English differ unimportantly from the original.

14. On Thomas to Palmer, cf. Thomas to Granger, ibid., 117. For Van Derveer, see ibid., 528. For Kämmerling, ibid., 536–37. Grebner's quotations of Van Derveer and Kämmerling deviate considerably from the originals.

15. Grebner's quotation, in English and reproduced exactly in the translation, seems inappropriate to the point being made.

16. Dana to Stanton, 25 Nov. 1863, in *Official Records,* Ser. 1, Vol. 31, Pt. 2, 68. Grebner quotes Dana in English. Dana's reference is probably to Hooker's vigorous pursuit of the retreating Confederates toward Ringgold, Georgia.

17. The Confederate figures add up to 6,687. Grebner errs by entering 2,180 rather than the correct 2,160 wounded. See Long, *Civil War Day by Day,* 438.

18. The Confederates, neglecting their duty as victors, had not buried many of the dead, leaving a "carnage field," strewn with all sorts of equipment, some whole, some broken; and with "full-length skeletons," skulls touching "like the cheeks of sleepers," and dismembered bodies "scattered about in promiscuous heaps." Dodge, *Waif of the War,* 118–19.

19. In the original, Thomas's words are in English.

12 February 22 to June 7, 1864

1. Chapter 8, pp. 163–73 of *"Die Neuner."*

2. *"Gewehr ab!"* That is, the command to bring rifles to the ground.

3. In point of fact, "veteranizing" (*Veteranisirung*) meant, not only the awarding of "veteran furloughs" for reenlistment (that is, retaining veterans and especially units of veterans by thus rewarding reenlistment), but also other procedures to keep and even increase veterans in the ranks. Details of officers and men were sent home from regiments, to bring back veterans, for example; and experienced men of all grades were recalled to duty. Nevins, *War for the Union* 4:147. Lerwill, *Personnel*

1:156, 170–73. As late as the Battle of Vicksburg, Sherman spoke of "the need to conserve these well-tried troops." Liddell-Hart, *Sherman,* 198. Unfortunately the absence of troops on veteran furlough posed its own problems. Ibid., 238–39. "Rearming" (*Wiederausrüstung*) is meant in the sense of all aspects of training and equipment. And not so much the fitting-out of unarmed troops as the arming of recruits and enhancing the fighting power of existing units—to carry the day against the Confederacy at last. See Nevins, *War for the Union* 4:146–47. On Sherman's organizing, equipping, and disposing his forces, and the Union/Confederate feints, ploys and maneuvers prior to engagement in northern Georgia, see Liddell-Hart, *Sherman,* 234–48.

4. Also called Buzzard Roost Gap. This action was one of two important ones here in 1864, the second occurring May 8–11, also referred to as Dalton and Rocky Face Ridge, respectively. At Dalton the so-called Demonstration on Dalton, led by John M. Palmer, was a probing attack on Johnston's Confederates, February 22–27, a prelude to Sherman's Atlanta campaign, which revealed that Johnston was too strong to be bested by less than a major assault. See Long, *Civil War Day by Day,* 467–69, and *The Union Army* 5:199, 340–42. Sherman had taken command of the armies in the West and begun the Atlanta campaign in March and April. The success of his forces in the second week of May was thus an early achievement of the campaign. See Liddell-Hart, *Sherman,* 231, 239–52.

5. The Ninth continued to reflect the skepticism, free-thinking, and downright atheism so strong among the Forty-Eighters, many of whom were now in The Ninth. Wittke, *Refugees,* 122, 123–46.

6. "L" is probably C. W. Hermann Lübbert of "*Die Neuner*'s" editorial committee.

7. "Remember," Carrington had already advised in his "familiar hints," remember that in preparing your superabundant rations, "half-cooked food is ruinous. Better use uncooked pork or bacon, hard bread and coffee, than eat victuals half cooked that need perfect cooking." Carrington, *Ohio Militia,* 23.

8. On this incident see also Bishop, *Story of a Regiment,* 142.

9. Grebner gives no reason, nor can any be hazarded (other than the desire to return home and resume civilian life, several times expressed infra and supra), for why The Ninth refused to reenlist when reenlistment was popular among regiments of the western armies.

10. That is, while Sherman drove into the southeastern Confederacy, his line stretched back into the West, at least to Nashville. So the Confederates' western strategy was to try to break the line anywhere between Atlanta and Nashville. Nevins, *War for the Union* 4:148.

11. Not only did the enemy gain strength "by picking up his detachments as he fell back," but he also "had railroads to bring supplies and reënforcements from his rear," he knew the terrain, and his forces were strong and well-generaled. Meanwhile, advancing, "we [of the Union] had to leave guards" at critical points, "diminishing [our] fighting force." Sherman, "Grand Strategy," 250. See also Liddell-Hart, *Sherman,* 252.

12. According to *The Union Army* (6:730), action at Resaca consisted of demonstrations, skirmishes, and engagements from May 8 to May 15: eight days. See the description of them in Liddell-Hart, *Sherman,* 244–51.

13. On the events of May 15–20, cf. Reid, *Ohio in the War:* The Ninth "participated in the battle of Resaca, May 15th . . ." (2:75). And "on the 20th [the regiment] entered on its last march against the enemy, moving from Kingston to the Etowah River." Ibid.

14. "All along the road stood [The Ninth's] fellow soldiers who cheered most heartily as the regiment moved away; and not any less hearty were the farewells returned by the boys of the Ninth Ohio." Reid, *Ohio in the War* 2:75.

15. Bishop, *Story of a Regiment,* 144. Grebner's quotation of Bishop's English is almost exact.

16. Keil, *Thirty-Fifth Ohio,* 189. Grebner's quotation of Keil's English differs but insignificantly from the original. "The separation was a sad one, as the Ninth and our regiment [the 2nd Minnesota] had been together for nearly three years. We had stood shoulder to shoulder in all of our battles and skirmishes, marched together day and night, suffered all the hardships together, and shared the pleasures alike. . . . We wished them Godspeed. . . ." Bircher, *Drummer Boy,* 115.

17. Germans, though numerically large and admired for thrift and hard work, nonetheless suffered nativist abuse in this era: especially for drinking on Sunday, free-thinking, political radicalism, and wanting to maintain their language rather than abandon it for English. See Leonard and Parmet, *American Nativism,* 95; Coppa and Curran, *Immigrant Experience,* 54–55; Billington, *Protestant Crusade,* 328–30; Beals, *Brass-Knuckle Crusade,* 113, 162, 167, 175.

13 The German Soldier in America

1. From the Appendix, pp. 273–77 of *"Die Neuner."*

2. In the original, McCook's words are in English.

3. In the original, this quotation is in English.

4. Nativism, notable in every generation of American history, prospered in that of the Civil War. "Germans received their full share of abuse and denunciation. . . ." Wittke, *Refugees,* 177–78. Germans and Know-Nothings, in nativist conflict, exchanged gunfire in Cincinnati in the 1850s. Writers' Program, *Cincinnati,* 42.

5. The reference is to the Battle of Chancellorsville, May 1–4, 1863, where German-Americans of the XI Corps, under Schurz and von Steinwehr, suffered heavy losses. A *New York Times* report (May 5, 1863) gained currency, that the Germans had cast off whatever nerve they might have had, fled in unjustifiable panic, and doomed the Union to defeat in the battle. The anti-German opinion endured, unfairly. See Trefousse, *Carl Schurz,* 133–35.

6. See Doubleday, *Chancellorsville and Gettysburg,* 25–27. Dodge, *Chancellorsville,* 100–105. See also Lonn, *Foreigners,* 512–21. Bates, *Battle of Chancellorsville.* Hamlin, *Battle of Chancellorsville.* Cf. Vocke, "Our German Soldiers," 348–57.

7. That is, in proportion to the total population, the Germans should have contributed 128,000 as "their share" but contributed 188,000. See Rosengarten, *German Soldier,* 195, and Faust, *German Element* 1:524–26. "The German population" of "the North-western States flocked to the Union standard" with "a noble unanimity." Frémont, "Command in Missouri," 280.

8. "Letter to the German Republican Central Committee of New York, February 25, 1862." Sumner, *Works* 6:377. In point of fact, however, neither the Germans nor the foreign-born together elected Lincoln. Pro-Lincoln feeling among Americans in general did it, not the votes of the foreign-born. Schafer, "Who Elected Lincoln?" 51–62 and especially 63.

9. Missourians divided between unionists and secessionists. Home guards and volunteer regiments, raised among turners in and around St. Louis, helped tip the scales to the Union by capturing Camp Jackson from Confederates and then fighting them in Missouri for the next ten months to save the state for the Union. Lonn, *Foreigners,* 489.

10. See Dodge, *Old Second Division,* 96–106, on German-Americans as "good soldiers."

11. On German regiments' "tremendous losses" see Lonn, *Foreigners,* 483–84.

12. An approximation of Grebner's German, of the first half of this quotation (up to the ellipsis), occurs in English in Vocke, "Our German Soldiers," 370. The ellipsis is Grebner's. The source of the second half has not been identified.

13. For example, when news of the bombardment of Fort Sumter arrived in Cincinnati, "a little incident . . . will show in what quarter the wind sets hereabouts. A gentleman ventured to express something like sympathy with the Secessionists. He was immediately confronted by a peppery adopted citizen [a German] who informed him that he did not like his principles, and could not tolerate their expression, and advised him to secede from the loyal states at once. The German was greeted with cheers, and cries of 'that's the talk,' and the tone of the 'unsound' American was considerably changed." *Cincinnati Daily Commercial,* 13 April 1861.

14. "There were, of course, on the surface, many Germans who rose early to a dangerous eminence, and some ended their career[s] with anything but credit to themselves or their countrymen, but these were soon thinned out by the actual experiences of real war." Rosengarten, *German Soldier,* 267. See "Knights-Errant and Soldiers-of-Fortune" in Lonn, *Foreigners,* 273–308.

15. "Why beholdest thou the mote that is in thy brother's eye, but considerest not the beam that is in thine own eye?" Matthew 7:3.

16. Cf. Lonn, *Foreigners,* 220: "When Wheeler called on him to surrender, he replied, 'I have been placed here to hold this post, not to surrender it.' "

14

1. Chapter 11, untitled, pp. 249–58 of *"Die Neuner."*
2. See *Constitution des neunten Regiments,* 5–10, 22–24.
3. "Meinhardt, F. L. Emmert, F[riedrich] Diester, Ch[ristian] Hafner, R.

Golde, F[riedrich] Bertsch, V. Weidlinger, J. Piesche, C. Hoffmann, and L. Mark." In the original this list is in the text.

4. "Col. McCook is represented in the undress uniform of a Colonel, with the overcoat thrown open and back. The Western rolling shirt-collar and plain knot tie complete the dress. The face is smooth, the long, abundant hair parted on the right side and thrown back. The features are strongly marked, and have a keen, determined expression, as if in the act of command. The angular jaw and firm set mouth contribute to the impression of determination stamped upon the face, which is approvingly vouched for as an excellent likeness by the surviving brothers of the favorite commander. The bust will rest on a square pedestal of gray granite, 12 feet high, making the whole height over 15 feet. . . . On the die, in raised letters, appears as inscription the name 'Colonel R. L. McCook.' Around the spire there are 34 stars, in bas-relief, the number of States in the Union the year McCook fell. Around the cap on which the bust rests are four laurel wreaths, and on the front the acorn—the emblem of the Fourteenth Army Corps, to which the regiment belonged." *Cincinnati Times,* 8 Aug. 1877, quoted in *New York Times,* 13 Aug. 1877.

5. In the original, the quotation of McCook's words is in English.

6. "Watch on the Rhine" refers loosely to *"Die Wacht am Rhein,"* a German national song written in 1841 and set to music in 1854.

7. A full description of proceedings, including photographs and speeches, is in Boynton, *Dedication.*

8. This is an extract of Schneider's speech, quoted in English by Grebner. A full text is in Boynton, *Dedication,* 349–51. The extract differs but slightly and unimportantly from the corresponding part of that text, 350–51.

15

1. Chapter 10, untitled, pp. 202–49 of *"Die Neuner."*

2. See Ohio Infantry, 9th Regt., *Descriptive Book,* and Ohio Roster Commission, *Official Roster,* in the bibliography, infra.

3. This sentence and everything that follows, up to the Muster Roll, have been moved here from the end of this chapter, pp. 247–48 of *"Die Neuner."*

Poems

1. Chukovsky, *Art of Translation,* 224.

2. From Chapter 9, pp. 181–83 of *"Die Neuner."*

3. From Chapter 6, pp. 143–44 of *"Die Neuner."*

4. That is, the Rev. Carl Türk (or Tuerck), pastor of the Lutheran church on the west side of Walnut between Eighth and Ninth in Cincinnati. Cist, *Sketches and Statistics,* 197.

5. From the Appendix, pp. 288–90 of *"Die Neuner."*

6. The only Jacker in the muster roll is Joseph Jacker, Company A.

Bibliography

Alexandre, Roger. *Musée de la Conversation.* 3rd Ed. Paris: E. Bouillon, 1897.

Amann, William Frayne, ed. *Personnel of the Civil War.* 2 vols. New York: Thomas Yoseloff, 1961.

Anderson, Nicholas Longworth. *Letters and Journals.* Edited by Isabel (Mrs. Larz) Anderson. New York: Fleming H. Revell, 1942.

Arndt, Karl J. R., and May E. Olsen. *German-American Newspapers and Periodicals, 1732–1955.* Heidelberg: Quelle & Meyer, 1961.

Atlas to Accompany the Official Records of the Union and Confederate Armies. Compiled by Calvin D. Cowles. 3 vols. Washington: Government Printing Office, 1891–1895. Reprint (3 vols. in 1) as *The Official Atlas of the Civil War.* New York: T. Yoseloff, 1958.

Bainton, Roland H. *Here I Stand: A Life of Martin Luther.* New York: Abingdon, 1950.

Basler, Roy P. *Abraham Lincoln: His Speeches and Writings.* Cleveland and New York: World Publishing Company, 1946.

———. *The Collected Works of Abraham Lincoln.* 8 vols. New Brunswick, N.J.: Rutgers University Press, 1953.

Bates, Joshua H. "Ohio's Preparation for the War." In *Sketches of War History* 1:128–41.

Bates, Samuel P. *The Battle of Chancellorsville.* Meadville, Pa.: E. T. Bates, 1882.

Battles and Leaders of the Civil War. Edited by Robert Underwood Johnson and Clarence Clough Buel. 4 vols. New York: Century, 1887–1888. Reprint. 4 vols. New York: Thomas Yoseloff, 1956.

Beals, Carleton. *Brass-Knuckle Crusade: The Great Know-Nothing Conspiracy.* New York: Hastings House, 1960.

Billings, John D. *Hardtack and Coffee: The Unwritten Story of Army Life* [in the Civil War]. Edited by Richard Harwell. Chicago: R. R. Donnelley & Sons, The Lakeside Press, 1960.

Billington, Ray Allen. *The Protestant Crusade, 1800–1860: A Study of the Origins of American Nativism.* New York: Macmillan, 1938.

Bircher, William. *A Drummer Boy's Diary . . . Second Regiment Minnesota . . . 1861–1865.* St. Paul: St. Paul Book and Stationery Co., 1889.

Bishop, Judson W. *The Story of a Regiment . . . Second Regiment Minnesota . . . 1861–1865.* St. Paul: Survivors of the 2nd Regiment, 1890.

———. "Van Der Veer's Brigade." *The National Tribune,* 9 and 16 June 1904. Reprint of paper read before the Minnesota Commandery of the Military Order of the Loyal Legion of the United States, 12 May 1903.

Boatner, Mark Mayo. *The Civil War Dictionary.* New York: David McKay, 1959.

Boney, F. N. *John Letcher of Virginia: The Story of Virginia's Civil War Governor.* University, Ala.: University of Alabama Press, 1966.

Boynton, Henry Van Ness, comp. *Dedication of the Chickamauga and Chattanooga National Military Park, September 18–20, 1895.* Washington: Government Printing Office, 1896.

———. *The National Military Park, Chickamauga-Chattanooga. . . .* Cincinnati: R. Clarke, 1895.

Buechler, John. " 'Give 'em the Bayonet'—A Note on Civil War Mythology." *Civil War History* 7 (June 1961): 128–32.

Burton, E. Milby. *The Siege of Charleston.* Columbia: University of South Carolina Press, 1970.

Byers, S. H. M. "Sherman's Attack at the Tunnel." In *Battles and Leaders* 3:712–13.

Carrington, Henry B. *General Regulations for the Military Forces of Ohio. . . .* 2d ed. Columbus: Richard Nevins, State Printer, 1861.

Carrington, General [Henry B.]. *Ohio Militia and the West Virginia Campaign, 1861. . . .* New ed. Boston: R. H. Blodgett, 1904.

Catton, Bruce. *Grant Moves South.* Boston: Little, Brown, 1960.

———. *Grant Takes Command.* Boston: Little, Brown, 1969.

Chukovsky, Kornei. *The Art of Translation.* Translated and edited by Lauren G. Leighton. Knoxville: University of Tennessee Press, 1984.

Cincinnati Daily Commercial, April-May, 1861.

Cincinnati Daily Gazette, Sept. 1863.

Cincinnati Enquirer, April-May, Nov. 1861.

Cist, Charles. *Sketches and Statistics of Cincinnati in 1859.* Cincinnati: n.p., 1859.

Cist, Henry M. *The Army of the Cumberland.* New York: Charles Scribner's Sons, 1882.

Clark, Charles T. *Opdycke Tigers, 125th O.V.I.: A History of the Regiment and of the Campaigns and Battles of the Army of the Cumberland.* Columbus, Ohio: Spahr & Glenn, 1895.

Cleaves, Freeman. *Rock of Chickamauga: The Life of General George H. Thomas.* Norman: University of Oklahoma Press, 1948. Reprint. Westport, Conn.: Greenwood Press, 1974.

Coddington, Edwin B. *The Gettysburg Campaign: A Study in Command.* New York: Scribner's, 1968.

Coggins, Jack. *Arms and Equipment of the Civil War.* Garden City, N.Y.: Doubleday, 1962.

Commager, Henry Steele. See *Documents of American History.*

Comte de Paris. *History of the Civil War in America.* 4 vols. Philadelphia: Henry T. Coates, 1888.

Cone, Stephen D. *Biographical and Historical Sketches: A Narrative of Hamilton {Ohio} and Its Residents. . . .* Hamilton, Ohio: Republican Publishing Company [1896].

Connelly, Thomas Lawrence. *Army of the Heartland: The Army of Tennessee, 1861–1862.* Baton Rouge: Louisiana State University Press, 1967.

———. *Autumn of Glory: The Army of Tennessee, 1862–1865.* Baton Rouge: Louisiana State University Press, 1971.

Constitution des neunten Regiments Ohio Vol. Infanterie, von Cincinnati, Ohio, nebst historischen Anhang. Cincinnati: Geo. Beinert, 1883.

Coppa, Frank J., and Thomas J. Curran, eds. *The Immigrant Experience in America.* Boston: Twayne, 1976.

Cornish, Dudley Taylor. *The Sable Arm: Negro Troops in the Union Army, 1861–1865.* New York: Longmans, Green and Co., 1956.

Coulter, E. Merton. *The Civil War and Readjustment in Kentucky.* Chapel Hill: University of North Carolina Press, 1926.

Count of Paris. See Comte de Paris.

Cox, Jacob D. "McClellan in West Virginia." In *Battles and Leaders* 1:126–48.

———. "War Preparations in the North." In ibid. 1:84–98.

Curry, Richard O. *A House Divided: A Study of Statehood Politics and the Copperhead Movement in West Virginia.* Pittsburgh: University of Pittsburgh Press, 1964.

Dictionary of American Biography.

Documents of American History. Edited by Henry Steele Commager. 8th ed. New York: Appleton-Century-Crofts, 1968.

Dodge, Theodore R. *The Campaign of Chancellorsville.* Boston: Osgood, 1881.

Dodge, William Sumner. *History of the Old Second Division, Army of the Cumberland.* Chicago: Church & Goodman, 1864.

———. *A Waif of the War; or, the History of the Seventy-Fifth Illinois Infantry.* Chicago: Church & Goodman, 1866.

Dornbusch, C. E. *Regimental Publications & Personal Narratives of the Civil War* [a Bibliography]. New York: New York Public Library, 1961.

Doubleday, Abner. *Chancellorsville and Gettysburg.* New York: Charles Scribner's Sons, 1882.

Dumbald, Edward. *The Declaration of Independence and What It Means Today.* Norman: University of Oklahoma Press, 1950.

Dunbar, Seymour. *A History of Travel in America.* 4 vols. Indianapolis: Bobbs-Merrill, 1915.

Dupuy, Trevor Nevitt. *A Genius for War: The German Army, 1807–1945.* Englewood Cliffs, N.J.: Prentice-Hall, 1977.

Eggenberger, David. *Flags of the U.S.A.* Enlarged ed. New York: Crowell, 1964.

Eidson, William G. "Louisville, Kentucky, during the First Year of the Civil War." *Filson Club Quarterly* 38 (July 1964): 224–38. Reprint in Harrison, Lowell, and Nelson L. Dawson, eds. *A Kentucky Sampler.* Lexington: University Press of Kentucky, 1974.

Faust, Albert Bernhardt. *The German Element in the United States.* 2 vols. Boston: Houghton, Mifflin, 1909. New ed. (2 vols. in 1). New York: Steuben Society of American, 1927.

Federal Writers' Project, Works Progress Administration (American Guide Series). *Kentucky: A Guide to the Bluegrass State.* New York: Harcourt, Brace, 1939.

———. *Tennessee: A Guide to the State.* 2d printing. New York: Viking Press, 1945.

Fick, H. H. "Constantin Grebner." *Deutscher Pionier-Verein: Vorstandsbericht* 39 (1907): 67–69.

Ford, Henry A., and Mrs. Kate B. Ford, comps. *History of Cincinnati, Ohio.* Cleveland: L. A. Williams, 1881.

Freidel, Frank. *The Splendid Little War* [of 1898]. Boston: Little, Brown, 1958.

Frémont, John C. "In Command in Missouri." In *Battles and Leaders* 1:278–88.

Friedenthal, Richard. *Luther: His Life and Times.* Translated by John Nowell. New York: Harcourt Brace Jovanovich, 1970.

Fullerton, Joseph. "The Army of the Cumberland at Chattanooga." In *Battles and Leaders* 3:719–26.

———. "General Grant's Comments on Missionary Ridge." In ibid. 3:727.

Galbreath, Charles B. *History of Ohio.* 5 vols. Chicago and New York: American Historical Society, 1925.

Gaynor, Frank, ed. *The New Military and Naval Dictionary.* New York: Philosophical Library, 1951.

Gould, Benjamin A. *Investigations in the Military and Anthropoligical Statistics of American Soldiers.* New York: Hurd and Houghton (for the United States Sanitary Commission), 1869.

Grant, Ulysses S. "The Battle of Shiloh." In *Battles and Leaders* 1:464–86.

———. "Chattanooga." In ibid. 3:679–711.

———. *The Papers of Ulysses S. Grant.* Edited by John Y. Simon. Carbondale and Edwardsville: Southern Illinois University Press, 1967–.

Gray, O. W. *Gray's Atlas of the United States. . . .* Philadelphia: Stedman, Brown & Lyon, 1873.

Greve, Charles Theodore. *Centennial History of Cincinnati and Representative Citizens.* 2 vols. Chicago: Biographical Publishing Company, 1904.

Hamlin, Augustus Choate. *The Battle of Chancellorsville.* Bangor, Me.: Augustus Choate Hamlin, 1896.

Hannaford, Ebenezer. *The Story of a Regiment* [6th Ohio]. Cincinnati: Ebenezer Hannaford, 1868.

Harlow, Alvin F. *The Serene Cincinnatians.* New York: E. P. Dutton, 1950.

Harrison, Lowell H. *The Civil War in Kentucky.* Lexington: University Press of Kentucky, 1975.

Hart, Albert Bushnell, ed. *American History Told by Contemporaries.* 5 vols. New York: Macmillan, 1929.

Heinrici, Max. *Das Buch der Deutschen in Amerika.* Philadelphia: Walther's Buchdruckerei, 1909.

Hill, Daniel H. "Chickamauga—The Great Battle of the West." In *Battles and Leaders* 3:638–62.

Hill, Jim Dan. *The Minuteman in Peace and War: A History of the National Guard.* Harrisburg, Pa.: Stackpole, 1964.

History of Cincinnati and Hamilton County. Cincinnati: S. B. Nelson, 1894.

Hooper, Osman C. *History of Ohio Journalism.* Columbus: Spahr and Glenn, 1933.

Howe, Henry. *Historical Collections of Ohio.* 2 vols. Cincinnati: C. J. Krehbiel, 1908.

Hunter, Louis C. *Steamboats on Western Rivers: An Economic and Technological History.* Cambridge: Harvard University Press, 1949.

Johnson, Robert Underwood, and Clarence Clough Buel. See *Battles and Leaders of the Civil War.*

Kagan, Hilde Heun, *et al.*, eds. *The American Heritage Pictorial Atlas of United States History.* New York: American Heritage, 1966.

Kaufmann, Wilhelm. *Die Deutschen im amerikanischen Bürgerkriege.* Munich and Berlin: R. Oldenbourg, 1911.

Keil, F[rederick] W. *Thirty-Fifth Ohio: A Narrative of Service from August, 1861 to 1864.* Fort Wayne, Ind.: Archer, Housh, 1894.

Kelly, R. M. "Holding Kentucky for the Union." In *Battles and Leaders* 1:373–92.

Klement, Frank L. *The Copperheads in the Middle West.* Chicago: University of Chicago Press, 1960.

———. *Dark Lanterns: Secret Political Societies, Conspiracies, and Treason Trials in the Civil War.* Baton Rouge: Louisiana State University Press, 1984.

———. *The Limits of Dissent: Clement L. Vallandigham and the Civil War.* Lexington: University Press of Kentucky, 1970.

Lamers, William W. *The Edge of Glory: A Biography of General William S. Rosecrans, U.S.A.* New York: Harcourt, Brace, 1961.

Learned, Marion Dexter. *The Life of Francis Daniel Pastorius.* Philadelphia: William J. Campbell, 1908.

Leonard, Ira M., and Robert D. Parmet. *American Nativism 1830–1860.* New York: Van Nostrand Reinhold, 1971.

Lerwill, Leonard L. *Personnel Replacement System in the US Army.* 2 vols. Mimeographed. Washington, D.C.: Dept. of the Army, 1954.

Leser, L. L. "Deutsche Dichtkunst in den Vereinigten Staaten." In Heinrici, *Das Buch Der Deutschen in Amerika,* 387–94.

Liddel Hart, B. H. *Sherman: Soldier, Realist, American.* New York: Dodd, Mead & Company, 1929.

Lieber, Francis. *Lieber's Code and the Law of War.* Edited by Richard Shelly Hartigan. Chicago: Precedent Publishing, 1983.

Lincoln, Abraham. See Basler, Joshua H.

Livermore, Thomas L. *Numbers & Losses in the Civil War in America: 1861–1865.* Boston: Houghton, Mifflin, 1900. Reprint. Bloomington: Indiana University Press, 1957.

Long, E. B. *The Civil War Day by Day: An Almanac, 1861–1865.* Garden City, N.Y.: Doubleday, 1971.

Lonn, Ella. *Desertion during the Civil War.* New York, 1928. Reprint. Gloucester, Mass.: Peter Smith, 1966.

———. *Foreigners in the Union Army and Navy.* Baton Rouge: Louisiana State University Press, 1951.

MacGill, Caroline E., *et al.* (under direction of B. H. Meyer). *History of Transportation in the United States before 1860.* Washington, D.C.: The Carnegie Institution, 1917.

McClung, D. W. "Cincinnati in the War of the Rebellion." In *History of Cincinnati and Hamilton County,* 387–412.

McDonough, James L. *Chattanooga: A Death Grip on the Confederacy.* Knoxville: University of Tennessee Press, 1984.

———. *Stones River: A Bloody Winter in Tennessee.* Knoxville: University of Tennessee Press, 1980.

McKinney, Francis. *Education in Violence: The Life of George H. Thomas and the History of the Army of the Cumberland.* Detroit: Wayne State University Press, 1961.

McMurry, Richard M. *John Bell Hood and the War for Southern Independence.* Lexington: University Press of Kentucky, 1982.

McPherson, James M. *The Negro's Civil War: How American Negroes Felt and Acted during the War for the Union.* New York: Pantheon Books, 1965.

McWhiney, Grady. *Braxton Bragg and Confederate Defeat.* New York: Columbia University Press, 1969.

Margedant, W. C. "Address of Capt. W. C. Margedant." In Boynton, *Dedication,* 350–54.

Miller, Francis Trevelyan, ed. *The Photographic History of the Civil War.* 10 vols. New York: Review of Reviews, 1912.

Millis, Walter. *The Martial Spirit.* Cambridge, Mass.: Riverside Press, 1931.

Moore, Alison. *The Louisiana Tigers. . . .* Baton Rouge: Ortlieb Press, 1961.

Morison, Samuel Eliot, and Henry Steele Commager. *The Growth of the American Republic.* 3d ed. 2 vols. New York: Oxford University Press, 1942.

Murdock, Eugene Converse. *Patriotism Limited, 1862–1865: The Civil War Draft and the Bounty System.* Kent, Ohio: Kent State University Press, 1967.

National Tribune, 9 and 16 June 1904.

Neeff, Gottfried August. *Vom Lande des Sternenbanners: Eine Blumenlese Deutscher Dichtungen aus Amerika.* Heidelberg: C. Winter; Ellenville, N.Y.: German Authors' Agency: 1905.

Nevins, Allan, James I. Robertson, Jr., and Bell I. Wiley. *Civil War Books: A Critical Bibliography.* 2 vols. Baton Rouge: Louisiana State University Press, 1967.

Nevins, Allan. *The War for the Union.* 4 vols. New York: Charles Scribner's Sons, 1959–1971.

New York Times, Aug. 1862, Aug. 1877.

Nicolay, John G., and John Hay, *Abraham Lincoln: A History.* 10 vols. New York: Century, 1917.

Nolan, Alan T. *The Iron Brigade: A Military History.* New York: Macmillan, 1961.

Nussbaum, Arthur. *A Concise History of the Law of Nations.* Rev. ed. New York: Macmillan, 1954.

Official Atlas. See *Atlas to Accompany the Official Records.*

Official Records. See War Records Office.

Official Roster [of Ohio Soldiers]. See Ohio Roster Commission.

Ohio Infantry, 9th Regt. *Descriptive Book of the 9th Regiment Ohio Vol. Infantry.* N.p., n.d.

Ohio Infantry, 11th Regt. *History of the 11th Regiment Ohio Volunteer Infantry. . . .* Dayton: W. J. Shuey, 1866.

Ohio Roster Commission. *Official Roster of the Soldiers of the State of Ohio in the War of the Rebellion, 1861–1866. . . .* 12 vols. Akron, Cincinnati, and Norwalk: Werner, 1886–1895.

Opdycke, Emerson. "Notes on the Chickamauga Campaign." In *Battles and Leaders* 3:668–71.

Paris, Comte de. See Comte de Paris.

Parrington, Vernon Louis. *Main Currents in American Thought.* 3 vols. New York: Harcourt, Brace, 1927–1930.

Phisterer, Frederick. *Statistical Record of the Armies of the United States.* New York: Charles Scribner's Sons, 1886. Reprint. New York: J. Brussel, 1959.

Porter, George H. *Ohio Politics during the Civil War Period.* New York: Columbia University Studies in History, Economics and Public Law [No. 105], 1911.

Porter, Horace. "Letter to the Editors." Footnote to Gillmore, Q. A. "Siege and Capture of Fort Pulaski." In *Battles and Leaders* 2:8.

Quarles, Benjamin. *The Negro in the Civil War.* Boston: Little, Brown and Company, 1953.

Randall, J. G., and David Donald. *The Civil War and Reconstruction.* 2d ed., revised. Boston: Little, Brown and Company, 1969.

Reid, Whitelaw. *Ohio in the War: Her Statesmen, Her Generals, and Soldiers.* 2 vols. Cincinnati: Moore, Wilstach & Baldwin, 1868.

Robertson, James I., Jr., "Military Aspects—Soldier Life." In Nevins, Robertson, and Wiley, *Civil War Books* 1:49–184.

Roseboom, Eugene H. *The Civil War Era.* Columbus: Ohio State Archaeological and Historical Society, 1944.

Rosengarten, J. G. *The German Soldier in the Wars of the United States.* 2d ed. Philadelphia: Lippincott, 1890.

Ryan, Daniel J. *The Civil War Literature of Ohio: A Bibliography.* Cleveland: Burrows Brothers, 1911.

Schafer, Joseph. "Who Elected Lincoln?" *American Historical Review* 47 (1941): 51–63.

Scott, H. L. *Military Dictionary.* New York: Van Nostrand, 1861. Reprint. New York: Greenwood Press, 1968.

Shannon, Fred Albert. *The Organization and Administration of the Union Army.* 2 vols. Cleveland: Arthur H. Clark, 1928.

Shaw, James Birney. *History of the Tenth Regiment Indiana. . . .* Lafayette, Ind.: [Burt-Hayward], 1912.

Sheridan, Philip H. *Personal Memoirs. . . .* 2 vols. New York: C. L. Webster, 1888.

Sherman, William T. "The Grand Strategy of the Last Year of the War." In *Battles and Leaders* 4:247–59.

———. *Memoirs. . . .* 2 vols. New York: C. L. Webster, 1891.

Sketches of War History, 1860–1865: Papers Read before the Ohio Commandery of the Military Order of the Loyal Legion of the United States. 4 vols. Cincinnati: Robert Clarke, 1888–1896.

Slocum, Henry W. "Sherman's March from Savannah to Bentonville." In *Battles and Leaders* 4:681–95.

Smith, Jacob. *Camps and Campaigns of the 107th Ohio Volunteer Infantry, August 1862 to July 1865.* N.p., n.d.

Smith, William Farrar, and Henry M. Cist. "Comments on General Grant's 'Chattanooga.' " In *Battles and Leaders* 3:714–18.

The Soldier's Guide: A Complete Manual and Drill Book for the Use of Volunteers, Militia and the Home Guard. . . . Philadelphia: T. B. Peterson & Brothers, n.d.

Stern, Philip Van Doren. *An End to Valor: The Last Days of the Civil War.* Boston: Houghton Mifflin, 1958.

Stewart, Charles D. "A Bachelor General [August Willich]." *Wisconsin Magazine of History* 17 (1933): 131–54.

Sumner, Charles. *Works.* 15 vols. Boston: Lee and Shepard, 1870–1883.

Trefousse, Hans L. *Carl Schurz: A Biography.* Knoxville: University of Tenneesee Press, 1982.

The Union Army: A History of Military Affairs in the Loyal States. 8 vols.

Madison, Wis.: Federal Publishing Co., 1908.
Urquhart, David. "Bragg's Advance and Retreat." In *Battles and Leaders* 3:600–609.
Vocke, William. "Our German Soldiers." In *Military Essays and Recollections: Papers Read before the Commandery of the State of Illinois, Military Order of the Loyal Legion of the United States* 3:341–71 (paper read 9 April 1896). 4 vols. Chicago: Dial Press, 1899.
Wandel, Joseph. *The German Dimension in American History.* Chicago: Nelson-Hall, 1979.
Warner, Ezra T. *Generals in Blue: Lives of the Union Commanders.* Baton Rouge: Louisiana State University Press, 1964.
———. *Generals in Gray: Lives of the Confederate Commanders.* Baton Rouge: Louisiana State University Press, 1959.
War Records Office. *War of the Rebellion: A Compilation of the Official Records of the Union and Confederate Armies.* 128 vols. Washington: Government Printing Office, 1880–1901.
Wheeler, Joseph. "Bragg's Invasion of Kentucky." In *Battles and Leaders* 3:1–25.
Wieck, William, and Constantin Grebner. *Höheres viertes Lesebuch für amerikanische Schulen.* Cincinnati and New York: Van Antwerp, Bragg, 1886–1887.
Wilczynski, Jozef. *An Encyclopedic Dictionary of Marxism, Socialism and Communism.* London: Macmillan, 1981.
Williams, T. Harry. *P. G. T. Beauregard: Napoleon in Gray.* Baton Rouge: Louisiana State University Press, 1954.
Wilson, Edmund. *Patriotic Gore: Studies in the Literature of the American Civil War.* New York: Oxford University Press, 1962.
Wittke, Carl. "The Ninth Ohio Volunteers." *Ohio Archaeological and Historical Publications* 35 (1926): 402–17.
———. *Refugees of Revolution: The German Forty-Eighters in America.* Philadelphia: University of Pennsylvania Press, 1952.
Wood, Thomas J. "The Battle of Missionary Ridge." In *Sketches of War History* 4:22–50.
Writers' Program, Work Projects Administration (American Guide Series). *Cincinnati: A Guide to the Queen City and Its Neighbors.* Cincinnati: Wiesen-Hart Press, 1943.
———. *The Ohio Guide.* New York: Oxford University Press, 1940.
Zimmermann, G. A. *Deutsch in Amerika: Beiträge zur Geschichte der Deutsch-Amerikanischen Literatur.* 2 vols. 2d ed. Chicago: Eyller, 1894.

Name Index

In the sequence of entries, the German umlaut has been disregarded.

Subject Index